Marion Shaw lived a̶ ̶ ̶ ̶ ̶ ̶ ̶for many years in the East Riding of Yorkshire and **UNIVER**sᴀᵗ at the University of Hull. Her previous publicatiᴏns include ᴮᴏᴏks on Tennyson and, as editor, *Man Does, Woman Is: An Anthology of Work and Gender* (1995) and *An Introduction to Women's Writing from the Middle Ages to the Present Day* (1997). She is also the editor, with Paul Berry, of *Remember, Remember! The Collected Stories of Winifred Holtby* (1999). Marion Shaw is currently Professor of English at Loughborough University.

Portrait of Winifred Holtby from a photograph painted in 1939 by Frederick Howard Lewis, now in Somerville College, reproduced by kind permission of the College. Vera Brittain thought it a 'remarkable' likeness and used it for the cover of the first edition of *Testament of Friendship*.

THE
Clear Stream

A Life of Winifred Holtby

Marion Shaw

A *Virago* Book

Published by Virago Press 2000

First published by Virago Press 1999

Copyright © Marion Shaw 1999

The moral right of the author has been asserted.

A CIP catalogue record for this book is available
from the British Library

ISBN 1 86049 810 8

Typeset in Berkeley by M Rules
Printed and bound in Great Britain by
Clays Ltd, St Ives plc

Virago Press
A Division of
Little, Brown and Company (UK)
Brettenham House
Lancaster Place
London WC2E 7EN

In memory of Edith Rutherford
1900–1976

Contents

Acknowledgements

My thanks are due firstly to the Leverhulme Trust for a grant which enabled me to have three months' paid study leave in which to begin the research for this biography.

I also wish to record my gratitude to the librarians of the University of Hull and Loughborough University. Permission to quote from letters of George Catlin has kindly been granted by the William Ready Division of Archives and Research Collections, McMaster University Library, Hamilton, Canada. Permission to quote from the Ballinger Papers has generously been given by the University of Cape Town. My thanks are also due to Pauline Adams, Librarian and Archivist, Somerville College. I am grateful too to the staff of Bridlington Public Library, and I am particularly grateful to the staff of the Local History section of Hull Library Services who have been unfailingly helpful and generous of their time. In this respect I owe an especial debt to Jill Crowther and her successor Jo Edge.

Many people have helped and encouraged me during the writing of this book, some of them friends and colleagues, some of them strangers whom I have solicited for information. I thank them warmly for their patience and co-operation. In particular, I would like to mention Kelvin Balcombe, Laurel Becker, Peter Bennett, Alan Bishop, Gill Brooke, Dr M.J.D. Cassidy of Nottingham City Hospital, Angela and Simon Dawson of Rudston House, Bill and Janet Duffin, Etaine Eberhard, Deborah Gorham, Geoffrey Handley-Taylor, Carol Heaton, Robert and Sonia Holtby, Mrs Hutchinson of East Witton, Heather Ingman, Eric Leazell, John Markham, Harriet Marland, Mr Pat Norton of Bridlington, Bill Overton, John Schad, Lizbie Shaw, Ron Shaw, the staff of St Margaret's School, Escrick, the late Martin Taylor of the Imperial War Museum, Sam Taylor, the late Mrs Margaret Waley, Diana Wallace, and, as ever, Angela Leighton and Patsy Stoneman. I am also greatly indebted to Tim Couzens for his assistance with the chapter on South Africa. Margaret Ballard, as one of the few who still remembers Winifred Holtby, deserves special gratitude for her willingness to share her memories and her photographs with me. I am fortunate in my editors at Virago Press; Lennie Goodings, Elise Dillsworth and Sajidah Ahmad have been consistently patient and encouraging.

My heartfelt thanks are also due to Mark Bostridge whose help in writing this biography, like his friendship, has been immensely valuable. And lastly, with great affection, I must thank Paul Berry. Unstintingly kind and trusting, he has been a source of strength, wisdom, encouragement and assistance. To visit him and Lea, to sit and talk with them in their sunlit garden, has been one of the delights of recent years and one of the rewards of writing this biography.

Winifred Holtby: a brief chronology

1898   23 June, Winifred Holtby born at Rudston House, Rudston, near Bridlington, North Yorkshire, the younger daughter of David Holtby, farmer, and Alice Holtby, born Winn.

1909   September, Winifred went as a boarder to Queen Margaret's School, Dulverton House, Scarborough, which she left in July 1916.

1911   December, *My Garden and Other Poems* by Winifred Holtby, published by A. Brown & Sons, Hull, at Alice Holtby's expense.

1914   Harry Pearson joined a West Riding Regiment. German bombardment of Scarborough from the sea.

1915   St Margaret's School evacuated to Pitlochry in Scotland.

1916   Edith de Coundouroff went to stay at Rudston House, remaining with the Holtby family until Alice Holtby's death in 1939.

        August, Winifred went to work in a London nursing home, to July 1917.

1917   October, entered Somerville College, Oxford to read Modern History.

1918   July, joined the WAACs as a private in the New Zealand Officers' Club. In September posted as hostel forewoman to a signals unit in Huchenneville, near Abbeville in France, where she met Jean McWilliam.

August, strike of agricultural workers at Rudston. David Holtby decided to retire from farming.

1919   February, David and Alice Holtby left Rudston House for 'Bainesse' in Cottingham, near Hull.

September, Winifred discharged from the WAACs and in October returned to Somerville College. Met Vera Brittain.

1921   Winifred graduated with a second-class degree. Writing *Anderby Wold*, published 1923. September, on holiday with Vera.

1922   Winifred and Vera took a flat in Doughty Street, London. Began lecturing for League of Nations Union and Six Point Group.

1923   Alice Holtby elected to East Riding County Council.

Grace Holtby, Winifred's sister, married Dr Peter Tolmie.

1924   Beginning of friendship with Margaret, Lady Rhondda. Writing *The Runners*, never published.

1925   June, Vera Brittain married the political scientist Gordon (George) Catlin.

1926   January to August, Winifred on a lecture tour in South Africa. March, met Clements Kadalie, Secretary of the Industrial and Commercial Workers' Union (ICU).

September, invited to become a director of *Time and Tide*.

1927   Recruited William Ballinger to help ICU organisation in South Africa.

Land of Green Ginger published.

1928   March, Grace Tolmie (Holtby) died.

Eutychus; or The Future of the Pulpit published.

1929   *A New Voter's Guide to Party Programmes* published.

October, *Women and a Changing Civilisation* published.

Vera Brittain began to write *Testament of Youth*.

1931   *Poor Caroline* published.

Autumn, canvassing for Gordon Catlin, unsuccessful Labour candidate in October General Election at which National Government came into office.

Onset of symptoms of renal failure; illness diagnosed spring 1932.

1932   February to April, on a 'rest-cure' at Monks Risborough, near Oxford. October, *Virginia Woolf* published.

1933   January, *Mandoa, Mandoa!* published.

March, David Holtby died.

May, *The Astonishing Island* published.

August, Vera Brittain's *Testament of Youth* published.

1934   Spring, Winifred in Withernsea, Yorkshire.

February, *Truth Is Not Sober* (short stories) published.

1935   February to April, lodging in Hornsea, finishing *South Riding*.

The Frozen Earth and Other Poems published.

29 September, died in a London nursing home. 2 October, funeral at Rudston.

1936   March, *South Riding* published.

1937   April, *Letters to a Friend*, edited by Alice Holtby and Jean McWilliam, published.

South Riding won James Tait Black Memorial Prize.

November, *Pavements at Anderby* (short stories), edited by Hilda Reid and Vera Brittain, published.

1938   Film of *South Riding* released.

1939   31 July, Alice Holtby died.

1940   January, Vera Brittain's *Testament of Friendship* published.

Introduction: the clear stream

In February 1935 Winifred Holtby, staying in Hornsea on the Yorkshire coast in order to escape the distractions and fatigue of life in London, wrote to her friend Vera Brittain to say that she had received a 'very nice letter from Virginia Woolf asking if I would like to write an autobiography for the Hogarth Press'.[1] She does not say if she was tempted by the invitation. In any event she would be dead within eight months, and during the time left to her she was occupied in finishing her last novel, *South Riding*.

South Riding is now the major reason Winifred Holtby is remembered, along with her friendship with Vera Brittain. But when Virginia Woolf wrote to Winifred,[2] *South Riding* was, of course, yet to be published. Vera Brittain's *Testament of Youth* had, however, recently been published to great acclaim but Winifred's presence in it towards the end would not by itself have justified an autobiography. So the Hogarth invitation rested on other claims. These related primarily to Winifred's reputation as one of the most successful and prolific journalists writing in London at the time. She was also well known as a feminist, particularly as a member of the

Six Point Group and a director of the feminist journal *Time and Tide*, and as an anti-war propagandist: she had lectured for years for the League of Nations Union and had recently contributed to Margaret Storm Jameson's powerful collection of anti-war essays, *Challenge to Death*. To a lesser extent, she was also known as the writer of the five novels, respectfully but unobtrusively received, which preceded *South Riding*. From the perspective of the Hogarth Press, she would also have been highly regarded as a campaigner for the unionisation of black workers in South Africa, Leonard Woolf being a member of the Labour Party Advisory Committee on Imperialism and having had considerable contact with Winifred over such matters.

Winifred's feminism, pacifism and socialism, her anti-racialist campaigns, and her intense commitment to the ideal of the woman citizen in the years after 1918 when women began to be enfranchised on an equal basis with men, make her an index of many of the progressive movements of the inter-war period. What was evident to Virginia and Leonard Woolf in 1935 was that Winifred was a representative and significant figure of the period, a 'woman in her time', according to the title Vera Brittain originally thought of for her biography of Winifred.[3] In addition, she strove to express this timeliness in the writing of imaginative literature, partly to exercise a talent for story-telling, and partly, as she came to realise and to bring to realisation in *South Riding*, because fiction itself can be a vivid historical record and a powerful agent of change; a novel can teach about sympathy, understanding and co-operation as well, or better, than a political tract or a deputation to the Prime Minister. Hers was an extraordinarily full and fulfilled life – 'Always rushing . . . and enjoying life and finishing my novel,' she wrote to Jean McWilliam in 1935,[4] three months before her death – but a life that faced outwards towards society rather than inwards towards personal needs and satisfactions.

A modern biography has, therefore, to address those various contemporary social and political issues that Winifred was so passionately concerned with. But there have been many women and men who lived equally useful and representative lives yet do not become the subjects of biographies. A biography of Winifred has therefore also to take into account the two reasons why modern readers might want to know more about her: her steady and enduring popularity as a novelist, particularly as the author of *South Riding*, which has never been out of print since its publication in 1936; and her friendship with Vera Brittain, celebrated at the end of *Testament of Youth* and throughout Vera's subsequent writings, as a model of female friendship, a 'noble relationship' equalling, as Vera maintained, the great male friendships of history. *Testament of Youth* has always been respected and valued, but it has also been reborn to generations of younger women in the years of second-wave feminism since the early 1970s.[5] As its reputation grew, so did Winifred's. The friendship became a feminist icon, an example of 'sisterhood' at its most admirable.

Winifred and Vera met for the first time in 1919 as undergraduates at Somerville College, Oxford. Both were returning there after periods of war service. When they graduated in 1921 they decided to live together in London, earning an income through lecturing, journalism and the writing of fiction. This thoroughly modern arrangement continued, with modifications, until Winifred's death in 1935. When the question of a biography of Winifred arose, there was no doubt in most people's minds that Vera was the person to do it. She took several years to write it, refusing to be hurried into a premature assessment, and it was published in 1940 with the title *Testament of Friendship*. It begins with the question of Winifred's autobiography:

In the last year of her life, three leading London publishers invited Winifred Holtby to write her autobiography. Half interested and half amused, she discussed the project with me during our Easter holiday. 'I don't see how I can write an autobiography,' she said. 'I never feel I've really had a life

of my own. My existence seems to me like a clear stream
which has simply reflected other people's stories and problems.'

Winifred's reported comment has not only given me the title for
this biography but has also provided me with a structure and an
organising principle for it. I have decided to take Winifred at her
word and write her story through the lives of the people who were
important to her, either in themselves, like her mother, or because
they represented aspects of her work which mattered greatly to her,
like William Ballinger in respect of South Africa, or Virginia Woolf
in relation to the world of fiction by women between the wars. It
is probably a biographical approach she would have found acceptable, being quite unusually lacking in self-centredness. It also
enables me to address her social and political concerns in more or
less discrete units rather than in fragments, as would have been the
case if I had told her life-story sequentially. This prismatic
approach has resulted in some loss of chronological structure to
the biography but I am not sure that in Winifred's case this is an
important loss because she did not, in fact, have a 'life of her own'
in the usual sense of a woman's life-story. She did not marry or
have children, and she had no great love affair or illicit relationship. There was also nothing obviously intense, climactic,
sensational or even tragic about her, except, of course, her early
death. Compared with others of her generation – Rebecca West,
Storm Jameson, Rosamond Lehmann, Stella Benson, and Vera
Brittain, for instance – there was an absence of the kind of emotional and sexual drama that is the stuff of biographies. Winifred
herself said that '[t]he things that happen to my friends are the only
things worth recording',[7] and this was in some respects true, at
least in regard to the 'human interest' element which usually con-
stitutes a life of one's own. As her remark suggests, neither did she
make a drama out of what experiences she did have; she was reticent about her disappointments and successes, didn't go around

sobbing on people's shoulders, writing vengeful letters, or pro-
claiming her triumphs and miseries. One has the sense that
although she considered she had an interesting life, she didn't
think she was, or even ought to be, particularly interesting as a
person.

This lack of the conventional structures of a woman's life-story
is a problem for a biographer, and so too are absences and obscu-
rities in the documentation of what life she did have. Many
important letters are missing, such as those to Margaret Rhondda.
Of the remaining letters and other personal papers and accounts,[8]
a great number are business-type letters, like the hundreds
Winifred wrote in connection with the Ballinger fund. There are
very few family letters, and of the letters to friends, those that she
wrote to Jean McWilliam were heavily selected and edited by Jean
and by Alice Holtby, Winifred's mother, and are therefore incomplete and inaccurate. The important, but also incomplete, cache of
letters[9] between Vera and Winifred are revealing but only to a limited extent because there was an element of censorship,
self-imposed, in what Winifred wrote. As will become clear,
Winifred felt very protective towards Vera, and her letters to her are
therefore less about her own feelings than expressions of support
and encouragement to Vera. When Winifred expressed happiness
to Vera, it was usually in relation to Vera's successes. On the few
occasions she did complain about being tired, harassed or upset,
this was quickly followed by an apology and a cheerful disclaimer
of any lasting depression or anger. As to diaries and journals, a few
remain, like the diaries she kept of the visits to Central Europe she
and Vera made in the 1920s, but these are records of places visited,
people encountered, lectures given, and are, in effect, business
jottings rather than intimate records. Of her conversations with
people, and their memories of her, by the time I started work on
the biography not many people remained who could remember
her; those who could, uniformly said she was a wonderfully warm
and radiant person. Vera Brittain seemed to voice the sentiments of

a whole generation in lamenting the loss to the world of Winifred's generosity, eagerness and 'lovely kindness' and this is the image which has persisted, a kind of nullifying sanctification of her memory. There is an empty space at the centre of Winifred Holtby's life which has to do not only with her reticence and self-effacement but also with what one must call her goodness. As all biographers recognise, good people are likely to be less interesting to read about than the wicked or even the ordinarily flawed; more importantly, they seem often to lack individuality, as though their unselfishness has indeed deprived them of selfhood.

And what of her fiction and journalism? Well, there are undoubtedly recurring preoccupations and themes in her work and I have referred to these in depicting her intellectual and political concerns. There is also a fair amount of personal information of an anecdotal kind. The journalist in Winifred could never resist a good story or an illustrative incident which could be made over into either articles or into fiction, even though some of these incidents related to painful episodes in her own life or the lives of others. Her journalism is rich in autobiographical anecdote and likewise much of her fiction can be mined for biographical information. Yet although in her writing she frequently used incidents and situations from her life, there is little which is straightforwardly revealing of her emotional life. Such as might seem to be so is displaced onto minor characters, like Lily Sawdon in *South Riding*, whose approaching death chillingly parallels Winifred's own situation at the time of writing the novel. But Lily is no self-portrait and her tragedy is only one not particularly important story amongst the many and varied stories in the novel. Winifred is fragmented into her numerous characters, and they only glancingly and tangentially reflect her. Even her poetry, which sometimes reveals a wistfulness her other writings do not show, is oblique or disguised in its expression of feeling, such as the poems she wrote about Vera's dead brother Edward. Such dispersal and reticence, which marginalises emotions and situations important to her own life, requires an answering reticence on the part of her biographer, at the very least a respectful caution in correlating the life and the work. Although I have used Winifred's fiction in suggesting what she might have believed or felt, I have tried neither to reduce the fiction to crude autobiography nor prescriptively to identify the author with her work.

Though also properly cautious in this respect, Vera Brittain's biography of Winifred, *Testament of Friendship*, for all its richness of personal knowledge and shared sympathies, tends to diminish its subject in other ways. There is no doubt that Vera very much wanted to pay tribute to Winifred but the biography has personal preoccupations which obscure many of Winifred's achievements. Vera was always the star of the relationship and Winifred seemed content to be the satellite, an arrangement tacitly agreed upon in all their dealings. There is a glimpse of this in the letter about Virginia Woolf and the Hogarth Press. After mentioning the invitation Winifred continues by saying, 'I take this to be an indirect compliment to *Testament of Youth*, which we know she loved.' Winifred's own achievements to this date, which included the first critical study in English of Woolf, are negated in order to sustain Vera's reputation as the writer of an important book, and to neutralise any jealousy Vera might have felt. The remark is disingenuous; Winifred cannot have believed her own minor role in *Testament of Youth* would have justified the invitation. Why mention it at all, unless she was preparing the ground to accept the invitation, or she wanted for once to boast but at the same time to take the sting from the boast?

For all its generosity towards her, its grief at her loss and remorse at the less than careful attention Vera paid to Winifred, *Testament of Friendship* and Vera's other writings about Winifred after her death maintain the structures of the relationship as it was lived, with Vera still as the star, even in her grief outshining Winifred. One of the ways in which this occurs is the emphasis Vera places on Winifred's unmarried, childless state. At the very beginning of *Testament of Friendship* their relationship is defensively cast in these terms, as a preparation for marriage:

> loyalty and affection between women is a noble relationship
> which, far from impoverishing, actually enhances the love
> of a girl for her lover, of a wife for her husband, of a mother
> for her children.[10]

Winifred's failure to marry, even her failure to be as attractive to men as Vera was, is subtly conveyed later on in *Testament of Friendship* when Vera describes her own wedding and Winifred's presence and appearance as a bridesmaid. Very tall, dressed in an imposing array of mauve draperies and wearing a large feathered hat, she looked older than Vera, when she was in fact four years younger. As she entered the church onlookers whispered ' "Who's that?" "Why, the bride's mother, of course, you silly!" '[11] This casting of Winifred as the plain one of the partnership, destined not to marry, is carried into *Testament of Experience*, Vera's account of her life in the decades after Winifred's death. Summarising Winifred's courageous attitude to denial and rejection, Vera says:

> How sadly conscious I felt that I had always accepted from
> her so much more than I gave, and now could give no
> more. None of her books published in her lifetime had sold
> well, so she helped mine to sell magnificently. The only
> man whom she really loved failed her, so she identified her-
> self with my married happiness. Her burdens were great
> and intolerable, so she shouldered mine which were often
> trivial. When she learned that she must never have chil-
> dren, she shared in the care of ours.

This makes Winifred out to be very selfless, almost saintly, but it also makes her seem pitiful, and a foil to Vera's more fulfilled and vivid life; it denies her, in fact, a life of her own. By the time

Testament of Experience was published in 1957, *South Riding* was an established success yet this posthumous fame has been eclipsed by Vera's need to maintain the friendship in the mode in which she wished it to be remembered. Correcting the typescript of *South Riding* in the first month after Winifred's death, full of admiration for what she read, Vera looked up at Winifred's photograph and thought: ' "Oh my dear love, I shall never do anything to equal this! I shall never produce work worthy of you, of your kindness and wisdom and pity! Oh, my poor dear love, my poor sweet." '[13] The urgency of new grief prompted Vera to acknowledge Winifred's achievements, even while grieving for her pathetic end but in the later, published versions Winifred's success, her reputation and standing in her own time are overtaken by Vera's needs, including an avowal of the noble friendship they created and, as will be seen later, a need to write a kind of love story for Winifred, a ghostly and rather shabby heterosexual narrative in which Winifred and her childhood sweetheart, Harry Pearson, finally reach a happy ending.

But in spite of the reservations one must have regarding *Testament of Friendship*, it remains a primary source of information on Winifred, written by someone who probably knew her better than anyone else, shared many of her aspirations, and loved her. Winifred and Vera were comfortable together with the familiarity of long-term friendship which often makes good behaviour or bad behaviour, or even liking and disliking, seem irrelevant. Vera wrote to someone who marvelled that Winifred should have put up with what seemed like Vera's exploitation of her that 'although we didn't exactly grow up together, we grew mature together, and that is the next best thing. . . . We were completely at ease with each other . . . I gave her rest and relief when she was at the end of her tether.'[14] Winifred endorsed this when she wrote to Vera that 'You are the only person I know in the world who does not prevent one work-ing.'[15] The truth of *Testament of Friendship* is real enough; it records the friendship of the two women over sixteen years and from it one can surmise the advantages of the relationship to each of them. But its emphasis is on the friendship, and those areas of Winifred's life which Vera either was not particularly interested in, like her directorship of *Time and Tide*, or disapproved of, like her affection for her mother, are not given full value. *Testament of Friendship* overwhelmingly reflects Vera's idea of Winifred and the dynamics of their relationship. But a more robust, humorous, independent, active and innovative person, even a more dislikeable person, still waits to be recovered. It is in her relationships with those other, shadowy figures of *Testament of Friendship* – Alice Holtby, Margaret Rhondda, William Ballinger, for example – that this other Winifred Holtby may be found, and it is with these that I, her latter-day biographer, must be concerned in an endeavour to colour the stream of her life with other tinctures of her personality, other facets of her experience. By reflecting other stories as well as Vera's, and by placing Vera's story in the context of these other reflections, I have tried to give Winifred more of a life of her own.

'. . . to be the daughter of Alice Holtby'

In May 1933, just before her thirty-fifth birthday, Winifred Holtby wrote to her mother Alice in response to a reproach that Winifred was too ambitious, too concerned with success, and not perhaps quite sure of her course in life. In her reply to her 'Darling, gallant, most understanding and wise of mothers,' Winifred admits that she doesn't really know what her life's aim is, except that she wants to see an end to inequalities of all kind, to persuade people 'to recognise the human claims of Negroes and Jews and women and all oppressed and humiliated creatures.' How she will achieve this, she doesn't know, nor whether she will ever achieve it: 'To learn, to practise, to work, to see all I can, to understand all I can. . . . And so, perhaps, one day be worthy of being used. And if not – it's an honour that comes to few; why should I expect to be privileged?'[1] The sentiments are characteristic and so too is Winifred's sense of responsibility towards her mother, not just as a loving and dutiful daughter, though she was certainly that, but as morally answerable to her too. Having set Winifred on an uncommon path through life, giving her independence of thought and lifestyle, Alice could never quite accept the full consequences of her actions. Proud though she became of Winifred, a part of Alice still expected from her not only a daughter's dutiful attentions in domestic crises but also a moral obligation to behave in ways that she, the mother, thought right. Winifred did not capitulate to all her mother's demands but she needed constantly to justify her actions when she did not do so, and she accepted almost without question an underlying moral imperative of service to others that her mother instilled in her. Alice was the first and perhaps the most important of the several strong women in Winifred's life who would seek, in different ways, to own and control her.

Alice was a large, vigorous, golf-playing, outspoken and opinionated woman, with youthful energy and enthusiasms even into old age. In 1925, when Alice was sixty-seven, Winifred described her as 'having taken to smoking and waving her hair, and . . . as full of vitality as a girl of twenty – much more so than most girls'.[2] She outlived her husband and her two daughters, dying in 1939 after an appendectomy[3] at the age of seventy-nine, on the day in which the manuscript of Vera Brittain's *Testament of Friendship* was completed. From a quite humble background she had become a woman of importance, having been elected in 1923 onto the East Riding County Council, and in 1934 becoming the first woman to serve as an alderman in 'this very conservative locality'. 'Splendid occasion,' Winifred observed of her mother's unanimous election: 'And the photographer & reporter from Leeds motored over this afternoon to interview & photograph us together, me sitting at her feet as she examined County Council papers! Most tasty'.[4] It was a characteristic pose, Alice confident and beaming, Winifred, already seriously ill, in attendance. Alice was the model for benevolent, autocratic Mrs Beddows in *South Riding* whom one of the other characters calls Deputy God and whose 'gaiety . . . kindliness [and] valour of spirit' console and encourage the novel's heroine.

Alice Holtby was born Alice Winn in 1858 and baptised on 17

April 1859 by her parents Christopher and Ann Winn of East Witton Mill, Christopher being described as 'farmer'. Alice was the fourth of six children. East Witton Mill, now no longer a functioning mill, lies about a quarter of a mile outside the village of East Witton, in Wensleydale. The Winns rented the mill and the farm belonging to it from the Marquis of Ailesbury as part of the Jervaulx estate in North Yorkshire. The estate, along with much property in the village, was sold in 1888. The mill was included in the sale but by this time, Christopher having died in 1882, Ann had moved into the village, the only son Francis taking over the mill and farm.[5] Alice may have moved away from East Witton before her father's death because family history suggests that by 1880 she had gone to work as a governess in the East Riding in the family of William Holtby at Rotsea, on the coast. It was there that she met tall, thin, silent, not very robust David Holtby and began the slow courtship which was to end with their marriage in 1892. In after years, with expansive cheerfulness, Alice liked to recall to a Holtby relative[6] how 'in this very room, David went down on his knees and proposed to me'. Grace, their first child, was born in 1896 when Alice was thirty-eight; Winifred was born two years later on 23 June 1898. Grace was a common name in the East Riding at this time but Winifred was not.

In a letter of 1927 to an unknown correspondent, Winifred said that she knew three areas of Yorkshire well and that these had featured in her three novels to date: Rudston and the wolds of the East Riding in *Anderby Wold*; Cottingham, a suburb of Hull, in *The Crowded Street*; and the Dales country where her mother was born in *The Land of Green Ginger*. Letherwick, the village in *The Land of Green Ginger*, was, she said, 'built like East Witton in Wensleydale' and Scatterthwaite farm was like many of the small, unrewarding holdings of the area where farming was, and is, harshly embattled against wind and poor soil. By contrast, the land of the East Riding in *Anderby Wold* was 'good land', with fertile soil that the heroine's 'grandfather and her father and [husband] had marled and manured and watched and waited as though nothing else in the world was of any importance'.

Thus Alice's story-book marriage to a man of property took her into a successful farming community and one in which David Holtby prospered more than most. There were, and still are, many Holtbys in the East Riding and at the end of the nineteenth century they successfully farmed across an area that stretched from upstream Humber to Bridlington. Robert Holtby of Elmswell, David's father, gave each of his three sons farming property and David seems to have made good what was given to him at Grindale so that by 1891 he had acquired farming land in Rudston,[7] six miles from Bridlington, and had bought Rudston House. He is first mentioned in Rudston All Saints Church records in 1892–3 as attending the vestry meeting and as a sidesman. When his and Alice's first daughter, Grace, was baptised in 1896, he is described as 'farmer' of 'Rudstone'; when Winifred was baptised on 15 July 1898 the entry is simply that of 'Rudstone House'. The impression is one of rising prosperity and of movement into a higher social class, and this is subsequently borne out by the parish magazines during the later 1890s which regularly record the Holtby contribution to church funds of 10 shillings as second only to that of £2 from the landed family of the Bosvilles. The census of 1901 records the population of Rudston as numbering 552.

Winifred described the countryside round Rudston as 'great undulating wolds, golden in harvest, chequered in spring with brown plough-land, bluish-green of turnips and the vivid emerald of winter wheat. Here and there on the slopes are scattered copses, sheltering the fold yards and gardens of outlying farms. It is one of the richest agricultural areas in England.'[8] The land has been worked by farming communities since prehistoric times, and Roman remains from the area, including a villa which was excavated during the 1930s,[9] indicate that it was heavily settled by them. The name 'Rudston', according to legend, comes from either 'red-stone' or, more probably, 'rood-stone' – the stone of the cross.

The village arranges itself in a rough triangle around All Saints Church and its churchyard, where Winifred is buried and where the ancient monolith stands, the twenty-six-foot high needle of grit-stone, the nearest source of which is ten miles away in the North Riding. The stone extends many feet under the ground and dates from the late Neolithic or Bronze Age. Possibly at one time it had a cross-head fixed to it by early Christian missionaries, hence the name Rudston. In one of her short stories, 'The Legend of Rudston', Winifred has the sexton recount to tourists the legend that the devil threw the monolith to halt the building of the church but the angels deflected its aim so that it pierced the earth and not the church. An alternative version of the legend, favoured by the sexton in the story, is that the stone is the hammer head of a gigantic Yorkshireman exacting justice from his Norman overlord.

Built in the early nineteenth century, Rudston House, looking now much as it did when David and Alice Holtby moved into it, is substantial, foursquare and imposing. When the Holtbys left in 1919, it boasted two kitchens and six bedrooms (but only one bathroom) amongst its many rooms, and also a cellar, a glasshouse, a vinery and extensive stabling, as well as farm buildings, a homestead, and 'ten cottages with gardens in the village'. The house stands on Long Street which forms the base of the elongated triangle of the village which has at its apex half a mile away the Bosvilles's seat, Thorpe Hall. During the early years of this century the triangle was completed on one side by the fast-flowing Gypsey Race, and at the other side by a Roman road. Rudston House is surrounded by a large, walled garden, with ash and beech trees; fields of wheat, or sometimes root crops, run up to the walls. Winifred recalled in 1934 what she described as her 'native country', the scene of her earliest memories:

[It] is a gravelled stable yard with golden jasmine starring the low grey brick buildings, and a gate facing westward inland to the wolds. . . . I lean against that gate in the ivied

wall under the ash tree, and hear the clump of farm-horse
hoofs coming from the drinking pond, and see the sun set
beyond the horse pasture and the sixty-acre stretch that
lies, dark plough-land, up to the flaming sky.[10]

Yet although she was imaginatively to return to this landscape in
her writing, intellectually her response to rural life was unsentimental and practical: 'almost every villager who has had the chance
has done what I have done about the countryside – escaped from
it at the first opportunity. [It] was not a place in which the poor or
moderately well off, the eager and ambitious and intelligent could
find life preferable to the life of the towns.'[11]

But the Holtbys were well off and life at Rudston House seems
to have offered Winifred as a child an ideal mixture of secure comfort and practical freedom. It is easy to see why Winifred later
would be surprised at the need for feminism. David Holtby managed the farm himself and the family home was the working centre
of the farm, where there were between eight to ten men employed
regularly with extra casual labour at busy harvest and lambing
times. In such a working community, especially with a powerful
mother like Mrs Holtby managing the household, there was less
demarcation between the world of women and that of men than
would have been the case in an urban or suburban middle-class
family, such indeed as the Brittain household. And with no
brothers to inhibit her, and neither her mother nor her father
inclined to curb her exuberance, Winifred ran about on the farm
'like a boy'.[12] She was later to write that she could plough and
milk, adding that she could also 'make my own clothes, speak in
Hyde Park, ride and dance'.[13]

Her relationship with her father's workers and their families
taught her social awareness and gratitude and even guilt at her own
privileged position. It also left her with a grudging respect for the
kind of hierarchical and paternalistic system which assumed
responsibility towards dependants at the same time as it demanded

unthinking loyalty. This was her parents' way of life and the way of life of a traditional rural community. She would criticise it in the managerial, Alice Holtby-like figure of Mary Robson in *Anderby Wold*, mourn its inevitable passing in the ruin and death of Robert Carne in *South Riding*, and it would inform her response to the black workers she met in South Africa and whose labour conditions she worked to improve during the last years of her life. The emotional roots of her fiction lay in the community of her father's farm, where people spoke 'with slow, considered intonation, the broad *o-s* and *a-s* of their dialect smoothed down by generations accustomed to wait upon the slow changes of wind and weather, unaware of the necessity for haste'.[14] The strength, humour and endurance of such people were exemplified for her in Welburn, the Holtbys' shepherd, whose children's births are recorded in the same register during the same years as Winifred and her sister Grace. His Christmas letter to Winifred of 1919, a year after the Holtbys had left Rudston, draws on shared memories and affections:

Dear Miss Winifred

Thanks for your letter which I received this morning which I was pleased to have. No, I have not got any lambs yet. It is too early for Rudstone, I oft wonder how I shall come on next lambing time, if it comes a rough night. . . . We have had the hounds over here two or three times this season but I have not been mounted yet, my horse is rather too fit. I have never been astride of a horse since poor old Matilda went away. I have driven round sheep last summer, in an old milk float. I was ashamed when I met any one I knew, but got bolder as time went on.

                                    Old Shepherd

According to a woman whose husband worked as a waggoner for the Holtbys before the war, Welburn would have earned between

£25 and £40 a year, possibly rising to £70 a year during the war. A waggoner – and with as many as twenty-four horses on the farm there were several of these – earned, she said, £26 a year in 1915. She had worked as a scullery maid for the Holtbys during the early years of the century, earning £5 a year, paid in arrears at Martinmas. This would rise to £20 during the inflationary war years, with a cook-general earning £30 or £35. The Holtbys had around six indoor staff, including two other maids, a cook-general and a chauffeur-gardener, with casually employed charwomen and washerwomen. What the scullery maid remembered most vividly was the endless ironing. Years later Winifred was to recall the 'nightmare' clothing of her childhood: 'long black cashmere stockings, woollen combinations (long-sleeved in winter, short-sleeved in summer), flannel knickers, "rational" corsets (though how irrational their platoons of buttons were, children alone can know), two petticoats, and a cotton "bodice", all to be covered by a holland frock, buttoned up to the neck and down to the wrist-band'.[15] Winifred didn't add ironing or cooking to her list of accomplishments and indeed she seems to have done little housework as a child. Many years later she recalled the 'fascinating novelty' of doing washing up during the maids' annual holiday in Martinmas Week when she and her sister could scatter soapy water around and dust the piano with a 'gorgeous rush up and down the keys'.[16] The servants at Rudston flowed over into Winifred's later life, long after she left the village, visiting the Holtby parents in Cottingham and regaling Winifred with all the latest Rudston gossip, or, more significantly, in the figure of Nursie, Winifred's nanny, supplying a housekeeper for Winifred and Vera during their days in a Maida Vale flat.

The largesse of the Rudston household, particularly at Christmas time when seventeen would sit down to dinner, is captured in Winifred's journalism and also in her fiction, most of all in *South Riding* where Christmas at Mrs Beddows's house echoes those at Rudston House: not only the fuss over the proprieties of present-giving but 'the real business of benevolence . . . orders of beef to every Beddows ex-maid and her husband . . . coals and blankets for ageing or invalid neighbours, toys, oranges, pennies and sweets for all the local children, and parcels of tea, cake and even whisky to dozens of often disreputable acquaintances who seemed to re-emerge in Mrs Beddows' consciousness only at Christmas time'. As well as Mrs Beddows's bustling managing manner, Winifred gives her another facet of her mother's behaviour: her flirtatiousness, her liking for men, finding them, as Vera noted, 'on the whole more congenial than women'.[17] Plump and ageing as she is, Mrs Beddows loves to wear nice clothes, her hands tremble at Robert Carne's kiss, she puts on perfume for his visits and lifts her skirt to show her shapely ankles. By all accounts, Alice Holtby liked expensive clothes, keeping a bolt of heavy purple silk for her exclusive use at the best Hull dressmaker's, and she loved to be driven around in solitary state by the local taxi man. She liked to flirt with tradesmen and workmen, to whom she was very generous, enjoyed banter with her fellow councillors, and, of course, liked to have Harry Pearson, Winifred's sort-of-boyfriend, around her. Never a pretty woman, she radiated enjoyment of life and the promise of solid comforts of the flesh.

By contrast, Winifred was a thin, physically timid, rather gangling girl. Although as a woman she grew to be imposing, she never reached her mother's grandeur of build but tended to be physically diffident and clumsy and to stoop, like her father. Her height was five feet nine inches, she weighed eleven stone and wore an eight in shoes. She was large-featured too, with a (slightly crooked) 'family nose', that is, her father's nose, for Mrs Holtby had a round face and broad nose. Winifred's height and strong features meant she could, and did, play male parts in theatricals, as in the Somerville going-down play, or as a sheikh at a fancy-dress party on board ship coming home from South Africa in 1926. As a man she looked glamorous, film star-like, for she was very fair and blue-eyed, a Viking in features as well as build, she liked to say, and in this respect was also her father's daughter. Margaret Ballard, who as Margaret de Coundouroff lived in the Holtby home as a child,[18] remembers Winifred sometime during the 1920s on a Christmas visit home from London, coming into the house from the train with snow on her hair, which shone and glistened like a halo. Joanna in *The Land of Green Ginger* is an idealised self-portrait, 'all the best of me, but without my academic side and with far more pluck'.[19] She is described as 'tall and grandly proportioned, like an immature young goddess. Soft golden hairs curled graciously against her firm, milky neck . . . her blue eyes, deep-set below heavy lids, laughed at a pleasant world.'

Joanna shared with Winifred a 'capacity for endowing the commonplace with transcendental qualities' and as being 'beyond all her other loves, in love with life'. This exuberance seems to have been inherited from her mother, in contrast to her sister Grace, two and a half years older, who although also tall and fair – like 'an elegant drooping lily on an over-long stalk', Vera Brittain described her[20] – was gentler, quieter, more languid, more like her father than her mother in personality. Grace had the reputation as the pretty one; Winifred recalled years later that their governess used to say to them, ' "That is the way of the world, you know, One is for use and the other for show," and which contemplating my pretty sister, I always thought unkindly apposite.'[21] Winifred's statements about her sister, and the sister relationship, are ambivalent. In writing of Virginia Woolf, she comments that Woolf cannot have been a lonely child because she had her sister, Vanessa, who 'seems to have been a special friend, and when sisters are friends the relationship goes deep to the roots of personality'.[22] But when they are not special friends, how does this affect the roots of personality? In 'The Grudging Ghost', a poem written after Grace's death, Winifred looked back with regret and guilt at the lack of close affection between them: 'unanswering heart to heart, / Lived we all our days apart, / Love was nothing in the mind / Save desire to be kind,' but the poem continues into a complaint that even now her sister is a burden: 'Must you still while season run / Cast your shadow on the sun? / I have nothing more to give. / Sleep, ah sleep, and let me live.'[23] Yet Winifred could write in 1920, about Grace's impending visit to her in Oxford, 'I love having her. Her peaceful presence makes small things insignificant and big things more worth while. Also she does my shopping and makes my tea.'[24] There is one surviving letter to Grace from Winifred, a brief, cheery, perfunctory letter, written in 1919 from London, which begins, 'Dearest old thing', gives her day's programme in the hostel where she was working as a WAAC, and concludes 'I'm awfully happy here . . . Lots of love, Babe'. What otherwise remains of Grace, who seems to have been Winifred's shadowy antithesis and who died after giving birth to her second child, is an impression of conventional femininity, of a woman who wanted marriage and children and not a career, although she did undertake some nursing before her marriage. 'Since she became engaged', Winifred wrote in 1923, 'she has found animation and beauty and a merry laugh – all the things she lacked before. . . . She will give way to him in everything, with a sort of obstinate submission.'[25] The impression Vera Brittain gives is that Winifred found this irritating and not at all in the spirit of the new woman citizen that she and Winifred were to espouse in the inter-war period, but the evidence is that the irritation was at least equally on Grace's side. On the day of Grace's death, 11 March 1928, Winifred wrote to Vera: 'She was slightly better last night; she knew me when I was there, but ironically true to our relationship, I irritated her even by going into the room, and her last words to me . . . were "Don't stare. You make me tired."'

Writing to Gordon, Vera's husband, after Grace's death, Winifred gave a harsh verdict on her sister:

The tragedy about Grace was not that she died, but that she never lived. . . . Grace never knew real happiness; she never knew that zest for life which may accompany even pain. She found life always a little too much for her, & in the end, too much for her altogether. But she wanted to go on living, because she was always hoping that the thing which she had missed was waiting for her round the corner of the next day. . . . I know that if she had lived, she would not have found what she wanted. . . . I know that her children will be better brought up by strangers than by her harassed & irritable kindness.[26]

In *Testament of Friendship*, Vera Brittain gave Winifred's sentiments cruel publicity in her remark that 'by dying Grace had perhaps served her daughters best'.[27] In her letter to Gordon, Winifred had stressed that hers was the kind of remark which should not be made public, not least because 'it mayn't be true. One learns how difficult it is to know the truth about people, however honestly one seeks it.'

Some of the tensions between the sisters' lifestyle and aspirations surface in Winifred's novel about 'a girl who never found romance', *The Crowded Street*. Its heroine Muriel and her sister Connie live in the well-off suburb of Marshington, a life of tennis-parties, charity work and elaborate domesticity that Winifred escaped from in not returning permanently to her parents' home in Cottingham after graduating. But Cottingham was where Grace succeeded in getting what she wanted, even though it meant enduring the ignominious competition for a diminished number of men: 'the girls had to wait for men to ask them, and if nobody came – they still must wait, smiling and pretending not to mind'. The desperation which leads a woman to accept any man who can be caught, as Connie does in *The Crowded Street*, is pondered carefully in this novel in which Muriel does not, finally, accept the most eligible man in the neighbourhood. 'I only hope he's good enough' Winifred wrote doubtfully about Grace's 'little Scottish doctor' of a husband: 'it is a great responsibility for a man to hold complete possession of a girl, as he holds her.'[28] Connie dies in *The Crowded Street*, from influenza aggravated by pregnancy, as Grace was to do four years later, leaving Muriel 'very weary but yet more bored [and with] a desolating sense of no purpose . . . now that she had not even a sister left who needed her.' Winifred's relation to her sister is a shadowy part of her life. In one who felt guilty towards the unfortunate of the world at large, who was obsessed with a sense of her own immunity from suffering, this coldness towards her sister and the apparent lack of grief and remorse at her death, was a strange aberration. Grace was a reminder of the historic fate of women to attend upon men and, as her later writings show, Winifred found such passive femininity a threat to the kind of feminism she and Vera professed. Grace and Vera were each other's opposite and the choice between sister and friend, and between the lifestyles they represented, may have been one Winifred needed to make in order to declare her own freedom from tradition.

There is no record of Alice Holtby's attitude to her elder daughter. Winifred made no mention of her mother's response to Grace's death in her letters of the time. Her father's response, on the other hand, she did comment on, as 'splendid – most stoical', as if in recognition of the greater bond between him and Grace, so alike as they apparently were in personality. It cannot have been easy for gentle and comparatively self-effacing individuals like David and Grace Holtby to hold their own amidst the exuberant company of Alice and Winifred.

By 1909 David Holtby's position in Rudston had become so respected that he was a school manager, along with the Revd Booty, vicar of Rudston church since 1876. There were two schools to be managed, Rudston Infants with around thirty-five children and Rudston Church of England with sixty-two boys and girls aged between seven and fifteen. The certificated headmaster of the latter earned £100 a year and the uncertificated headmistress of the Infants' school earned £60 a year. The professionalisation of the teaching profession and the long struggle to gain equal pay for women teachers were issues Winifred would become involved with during the 1920s. But in Rudston, as the daughters of well-off parents, there was no question that she and Grace would attend the village schools, although they did attend the Sunday school and became teachers in it as they grew older. They had governesses, including Maud Nudd, 'Nuddie', who joined them when Winifred was four and remained until she was eight. Surviving letters from Winifred to 'darling dearest Nuddie' from around the age of seven illustrate two enduring characteristics: a delight in writing and acting stories, and weak spelling: 'We went to the Vicerage and Miss Bosville & Miss Booty acted "The Backward Child" and "Cheerfull & Musical." Are you going to have theatrecils this year? With much love from everybody, and some speachle from me, Goodbye, Nuddie, Goodbye.'[29]

From these governess days Winifred remembered hearing read aloud Tennyson's 'The Lotos Eaters', discovering the border ballads of 'Chevy Chase' and 'Fair Helen' for herself, and then on to adventure stories like *The Scarlet Pimpernel* (her favourite), *Westward Ho!* and *Rob Roy*. A precocious and omnivorous reader, she had to make do with the limited resources of a home where 'the most conspicuous element of our library consisted of two solid rows of bound volumes of *The Ladies' Realm* and *The Quiver* [which Winifred would write for herself in the 1930s], with two novels, chosen by the local librarian, arriving weekly in a green baize bag.'[30] Her history lessons with Nuddie were of the Alfred-and-the-cakes kind and this concentration on national history was continued at school where she could remember doing the civil war three times: 'I had been to Oxford for two years before I realised anything about other civilisations.'

But Winifred's warmest memories were of writing more than reading. 'Most small children find their way into literature by trying to make it for themselves. They tell stories before they can read them,' she wrote in 1933 and this was her own experience. She was particularly keen on writing dramas, having seen a performance of 'The Yeoman of the Guard' at the Grand Theatre, Hull, which led to her and Grace writing melodramas, performed in the big stone front kitchen, 'with curtains hung from the bacon-hooks . . . the stage plentifully [strewn] with corpses, and a toasting-fork, which would contract by pressing in upon itself [making] so effective a dagger that its frequent use was irresistible.'[31] But her first taste of real fame came through poems rather than plays. Christmas shopping in Hull with her school matron in 1911, she saw in a bookseller's window a display of 'elegant little pink and pale-green gift books' entitled *My Garden and Other Poems*, by Winifred Holtby. It was Alice Holtby's Christmas gift to Winifred and cost her £11 9s 9d, a not inconsiderable sum for the time. Winifred was ecstatic: 'I have known since then countless moments of pleasure, several of rapture and a few of pride but as I walked back to school with my first published work I knew so dazzling an ecstasy of achievement that nothing experienced since has ever approached it.' It was a fine motherly gesture, and the false modesty of its Foreword, by Alice, could not disguise her pleasure and pride in her daughter's achievement:

> The twenty-five poems contained in this little book are the spontaneous outbursts of one of Nature's youngest songsters. The earliest of them was written at the age of ten, the latest at the age of thirteen, and most of them found their inspiration in an East Riding garden, to which blows freely 'The Wind O'er the Sea'.
>
> As gleanings from a waste-paper basket, found crumpled up and cast aside, they have been here put together; and as such discarded trifles they must be judged by those lovers of poesie into whose hands they may chance to fall.

Winifred continued writing poetry all her life and none of it ever really became more than poesie, although in the context of her life much of it is expressive and moving. The significance of *My Garden and Other Poems* lies rather in its indication of literary aspiration by Alice Holtby on Winifred's behalf, an uncommon ambition in a

Yorkshire farmer's wife of the period, even a prosperous one.

In September 1909 Winifred, unlike Grace, went as a boarder to Queen Margaret's School, Scarborough, going into class IIIA where the average age was thirteen (throughout her schooling she seems to have been younger by between one and two years than her class mates). Not surprisingly, she came eleventh out of a class of thirteen, and her school report comments on her untidiness and poor spelling, that her conduct is good but 'she must try to be less dreamy and forgetful' and that her dancing is 'very stiff' and her deportment in general needs special attention. The next year the comment is that she 'must make a great effort to put more energy into all she does and be more thoughtful for others'. But by 1911, although the comments on poor spelling and absent-mindedness persist, she had moved to third place in the class: 'Her work shows originality, but style needs more care'. By 1912, now known as Winnie, she is described as 'always hopeful and cheery . . . full of loyalty and sympathy'. A later comment says that 'she must be careful not to allow herself to become too critical or give her opinions too freely'.[32] Writing in the *Yorkshire Post* in 1929 Winifred recalled the conventions and proprieties that governed life, formally and informally, at school: 'Gulfs of social ostracism yawned before me because I spoke to a prefect before she spoke to me. I took three biscuits at eleven o'clock instead of two. I did not understand the formula, "May I have your knees?" [There were even] correct and incorrect psychological conditions. It was all right to be practical, quick tempered, down-right and sporting; it was all wrong to be dreamy, speculative, moody and shy. It was wrong to enjoy lessons; it was essential to think games important; it was necessary to be public spirited, though less clear what this meant.'

Queen Margaret's School was a Woodard school, one of a group of eight girls' boarding schools originally founded, with some reluctance because he was not a wholehearted supporter of girls' education, by the high church clergyman, Nathaniel Woodard

(1811–91), as sister schools to the boys' schools he had introduced in three categories, according to his ideas on the class segregation of aristocratic, middle or merchant, and artisan classes. To some extent his girls' schools followed this segregated pattern and the two Yorkshire schools, Queen Margaret's in Scarborough and Queen Ethelberga's in Harrogate, were of the middle category, designed to equip girls to earn a living, preferably in the professions. Queen Margaret's was founded in 1901[33] and like many boarding schools of the time adopted a spartan regime, and, in the case of Woodard schools, a model of behaviour based on notions of responsibility and of practical usefulness to society. Its school motto, *Filia Regis*, daughter of the king, tells much of the school's Anglican ideals, echoed in Psalm 45 which the school used on ceremonial occasions: 'Thou lovest righteousness and hatest wickedness: therefore God, thy God, hath anointed thee with the oil of gladness above thy fellows. . . . Kings' daughters were among thy honourable women.' This psalm was sung at Winifred's Memorial Service in St Martin-in-the-Fields on 1 October 1935.

According to her own account, Amy Francis, who with her husband Charles Burnett, came to look after the Brittain–Holtby–Catlin household in the 1930s, was the model for the schoolgirl Lydia Holly in *South Riding*. Amy had told Winifred about her struggling family background and her attempts to gain an education through the scholarship system. But the details of Lydia's school work were surely Winifred's own: 'Twenty-six spelling mistakes. No punctuation. Five blots, and seventeen crossings out. . . . At the same time, it's much the most interesting piece of work I've had in from this form . . . indeed, it's really one of the most interesting school essays I've read.' Similar also to Lydia Holly's adoration for the headmistress Sarah Burton was Winifred's response to the headmistress of the school from 1913, enlightened, feminist Rosalind Fowler who encouraged her girls into higher education and who would remain Winifred's friend throughout her life. Like Sarah Burton she was one of the many dedicated women teachers of the early and interwar years of this century, unmarried by virtue of the marriage bar, who used their university education to staff the girls' grammar and public schools of the time. Rosalind Fowler came from the Diocesan School for Girls in Grahamstown, South Africa, with which Queen Margaret's had a long-established link, one of the many connections that were to flow into Winifred's later commitment to that country. It is a nice irony that another 'Rosalind' would go to South Africa in 1920 eventually to become a headmistress, a red-headed one like Sarah Burton; this was Jean McWilliam, the 'Rosalind' of *Letters to a Friend*.

Winifred's contributions to the school magazine and entries in notebooks from her schooldays are humorous poems like 'How I watched the hockey match' (by not being able to take part in it through having lost a jersey) and action-packed stories and plays like 'Espinage: A Drama of 1914' in which a German visitor is suspected of taking some papers which have actually been taken by the daughter of the house; it isn't clear why.[34] It is racily written with a deftness of characterisation, and the whole output is cheerful and robust, not particularly subtle, the work of a journalist in the making. It is also lacking any romantic element, perhaps because of school and home censorship or simply because Winifred, young for her age, was not interested in romance. Annotations and transcriptions by Alice Holtby indicate her continuing involvement with her daughter's writing career. And it was she who painstakingly transcribed for publication in the *Bridlington Chronicle* Winifred's account of the shelling of Scarborough by German gunboats in December 1914. Prints were taken of this eager, slightly melodramatic, self-consciously literary account and sold by Winifred and her mother to raise funds for the Red Cross. The bombardment would be used ten years later in Winifred's second novel, *The Crowded Street,* and ironically transformed, so that what had been of great excitement at the time becomes in fiction coloured by the disappointments and failures in the life of Muriel, the novel's heroine. The escape from the shelled town seems like a dream to Muriel in which she cannot seize the opportunity of love: 'Her hour had come and passed her. She did not honour love less, but knew herself to be unworthy of it.' Even the bombardment had not resulted in the excitement of invasion, 'the supreme adventure dwindl[ing] into an uncomfortable wandering among the smells and indecencies of a refuse camp on the outskirts of Scarborough'. The disappointed love scene, where accident, ill health or failure of will prohibit both sexual and emotional commitment, is one which almost all Winifred's novels would feature. Friendship is shown as more lasting and *The Crowded Street* ends with a future of work and usefulness for Muriel which has been motivated by her friendship with Delia, the character based on Vera Brittain.

But before Vera–Delia, in life as in the novel, there were school-friends like Edith Mannaberg and Osyth Harvey, amalgamated in *The Crowded Street* into the glamorous, musical Clare Duquesne who bewitches both Muriel and Muriel's wished-for lover, and then disappears to South America. Muriel thinks to herself how she cannot help loving Clare, even though she has been told by the headmistress that such passionate friendship between girls 'was usually silly and frequently disastrous. If carried too far, it even wrecked all hope of matrimony without offering any satisfaction in return.' That Winifred, like many girls, particularly at single-sex schools, had passionate friendships of this nature seems very likely, though the evidence lies only in her novels (*The Land of Green Ginger* features such friendship too) and in a poem, 'To Winifred', by someone called Quetta Maude, probably a pseudonym since no such pupil attended the school:

> Straight her form as grow the pines
> . . . And her hand how strong,
> In fixed purpose to engage:
> In her heart ever a song –
> Pain & sorrow to assuage:

Fragile, chaste ah! fair to see
God's rare masterpiece is she.

There is also no evidence that Winifred found school frustrating and limiting, as Muriel did, but it certainly didn't improve her health. It was dark and gloomy, the food was poor, the sleeping accommodation lacked warmth and privacy, and Winifred, never robust, was frequently ill. As an after-effect of mumps she had infected glands of the neck, which were removed, leaving a scar, and more seriously she had scarlet fever when she was fifteen, which is caused by bacteria associated with nephritis, the illness she would die from. The contrast between the comfort of Rudston House and the discomfort of school was considerable and it is a little puzzling that Alice Holtby was not concerned at her daughter's ill health to the extent of removing her from the school. But since most public schools were uncomfortable places at this time, the privations endured by Winifred were perhaps seen by her parents as nothing out of the ordinary.

After the bombardment, the school was evacuated to Pitlochry in Scotland where Winifred's health improved and where she became more active, writing for the school magazine and winning prizes, including a nurse's wallet for an essay on ambulance work. When she left the school in 1916 she won the VI Form prize that year, though, surprisingly in view of her popularity and energy, she was not head-girl but only a prefect. By this time the school magazine was regularly reporting accounts of war service by brothers and fathers of the girls and of war work by Old Margretians: secretarial, nursing, munitions, canteen work, looking after prisoners. After she left, Winifred kept in touch with the school through the Old Margretian Association, of which she was a life member, and which had its own magazine. In 1927–8, and perhaps for other years too, she was a committee member. When she died she bequeathed her books to the school, almost 2,000, including thirty by or about George Bernard Shaw.[35]

The war years which disrupted Queen Margaret's School also brought irrevocable change to the quiet, settled community of Rudston. Farming conditions during the war were generally difficult, particularly so in the 'big push' of the spring and summer of 1918 when the military age was raised to fifty-one. Exemption from service was by now no longer generally available for agricultural workers and in 1918 they were not released from war service even for harvest work, as in the previous years. The country badly needed home-grown food and farmers were under pressure to produce it but they had to do so without the customary supply of cheap and docile labour. The position of those workers who remained on the land was unprecedentedly strong and their grievances both long-standing and pressing: 'how is a man to do hard work if he has a family of five to keep out of 30's. a week? . . . Nothing under £2 per week can be called even a fair wage today.'[36] The debate concerning wages was conducted on three sides between the Agricultural Wages Board, attempting to regularise a system of payment essentially feudal in origin, the National Farmers' Union, resentful of government interference and outraged by the 'ingratitude and presumption' of their employees, and the rapidly strengthening Agricultural Labourers' and Rural Workers' Union. In the East Riding the unrest came to a head over payment for harvest work, traditionally involving longer hours and higher pay than at other times of the farming year. On 17 August the *Hull Times* reported that 'the Rudstone labourers who recently joined the Agricultural Labourers' Union, and number 35 members, came out on strike on Monday morning and are all out with the exception of two whose names were struck off the roll. . . . The men ask for 60's. [with board] or 80's. [without board] but the farmers held to the offer of 50's. or 70's.' The dispute was finally settled by arbitration but the men did not return to work until mid-September. By then the Holtbys had decided to give up farming and leave Rudston House 'next Lady Day'. The reason given in the *Hull Times* was 'the continued ill-health of Mr Holtby' but, as

Winifred's letters home at this time indicate, he found the strike 'heart-breaking'. Delicate and nervous as he was, and 'equipped neither by temperament nor training to deal with unfamiliar situations', he could not contemplate with ease the changing labour relations of the post-war years. In a letter of 1920, when the issues involved in the removal were fresh in her mind, Winifred commented that the courage of the pioneer is always celebrated but that 'it seems not out of place to talk for a little of the courage of those who, seeing the things they have given their lives to, passing, raise no hand to prevent the coming of the new, that may mean for the world salvation, but for themselves, and all they stand for, certain destruction.'[37]

The story of the Rudston strike is told in Winifred's first novel, *Anderby Wold*, written when Rudston was some seven years into her past life, and when it was clear that neither she nor her parents would live there again. She had heard of the strike only after the decision to leave the farm had been taken. A slightly sad letter to her father, from 1918, acknowledges that, however loving the bond between her and her parents, she and they have separate lives and that each must make their own decisions in life:

> My own dearest Daddy,
> . . . Thank you very much, dear, for writing and telling me what you have planned. I quite understand your decision, and for me whatever you think best is right. Of course I shall be sorry in many ways to leave Rudstone, but for me Home is where you and Mother are, and wherever you two will be happiest will please me best. . . . I can't be with you both always in body, but in my love and sympathy I will always be – best of Fathers – your loving Babe.[38]

To her mother she wrote more emotionally:

> Dear heart, don't I know what you must be going

through. . . . I suppose their [sic] are few people whose absence will leave such a big gap behind (you aren't a very little body any way, are you Mums?) I guess that that is one of the hardest things to deal with for you, who in your large-heartedness cant help feeling sorry for the Lucies and Smiths and others, to whom your strength and courage gave them some confidence and respite when life seemed almost too much for them. And I guess that it has not made it any easier having to stay in Yorkshire as Father wishes.

In *Anderby Wold*, Mary Robson, surely modelled on her mother, resents having to leave her sphere of influence and grieves at the things she will miss when she and her ailing husband move from the farm: 'the smile of the labourers as she passed them by the stackyard gate, the brown full-bosomed curve of the hills, and the scent of cream and butter in a red-tiled dairy'. But if Alice Holtby did have regrets of this kind, she would soon find compensation in the new life awaiting her in Cottingham.

The prefatory page of *Anderby Wold* states 'To David and Alice Holtby is dedicated this imaginary story of imaginary events on an imaginary farm', but there was an earlier dedication which laid no stress on the inventedness of the story: 'To my two dears, to whom the book is dedicated, with the love that I am quite unable to express & gratitude for the tenderness & consideration without which the story, such as it is, could never have been told.' It is possible that Alice Holtby, always to be nervous lest connections might be made between Winifred's fictions and Holtby biography, censured the early version. Certainly, *Anderby Wold* is based on facts in as much as there was a strike, and there were, according to a letter from a local farmer in the *Hull Times*,[39] 'paid agitators . . . inciting not only labourers but also the men who are under a legal contract for a year to strike and refuse to gather in the harvest unless most unreasonable terms are conceded'. The letter notes that 'in all great upheavals, the scum comes to the top. We see this in Russia at the present time.' Two weeks later, the paper mentions Danish labourers employed on the land, and also that one of the Holtbys' waggoners, George Walker, has died of wounds in France after serving for two years. *Anderby Wold* is set in 1912, before the war, the strike or the Russian revolution, but it gropes towards a historical awareness of these 'upheavals' in its ranging of the conservative, traditionalist community, headed by Mary Robson, 'the serene mistress of bountiful acres', against the socialist agitator David Rossitur preaching the nationalisation of the land who is killed 'horribly, wastefully, wantonly' by fanatical forces. The challenge of democracy to established practices, and the losses as well as the gains entailed in this, is a theme Winifred will develop in all her fiction. Politically, of course, she and her mother would grow far apart, Alice remaining staunchly Conservative, Winifred moving steadily towards to the left, through a confused and comical membership of all political parties during her early years in London, to membership of the Independent Labour Party in the early 1930s. Disagreements would arise between mother and daughter, over, for instance, the miners' strike of 1926. Winifred was sympathetic to the miners but, she wrote to Vera from South Africa, 'Mother will be grieving. She loves a vague abstraction called England amazingly. . . . Damn the capitalist Press. Damn the contradictious imperfection of things.'

In July 1923, the same month as *Anderby Wold* was published, Winifred visited Rudston with her mother nearly four years after the Holtbys left the farm on 1 March 1919. 'I don't know whether I liked it or disliked it,' Winifred wrote. 'My mind was a confused muddle of emotions and memories. . . . It was lovelier than I had remembered, and smaller and more hilly.'[40] But her mother seems to have found the visit stressful: 'Everyone was very kind but coming back on the train Mother had a sort of fainting fit.' By this time Alice Holtby was actively engaged in local politics in Cottingham, and finding in her new life a greater opportunity for the exercise of power. The house she and David Holtby had retired to, which they called Bainesse,[41] now owned by the University of Hull and named Holtby House, was built in 1871 and was as large as Rudston House, and not dissimilar in its yellow-grey brick and solid, comfortable appearance and pleasant garden, but its setting was suburban and Winifred disliked what she thought of as the complacency and snobbishness of the area, compared with either the rural world of Rudston or the city of Hull. But Bainesse suited Alice Holtby; its closeness to the railway station at Cottingham meant she could easily go shopping in Hull or to council meetings in Beverley. The house was large enough to accommodate her 'collection', as Winifred called it, of dependants and unfortunates: 'She has at present [a] sick nurse, a tubercular baby of nine months, an unemployed boy from South Africa, and a family of four children and their mother – who are sort of distant cousins of ours. The son is a cripple, and the eldest girl twelve. She seems to manage them all quite unperturbed, and grows younger and more delightful to live with every month.'[42] The house's handsome and prosperous appearance also suited Alice, along with its proximity to the chief families of the area. Life in such a household could be pleasant for a daughter at home: 'I have breakfast at nine-thirty,' Winifred wrote in 1921, 'do a little vague housework, such as washing breakfast things and tidying my room, drift down the village on an errand, or put on my second-best hat and meet the Hull train, bearing its load of Cottingham ladies back from a pre-lunch shopping. In the afternoons I play tennis; in the evenings, bridge. It's very delightful – for a week.'[43] But beyond a week it was a stifling environment: idle, gossip-ridden, complacent and very conservative: 'Cottingham is refreshingly shocked by my pink finger nails,' Winifred wrote to Vera in 1933.[44]

Cottingham is Marshington in *The Crowded Street*, and its routine of tennis and bridge parties reduces the novel's heroine, Muriel, to a state of 'frigid and self-conscious terror'. By the end of the novel she has rejected Marshington and all it represents: 'I loathe it with all my heart and all my soul and all my spirit.' Less vehemently stated, this was Winifred's response; to visit frequently, to be there at times of need, to fit in with its demands and routines when she was there, all this Winifred did but to live there permanently as a daughter at home she could not do.

Yet to escape from the influence of home, particularly Alice Holtby's influence, was less easy. Writing to her mother from France in April 1919, Winifred said that when she was in doubt or difficulty, 'the one thing I have to help me . . . is – if Mother could see or hear me, would she be glad or sorry?'[45] Though thousands of daughters must have written or said this to their mothers, what follows afterwards in Winifred's life strengthens the impression that her mother was a moral touchstone and her influence unusually profound and lasting. This influence was not silent; Alice Holtby seems to have frequently reproached Winifred, probed her motives and called her back to the principles of service and self-sacrifice instilled into her as a girl. Alice Holtby's letters to Winifred have not survived but it is possible to read the mother's questions and admonitions in the daughter's answers and self-justifications. In an undated letter of 'about 1923'[46] Winifred is defending to her mother her refusal to take the sacraments. It is the defence of a daughter newly graduated in History, whose studies have made her sceptical of church authority, replying to a mother whose position is deeply entrenched in church tradition: 'I have loved the church,' Winifred wrote, 'But it is bloodstained. . . . It is darkened by superstition and fear. It stands between the world of the thing I long for most, the coming of the Universal Kingdom of God. So I will not take its sacraments nor support its organisation.' In the same letter Winifred defends her writing and lecturing against charges of ambition by saying that these are what she does best: 'I believe that service lies in this – that each of us should use in the highest way, to the very widest possible extent, the abilities or powers they have been given.' The letter is intense, overwrought, vehemently answering accusations of selfishness and carelessness, and equally vehemently protesting her love for her mother and sorrow that she must anger and disappoint her.

In *Testament of Friendship* Vera Brittain describes a crisis of faith Winifred experienced in 1921 during their final year at Oxford: 'All that evening I sat in front of her fire while she knelt beside me with her face in my lap, and poured out the pent-up torment of her religious conflict.'[47] Winifred's letter to her mother was written not long after this, perhaps a release of some of the 'pent-up torment' of religious conflict Vera speaks of. Yet the torment was relatively short-lived and should perhaps be seen more as a rite of passage for a post-war, modern young woman than a sustained theological crisis. In any case, a goodly part of the torment lay not so much in doctrinal doubt, though that to some extent was present, as in the rejection of the habits and beliefs of her childhood, and of her mother's way of life. Certainly, in her later years Winifred seemed little concerned with questions of faith and doubt. After *The Runners*, her unpublished fictional study of the fourteenth-century priest Wycliff, which she began in early 1924, soon after this period of religious conflict, and which tried to express 'the agony of a fierce intelligence confined by the crabbed logic of the Schools',[48] Winifred never seriously wrote about theological issues again. She sometimes used mock-religious situations to explore moral questions, particularly those relating to the haunting sense of immunity from suffering and deprivation she harboured all her life. In one of her short stories, 'The Comforter', written in 1934, a man who was esteemed on earth as 'a staunch upholder of the righteous cause', has recently died and finds hell rather than heaven is 'his natural element' because 'Heaven is only tolerable for those who have learned to forgive themselves. [In hell] we may at least share the pain we have inflicted. We are not called upon to suffer the horror of immunity.'[49] Only seven pages long, and written in a snappy, journalistic style, the story jokingly uses religious points of reference – heaven and hell – as a means to express a quite profound sense of moral communism. Even *Eutychus; or The Future of the Pulpit*, her 'short treatise in the form of a plain dialogue' published in 1928, was a survey of moral alternatives open to the 'common man' rather than a religious exposition. Whatever impact the Anglican doctrine preached in All Saints Church, Rudston, had on her as a child, it seemed to fade into affectionate memories of social occasions, such as the visits of carol singers or harvest festival suppers. What remained was a religious sense of service, guilt and obligation which, as she grew increasingly agnostic, became ever more fiercely and fervently secularised into strivings after social reform.

But even in this respect, there would come to be differences between Winifred and her mother, relating particularly to women's role in the community. Although Alice Holtby's service on the East Riding County Council involved her with public concerns such as mental health (she was particularly active in the setting up of the new mental hospital, Broadgates, just outside Beverley), maternity clinics, sanitation and roads, the closeness of these concerns to the kind of private philanthropy she practised at home made them entirely acceptable. Winifred's London life, particularly her life as a writer, seemed unnervingly ambitious to her mother, and also public in a glamorous and self-advertising way. In the Prefatory Letter to *South Riding*, written to her mother, Winifred pays tribute to Local Authority work as 'the first-line defence thrown up by the community against our common enemies – poverty, sickness, ignorance, isolation, mental derangement, and social maladjustment'. But it remained for her a first-line defence; she wanted a more assertive and far-reaching role: 'To learn, to practise, to work, to see all I can, never to let my personal preoccupations come between me and the thing (whatever it is).'[50] The difference was between the Victorian mother and the daughter born at the very end of the Victorian age and moving into new freedoms and responsibilities. *South Riding*, which is Alice Holtby's book in ways other than its Prefatory Letter, dramatises this debate in the relationship between Mrs Beddows and her 'daughter' Sarah Burton. At the Beddows's Christmas family party that Sarah interrupts, she thinks angrily that even when the women of Mrs Beddows's generation 'gave one quarter of their energy to public service they spent the remaining three-quarters on quite unnecessary domestic ritual and propitiation. The little plump woman with the wise lined face might have gone anywhere, done anything; but she would always set limits upon her powers through her desire not to upset her husband's family.' The ensuing conversation about Lydia Holly opposes the older woman's resignation to the domestic sphere – 'There'll be one school teacher less, and perhaps one fine woman and wife the more' – and the younger one's belief 'in being used to the farthest limit of one's capacity'.

Alice Holtby's strengths and weaknesses were particularly evident to Winifred, and also particularly trying to her, at the time of David Holtby's death. Ailing for a long time, from a lung complaint which may have been tuberculosis, he entered a final stage of illness towards Christmas 1932, dying on 9 March 1933. Winifred was chronically ill herself by this time, yet she spent most of those months in Cottingham, 'being bored and sad [which] is better for me than feeling eager and alive as I do in London'. She did some writing (*The Astonishing Island*, in particular), planned *South Riding*, and generally was there for her mother's sake: 'Father is now very little conscious – under morphia most of the time. I am sitting by him now. . . . I sit here a few hours a day, I amuse Mother at meal times, and I live in a dream world of books, reviews, etc. . . . Mother does not seem keen for me to go. I think she is frightened herself of collapsing when the end comes, and wants me by her. After all, I do understand her better than anyone, and am prepared therefore to stand more from her strained nerves than anyone else.'[51]

What Winifred had to stand after her father's death was quite considerable and it took a form characteristic to Alice Holtby of energetic, efficient but exhausting organisation. The funeral involved a thirty-mile drive, in brilliant sunshine, to Bridlington. All the remaining Rudston farm servants came; it was solemn and fitting: 'Mother stoical & full of organising ability as usual but arranged a perfect memorial service, with *Nunc Dimittis* sung as they carried the coffin down the church between banks of flowers into the spring sunshine. All very touching.'[52] But after this Alice plunged into frantic activity as though all the slow months of illness and nursing had frustrated her usual energies which now spent themselves on modernising the house and on a holiday, accompanied by Winifred, in Scarborough: 'We are having the house all painted & electric light put in *now!* Swarms of people, workmen & relations all day. . . . Like a sort of factory of post-mortem activity,' Winifred wrote to Vera three days after the funeral. And three days later she wrote from Scarborough, an unusually complaining letter saying how tired and ill she felt, and how her mother's regime left no space for her own grief:

> to be the tactful go-between & lieutenant, never to be able
> to say *just* what one thinks, to compromise between con-
> flicting interests . . . to talk to relatives with whom I have
> not one thought in common, to write letters to people who
> are vague names to me – All this, combined with a blind,
> streaming cold, a small succession of quite trivial
> headaches, & the knowledge that if the heavens fall, my
> Schoolmistress, News Chronicle, & Notes on the Way arti-
> cles must be got off to time – have left me no ounce of
> energy for personal feelings. I have been an institution, not
> a person – never done except in bed, writing usually in a
> room full of people so that I can be on the spot if needed.

Three days later she apologised for this querulousness, but still the necessity for staying at home continued, amongst the chaos of a house ripped up by workmen, spring cleaners and painters and the need to visit relatives in Middleham, a 'nightmare' scene of an uncle 'drinking himself to death, the cousins quarrelling, Aunt Jane paralysed, Aunt Mary complaining', and in Bridlington

Grace's little girl, Anne, with congestion of the lungs. On one occasion, her mother being too tired to make a speech, Winifred had stood in for her impromptu at a mental home, and on another she and her mother took an old, impoverished ex-schoolteacher to a home in Bridlington to be looked after very inexpensively, on Alice's persuasion. Altogether it was 'a catalogue of disasters', 'an unending war of mortality against man's brittle life'. It was also the material she would draw on in *South Riding*, a novel freighted with all the disasters that can afflict a 1930s community: tuberculosis, cancer, death in childbirth, madness, paralysis, heart disease, and rural bankruptcy. But however valuable for her fiction, it was an experience which exhausted Winifred. Alice appears to have expected from her daughter all the attention and patience which a healthy person could give, and also one whose own life, as a single woman, must be subservient to the needs of her parents. Winifred tolerated – was glad to tolerate – her mother's demands knowing that she could eventually escape, that she did not have to be permanently her mother's companion. That role was filled by Edith de Coundouroff, now more than ever to be Alice's adopted daughter. If Edith had not been there, Winifred would have found escape less easy.

Alice Holtby's phenomenal energy, her managerial and autocratic tendencies, would be displayed again at the time of Winifred's death. Vera Brittain wrote bitterly about Alice 'holding court' in the room next to where Winifred lay dying, about her mania for 'arrangements', her insensitivity to the 'intense beauty and pathos' of the dedication to *South Riding* which was given to her five days before Winifred died,[53] and her attempt to prevent anyone being with Winifred when she actually died – ' "We can't do anything, and we should only be in the nurses' way. . . . You do agree about not being called," ' she said to Vera.[54] The determined cheerfulness and matter-of-factness of Alice's approach to life and to death – qualities Winifred of course shared with her mother – are unmistakably present in a letter she sent to the *Yorkshire Post* (very much *her* paper, as opposed to the London papers Vera valued):

> I should like everybody to know of the utmost joyous last days and hours. Winifred was so gallant, so determined there should be no 'sadness of farewell'. . . . For some days before the end she had no pain. . . . If the world is a happier place because she has lived in it, may I say to the many young people who have sought her help and advice that what she has done they can do – and she calls them to bear the torch which she may no longer hold. I can finish on no better note than was written by Annie Swan in her 'We Travel Home', just published:
>
> > *'God give me work till my life shall end*
> > *And life till my work is done.'*
>
> To you, each one, who loved her, just the thanks of
> > > Winifred's Mother.[55]

The Annie Swan quotation was used, at Alice Holtby's behest, as the epitaph on Winifred's tombstone in Rudston churchyard. '(But *was* her work done? No, oh *no*!),' as Vera pointedly remarked.[56] What else is odd and sad about Winifred's epitaph is the absence of any mention of her writing. Although the tombstone is in the shape of a book – but then so are many tombstones – the 'beautifully carved' words facing the Annie Swan quotation read: 'In loving memory of Winifred daughter of David and Alice Holtby. Died in London Sept 29th 1935 aged 37 years.' After all Alice's early promotion of Winifred's writing career, in death it is Winifred's role of daughter that is reclaimed.

This was the public face of grief that Alice showed. It is difficult to gauge her private response to Winifred's death. The few of her letters that survive describe how she 'suffered in Gethsemene &

stood by the Cross two years ago' but more vehemently they express her suffering at the embarrassment *South Riding* had caused her, an embarrassment so acute it seems to have been a major factor in her resigning her seat on the County Council:

> Nobody but Edith (& not even she fully) knows what price
> I have paid for all S.R. is doing in the world – educating
> women – employing hundreds of film people, printers &c
> &c &c it is such a travesty on any C.C. & on E.R. in partic-
> ular – 72 people without officials feel it to be so – & have
> been more than kind to me, but I could never have sat
> among them again – if only I could have seen it and made
> the book more like the film is[57] – & taken out parts (I don't
> mean the sex & vulgarities) but the parts that are . . . too
> near the truth *what* a difference it would have made & the
> book would have been just as popular – however I suffer
> alone, and have so many mercies that I may well bear it –
> *but* Hilda [Reid] darling I dont feel I can risk any more –
> Gladly have I suffered that she might be glorified & by her
> death speak to so many millions.[58]

To Alice, Vera was 'merciless' in her belief that 'literature must be served' and 'truth must be served' and she was apprehensive that the biography that Vera was writing would be as scandalous as she believed *South Riding* to have been. 'Vera *is* going to let you see what she writes is she not?' she wrote to Hilda Reid. 'Oh! that you were doing it – if it is to be done at all.'

For her part, Vera was only too well aware of Alice's opposition to the publication of *South Riding* which she attributed not just to fear of libel action but to Alice's jealousy of Winifred. 'Another letter from Mrs Holtby to Collins generally grousing at Winifred's prefatory letter [to *South Riding*] because it refers to her, and her public work that is apparently sacrosanct,' Vera wrote in 1936, having noted the year before, during the final days of Winifred's life, that Alice thought there was '"too much having been said" about W. in the papers already, and that when Grace and Mr Holtby died they were "Winifred Holtby's sister" and "Winifred Holtby's father" instead of themselves.'[59] What Vera describes as Alice's 'tendency to resent the importance of Winifred' must be viewed cautiously in the light of Vera's own resentment of Alice. Nevertheless, it does accord with aspects of Alice's personality and her outlook on life. As one powerful woman in relation to another, she may well have been envious of Winifred, as mothers sometimes are of their daughters, and this would have been exacerbated by the difference in their lifestyles. Winifred's success was alien to Alice; it was London-based rather than Northern, intellectual rather than practical, national and international rather than local. Their old conflict about ambition and notoriety was inevitably continued over Winifred's posthumous publications. Only Vera's determination to see *South Riding* through the press, and perhaps also Winifred's foresight in appointing Vera as her literary executor, rescued it from censorship or even non-publication.

When Alice died in 1939, Vera was busily finishing *Testament of Friendship* and arranging for a portrait of Winifred to be painted from photographs by Howard Lewis, to be reproduced in colour in the biography. She was also buying gas-masks for herself and her children amidst the increasing gloom of the international situation, and arranging to buy a country cottage at Lyndhurst in the New Forest. On 31 July, came a telegram from Edith de Coundouroff to say that Alice had 'died in her sleep early that morning'. It was, Vera wrote, 'very strange that Winifred's mother should die on the actual day that I completed my biography of her when I had been working on it for three years'. She and Gordon attended the funeral on 3 August at the Priory Church, Bridlington. Alice was buried with David and Grace; the inscription on her gravestone reads: 'She hath outsoared the shadow of night.'

CHAPTER 2

'A war casualty of the spirit': Harry Pearson

In *The Crowded Street*, war is described as coming to Marshington 'with the bewildering irrelevance of all great catastrophes'. The coming of war must have seemed an equally irrelevant catastrophe to Rudston, its impact registering slowly as men volunteered and were conscripted. The War Memorial in Rudston lists eleven men killed in the war, nine of them Rudston-born, the other two merely 'living in Rudston'. Winifred was sixteen and at home for the school holidays when England declared war on Germany on 4 August 1914. By the time she returned to school in September the battles of Mons and the Marne had been fought.

Winifred always maintained that she had a fortunate war; nobody close to her was killed and her war service with a signals unit saw none of the horrors of the front line. Her easy passage contributed to her sense of immunity from suffering and provided the greatest contrast, so she thought, between her life and Vera Brittain's. But the war did affect her in one important respect in its influence on Harry Pearson, the boy who had been a regular visitor to Rudston House with his younger brother, Wilfred, from the nearby town of Driffield.

Born in March 1897, and therefore a year older than Winifred, Henry Lindam Pearson was the son of a bank manager, and it was probably through the bank that he and his family got to know the Holtbys. He and Wilfred came to play games in the stackyard, to take part in the theatricals Winifred devised, and generally, as Vera Brittain deseibes it, 'took the place of brothers at the farm'. Even when Harry and his brother left their local school to attend Rossall School, near Fleetwood in Lancashire, the visits to Rudston continued during the vacations. Like Winifred, Harry had literary aspirations. Twenty years later, Winifred recalled how he and she had visited the vicar's wife in Rudston to meet her sister, the classicist and anthropologist Jane Harrison: 'She was the first Great Woman whom I had ever met. . . . Together with a schoolboy friend, I was invited up to tea with her. The schoolboy friend wrote good boyish verse, which had been shown to the Great Jane. . . . She said that he had an "unusual gift of language." Then we were both delighted with the compliment. Had we understood further her passion for linguistic beauties, we should have been further pleased.'[1]

The public school Harry attended, Rossall School, was founded in 1844, with the intention of being the 'Northern Church of England Public School',[2] for the sons of clergy and laymen who sought a modern as well as a classical education. In an exposed, sea-blown position, the school was renowned for its 'bracing atmosphere' and its orderly, even regimented, discipline. Like many boys' public schools of the time, Rossall repressed sexuality of all kinds – housemasters were not allowed to marry, for instance – although comradely and even romantic feelings between boys were encouraged, along with the hero-worship of men of action and of sporting prowess. The homosexual writer Joe Ackerley was a pupil there shortly before Harry and described as typical his own confused adolescent experiences:

[I was] more repelled than attracted to sex, which seemed

to me a furtive, guilty, soiling thing, exciting, yes, but nothing whatever to do with those feelings which I had not yet experienced but about which I was already writing a lot of dreadful sentimental verse, called romance and love.[3]

Harry entered Rossall in the second term of 1912 when he would have been almost fifteen. He spent three years there, leaving in 1915 having passed the Cambridge 'Little Go' and securing a place at Selwyn College. According to his school records, he was a monitor, had colours in rugby and hockey and played for a school cricket team. A surviving photograph of him as a young man shows him in open-necked shirt, fair-haired, lean and bronzed. In 1913 and 1914, he won the school prize for English verse. The school magazine, 'The Rossallian', printed his poems: a group about Scott's Antarctic expedition, another group about Ulster, and several single ones, all of a patriotic and religious cast. A typical example, printed alongside a prose piece commemorating a Rossallian killed in action, is 'Self-Contemplation', dated February 1916, by which time he had left the school:

> O Youth of mine! To live, to laugh, to love,
>   Whilst all my boyhood rises into song,
> And – the fair earth beneath and heaven above –
>   Its wild pulsation drives my heart along . . .

> O Life of mine! so dread and mystical!
>   Thy peace, the faith in fuller things to be;
> Thy joy, the hope illuminating all;
>   Thy tears, the birthpangs of Eternity:
> And, binding all to Heaven, a mystic span,
>   Fixed and omnipotent, the Soul of Man.

Harry would write poems all his life, including, crucially, a group of romantic poems to Winifred during 1916, which she did not at

the time take seriously. He was, according to Vera, 'deeply, irre-
trievably wounded' at her 'breezy schoolgirl scepticism' and
Winifred came to think that perhaps he never forgave her for this
slight. But it is difficult to believe that even if she had responded
more positively, the progress of their love story would have been
different. Harry's restless character, an impractical mixture of
idealism and cynicism, the kind of education he received and his
experiences of the war, combined to make him unreliable and
nervous of commitment, 'as wary as a bird in a bush', in the words
of one of his friends.

Rossall School had strong military connections and a thriving
OTC and it was almost inevitable that Harry would enlist as soon
as he left school rather than take up his place at Selwyn College.
He apparently told Winifred in 1916 of 'all the enormities he had
seen at the front' but though he may have heard about enormities,
he had in fact seen little front-line action by 1916. The Army
Lists show that he was commissioned as a 2nd Lieutenant in 4th
(Extra Reserve) Battalion, the Prince of Wales's Own (West
Yorkshire Regiment) on 10 June 1915. Extra Reserve Battalions
were used for training men for overseas service and the 4th
Battalion remained in Hartlepool throughout the war. Harry was
probably posted from it to 1st Battalion of the West Yorkshires
which had been in France for nearly a year. At this early stage of
his war service, he seems to have been stationed in France for only
a few weeks, returning home with a wounded shoulder 'in the
Easter holidays of 1916'.[4] He thereby missed the 'minor enterprise', as it was called in official language, in which the Battalion
was involved during late May along the Yser Canal, north of Ypres;
losses were quite heavy for a relatively small undertaking, with
eleven killed and twenty-six wounded.[5] By 1917 he had been
posted to the 11th Battalion, and may well have taken part in June
in the Battle of Ypres in which the Battalion suffered the heavy loss
of 260 men killed. It could have been here that he sustained the
second injury that Vera Brittain mentions, a bullet wound 'which

barely avoided permanent damage to one of his eyes'. Harry was promoted to Lieutenant on 1 July 1917, and then probably went with the Battalion to Italy in the early part of 1918 where it remained until the end of the war. The main offensive for the Battalion was the Asiago front, with particularly fierce fighting in June and July through to October. It was on the Asiago plateau that Vera Brittain's brother Edward was killed in June 1918. The fact that she doesn't mention this in describing Harry's war service could suggest that he wasn't with the Battalion at this time; or perhaps, by comparison with Edward's death, Harry's presence seemed not worth mentioning. The 11th Battalion was disbanded in 1919 and Harry was transferred back to the 1st Battalion and then to 4th Battalion. His last appearance in the Army List is in 1920. During these last months in the army he is likely to have been based in York.

After the war Harry became the restless 'war casualty of the spirit' of Vera's description, refusing to take up his place at Selwyn College, making little attempt to find an occupation in keeping with his education, always short of money, disaffected and rootless. In the Rossall School register for 1923, the entry says 'Forestry in Nova Scotia' and in the Club book for 1924 he gave an address in Mexico, calling himself 'tutor'. This confirms Vera's account, although in reverse order, that after a period of 'half-heartedly exploring the discouraging possibilities of free-lance journalism . . . he accepted the post of tutor to the two nephews of a Mexican bishop, and sailed for South America'. She continues: '[He then] worked his way intrepidly to a Canadian lumber camp, and for a time disappeared so completely that Winifred did not know whether he was alive or dead.'[6] There is indeed a telling silence surrounding him in Winifred's correspondence during the early 1920S, but after 1924, when he had returned to England, he starts to feature in the letters between Winifred and Vera, partly because of their attempts to settle him into work, and partly because he became a frequent if unreliable visitor, both in London and

Cottingham. An example of his unreliability was his failure to attend Vera's wedding in 1925, after promising to be there. Apparently he had arrived at the church door but seeing how 'posh' it was, 'I decided I couldn't live up to it, so I went back to Peckham,' to his lodgings.

In 1926 he joined the Royal Air Force and served as an aircraftman on the north-west frontier of India. By his own account, he was in the same squadron in Peshawar in India as T.E. Lawrence – 'I knew him well. He lent me books and discussed them with me' – but Lawrence was posted to Peshawar for only two days and it seems unlikely that Harry knew him other than as a passing acquaintance.[7] He apparently wrote to Winifred about this meeting: 'Harry is in India with Colonel Lawrence – now with the flying corps in Karachi,' she told Gordon Catlin,[8] in January 1927; and the next month she told Jean McWilliam that 'H. is in India with Lawrence of Arabia, so he has found his romance at last. He is happier than he has ever been, he says; and is writing a series of pseudo-Blake prose poems about God. He has the detachment of a genius without the creative power. Sometimes I think that will come . . . He says Lawrence denies "time and space."'[9] Harry's own comments, delivered nearly thirty years later, are not informative about his relationship with Lawrence: 'But [Lawrence's] troubles were his own fault, you know. He was a bit daft. I mean, fancy suddenly appearing in a Service mess dressed in Arab costume. Well, the chaps would think, "Who's this wog?" And if they said anything to him he would be likely to reply with a joke in Greek. He was a difficult man to like.'[10] Whatever the facts of Harry's relationship with Lawrence, by the time John Catlin, Vera's son, published *Family Quartet* in 1987, the legend of Harry's friendship with T.E. Lawrence was fully established. 'Harry became a loner,' Catlin wrote; 'it is significant that his best friend in the R.A.F. in India was T.E. Lawrence, another, if more spectacular loner.'[11] To a man of Harry's romantic disposition, it must have been tempting to exalt a passing acquaintanceship into friendship. Lawrence during the interwar period and in the 1940s was indeed a romantic figure, a 'lost leader', who many thought might have saved Europe from another war. In a review[12] in April 1934 of an early biography of Lawrence Winifred herself suggests as much, agreeing with the book's conviction that Lawrence 'could, if he would, be a light to lead stumbling humanity out of its troubles'. She makes the contrast between Lawrence and Hitler, whose leadership ambitions had been celebrated in Goering's recently published *Germany Reborn*. The best men, like Lawrence, she says, are reluctant to lead, leaving the world to be dominated by the worst.

Winifred's relationship with Harry, begun in childhood when he came to play at her father's farm, seems to have been subject during their adolescence to some pressure or expectation, particularly from his family, that they would eventually marry.[13] Winifred certainly met him occasionally in London during 1918 when she was working as a WAAC at the New Zealand Officers' Club in Hill Street, and when he, presumably, was on leave from his Battalion. In a letter to her parents[14] she mentions getting a pass to be allowed out with him from 12.30 to 7.30 in a manner which suggests this is not an exceptional occurrence. According to expectations of the time, this would mean that he was her 'boy friend' (a term Winifred would herself use about him for the rest of her life, although often ironically) and that an engagement would be likely to follow. But instead, in late 1920, Harry left for Nova Scotia and on the boat going out there he became engaged to a young woman pianist whose 'pretty, fragile, penniless, dependent' state appealed to him more than Winifred's sturdy self-sufficiency could do. Harry's engagement was short-lived but its effect on Winifred was cautionary – Harry could never quite be trusted again – and painful. Her reaction was given to Vera Brittain in a letter written from Cottingham during the Christmas vacation of 1920–1, only some of which Vera quotes in *Testament of Friendship*. The letter is a brave attempt to be generous, unsentimental, to believe all is for the best, and, understandably, to shrug off the role of abandoned woman. Nevertheless, it is full of hurt, and of the painful cheerfulness and altruistic stoicism that will characterise Winifred's responses to misfortune and unhappiness in the years to come.

> He never gave me any sign that he cared for me beyond other people, except the poems & one conversation with mother about four years ago. These I deliberately laughed at – told him to his face he was soppy – & quite firmly and definitely quashed any romance that might hang round me. Even then I knew, you see, in my heart of hearts, that what he loved was a dream woman whom he called by my name because he knew no-one else. And I would not accept his identification of me with his dreams until we had both proved ourselves; for, if he was uncertain of his love for me, I was still more uncertain of mine for him. And we have proved ourselves. I've seen a photograph of Irene [Harry's fiancée] & she is far more like the girl he dreamed of than I could ever be – not only because she is small & slim & dark & wistful, but because . . . she loves him as I should never have done – as a wife should – not as a rather patron-ising & superior friend, who, while she reserves the right to criticise, still harbours a secret desire for all the romantic trimmings of life.
>
> He was right – he had a perfect right to love whom he liked. I set myself at work to leave him perfectly free from the first moment I knew he loved me. The most incriminat-ing thing I ever did was to send him that poem, & by the time that came he had been rendered invulnerable by a real love, not a broken dream. . . . And I realise now what I sus-pected before, that I had no more love for him than for a friend – & that I still have, only stronger because it is clear of all illusions – about myself, not him. I only wanted romance. I felt a bit 'Dead Mannish', so played with the

most romantic thing that ever happened to me, until I
almost believed it was real – almost, not quite.
    All the same, I meant my poem, & I'm glad you like it.

The letter continues with a hectic account of Christmas festivites
and of her intention to avoid some of them because of the need to
work for examinations. The poem she mentions as having sent to
Harry was 'The Dead Man', which was published in the 1920
number of *Oxford Poetry*:

> I see men walk wild ways with love,
> Along the wind their laughter blown
> Strikes up against the singing stars –
> But I lie all alone.
>
> When love has stricken laughter dead
> And tears their silly hearts in twain,
> They long for easeful death, but I
> Am hungry for their pain.

Vera described this as 'entirely typical of the disillusioned, sar-
donic element in [Winifred's] character which always lay beneath
the benevolent surface but only began to reach its full intellectual
expression in her final years'[15] but this seems to misread both the
poem and Winifred's struggle in the next few years to come to
terms with Harry's defection. The lessons she taught herself from
the experience were several: that love should not be importunate,
that love denied could be sublimated into work or an appreciation
of moral beauty, that it is more fulfilling to love than be loved, and
that rejection should be faced stoically and without spreading
misery to others. Winifred worked through these lessons in her
writing; even, perhaps particularly, in *South Riding* they are dwelt
on in the failed love affair of Sarah Burton and Robert Carne: 'If he
had loved me, even for an hour, she sometimes thought, this [her

grief at his death] would not have been unendurable.' But some of her early stories harboured an optimism about a union with Harry and blamed his apparent indifference, as women's love stories often do, on misunderstanding and on reticence on the man's part. 'When Brenda Came Home', one of the chapters in her unpublished wartime sequence 'The Forest Unit', follows a triangular relationship in which Brenda, a WAAC, brings an Australian soldier friend home with her from war duty, creating gossip amongst the villagers and dismay in Captain Cartwright, the badly wounded war veteran who had been Brenda's boyfriend before the war. All works out well in the end; the Australian has a fiancée back home, Brenda and Cartwright overcome his reluctance to burden her with a cripple like himself, and the story ends with their engagement.

Winifred's relation to Harry during the mid-1920s, after his return from abroad, was carefully non-possessive yet also anxious to be helpful, to give him some anchorage in life and prospect of a career. She made several attempts to find work for him, rarely successful, primarily because he didn't want to be managed by her, or by Vera either. 'I'm having a rough crossing with him at the moment,' she wrote to Jean McWilliam in April 1925. 'This boy's older than I, and has such a sensitive pride, and I find it so damned hard to persuade him a) that he is getting on splendidly all on his own; b) that I'm not falling in love with him.' If only she were, she protests with her customary bravado: 'I'd be quite grateful if he or any one else would raise a flutter in my heart. I really shall be disappointed if I go through life without once being properly in love.'[16] Her attempts to rationalise her attitude to him prompted her to begin 'germinating in my head' a play to be called ' "The Public Woman" . . .with its subtle suggestion of the improper.' This germ of a play both analyses her feelings for Harry after his return to England and foretells their future relationship. The heroine of 'The Public Woman' is thirty-five, university educated, has been a teacher until left money by her father when she moves to

Hardrascliffe (the name Winifred habitually gave to a composite version of Scarborough and Bridlington) to take up public work, and become Alderman and Mayor:

> And then the lover of her youth – the clever boy, musical, a
> poet, son of a small solicitor, to whom she was secretly
> engaged until the war – who has never had a job since the
> war, but been tossed from place to place, sensitive, artistic,
> slightly cynical, drinking a little but gracefully enough –
> returns 'broke' to Hardrascliffe on the night of the banquet
> & comes to the reception with his parents who are trying
> not to be ashamed of him. You must have the surge of her
> pity, maternal instinct and strongly passionate nature – for a
> long time suppressed and stifled by public work – all sud-
> denly aroused again by the sight of him. He, slightly bitter,
> cynical about both of them, yet finding strength and ease in
> her confident self-sufficiency, balm for his tortured nerves
> in her calm security. Her attempts to get him a job in the
> town – His inefficiency & embezlement.[17]

After stormy scenes, he disappears again, 'taking with him some gift of warmth and beauty & tenderness, & she returns to her committees, her uplift, her safeguarding of the town's morality'. There won't be a resolution, only the portrait of a clash 'that should not be a clash'. It would be a comedy, she insisted, '& you shall laugh at my poor tortured creatures with their loves and con-sciences, even while you weep for them'.[18]

During his six years in the Royal Air Force, Harry kept in touch with Winifred, visiting the Holtby home at Cottingham when on leave. By this time Winifred could be both more relaxed and more realistic in her accounts of him: 'He is charming, inconsequential, loveable and unstable.' She thought he was throwing himself away into a life which lacked intellectual companionships, and of which, 'in theory, he disapproves'.[19] Perhaps this is why she dedicated *The*

Land of Green Ginger, published in 1927, to Harry: 'To a philosopher in Peshawar who said he wanted something to read.' In July 1932 he left the RAF to return to England, to base his life in his mother's home in Driffield, although often to wander around the country living rough, and apparently keen to re-establish some kind of relationship with Winifred: '[He] has written suddenly the most charming letters. He's beyond me,' she wrote to Vera. What occupied her now more than ever in the relationship was the need to find work for him, and a settled life of some kind. 'Collins [the publisher] rang last night,' she wrote in December 1932. 'He had been so personally charmed by Harry that he now wants to try to lure him into the London office. He said, "I suppose it's no use trying to persuade him to come to Glasgow again. But we all liked him so much that the loss is ours". In these days of unemployment, I could *slap* Harry. But what it is to have charm.'[20]

Her concern for Harry's future, and also an acceptance on her part that he was unlikely to marry her, and even that she no longer wanted to marry him, is present in her novel *Mandoa, Mandoa!*, where he features as Bill, the elder of the two Durrant brothers, his mother's favourite, whose body is 'temporarily disabled' by the war and his nerves 'permanently deranged. . . . He walked with a slight limp, talked wildly, drank too much, [and] expressed the most outrageous opinions about war, politics, morals and the academic life.' Winifred wrote this novel during the onset of her fatal illness and Harry's renewed presence in her life at this time therefore coincided with a period of introspection and of assessment of what was important in the remaining time she might have. In its depiction of the Bill/Harry figure, *Mandoa, Mandoa!* is full of contradictory impulses and analyses. His physical appeal is registered – the 'tall, wiry figure, the finely-drawn features [and] light, curving smile' – but so is his dissipation, 'finally accepted as a ne'er-do-weel'. He is also seen as exploitative, particularly of the Jean/Winifred character, 'feeding upon her, demanding from her, yet always remaining just sufficiently detached to give her nothing in return, to place upon her all initiative for greater intimacy'. Yet the inconclusiveness of their relationship is partly her fault too: 'though she had not sent him away, she could never yield completely. Always, even while lending him her knowledge and her practical sense, she had felt the unsleeping clock of criticism beat in her brain . . . marking his faults, her withdrawals, the time that both were wasting, the energy they spilled.' But the feckless Bill Durrant in *Mandoa, Mandoa!* is transformed into a useful servant of the new state of Lolagoba, 'upheld by no ideal of ultimate perfection' yet with the almost god-like powers of bringing 'the three great gifts of civilisation – Profit, Power, Pity'. It is as though to Harry's physical and temperamental characteristics Winifred added a touch of T.E. Lawrence, ennobling with a sense of purpose the story she makes out of Harry's life in *Mandoa, Mandoa!* The idealism he had as a boy is given a fictional realisation.

But in life, whatever was found for him seemed either not to be taken up or not to last. This did mean that he was frequently to be found in Yorkshire, and a frequent visitor to Cottingham, something of a son to Alice Holtby, or perhaps a grandson because, like Vera, he called her Granny. He was on hand and particularly helpful during the period of David Holtby's last illness and death in the early spring of 1933: he was, Winifred wrote to Vera, 'running errands & being a general lamb'. In the period after her father's death, Harry's charming and slightly irresponsible company soothed and refreshed her, and though his solicitude was in the way of small impersonal attentions, and he treated her as 'a cross between a queen & a prize pekinese', there were some golden times. One day in particular she wrote of to Vera:

> an exquisite day – the sort of thing one only expects in
> youth, & never hopes for at Cottingham. . . . Harry took
> me by train to Beverley, & we arrived too early for tea, so
> went to look at the carvings in St Mary's – & he told me
> absurd stories of what all the carvers were thinking about

when they made the pictures on the pews. Then to his
cousins [and afterwards] for a walk on the Westwood to an
oakwood I never knew existed, full of wood anemones –
lovely – & stayed till the moon rose & talked nonsense.
Then went back to supper . . . Nothing in it perhaps, but a
lovely & happy time – perfectly at ease & Harry completely
himself.[21]

But the next month he was far away in Cornwall, 'writing, & for
the first time really placing articles, & happy, I think'.

During the last two years of Winifred's life, she and Harry
seemed to draw closer together. Winifred's three-month sojourns
on the East Coast – Withernsea in 1934 and Hornsea in 1935 –
made it easy for him to visit her. She chose these places because
she needed time to rest and write away from London and they
were conveniently near to her mother in Cottingham and the tribe
of Holtby and Winn relations who always seemed to be in need of
attention. But there must surely have been the hope that the
Yorkshire environment, not Rudston itself but not far away, might
recreate their early intimacy. And to some extent it did. In April
1934, she wrote to Vera that Harry had been to stay and had gone
away that morning, as footloose as ever:

I am a fool to want more than I get from him. What I have
is so gay, foolish & charming – something everyone needs –
a frivolity, an enchantment, a relaxation. Then, in his black
moods, he revolts both against & towards me, does & does
not want me. Is not going to Spain. Is going to Norway.
Took me to Hull, to the Tivoli. We heard an idiotic music
hall show. He introduced me to a bar maid of 57, a friend
of his, & the assistant manager of a 3rd rate provincial
music hall. Well, I have got out of the episode a red rose &
another scene for South Riding. . . . I can't pretend I don't
owe him far more than he owes me. I love every tone of his

voice, every movement of his hands. And I wouldn't *not* love him for anything. But it is, I suppose, a humiliating & ridiculous situation for a woman of my age, intelligence & interests.[22]

In her journalism that year she records something of his anti-bourgeois philosophy, and also gives a glimpse of the kind of conversations they must have had:

I have a friend who would, he declares, abolish by law those curtains and clusters of aspidistra leaves which veil the great majority of our private apartments from the public eye. He declares that . . . the close corporate intimacy of an Indian village is far more human, than the exclusive, private, keep-ourselves-to-ourselves life of the English suburb. . . . He would tear down curtains and garden hedges, make every citizen live in the full light of sociable publicity and cure us for ever, he declares, of the furtive reticences, our mean economies of imagination, and our narrow niceness of detachment.[23]

Perhaps emboldened by this kind of permissive talk Winifred seems to have forced their relationship towards a sexual resolution during her stay in Withernsea. It may be that she had attempted this earlier, in 1932, telling Phyllis Bentley that she had spent a depressing evening with 'my-young-man-who-will-never-be-more-than-my-young-man'. She suddenly knew, she said, what her next novel (*South Riding*, in fact) would be about.[24] It is possible that the idea for the unconsummated sexual relationship in the novel sprang from this depressing evening with Harry. The evidence is clearer on the later occasion. Writing in November 1934 to Vera, who was at the time physically attracted to George Brett, her American publisher, and wondering whether she should tell him so, Winifred said that her own 'situation with Harry' had had no such 'maidenly hesitations' as Vera describes. 'We had a complete crisis at Withernsea – my doing. I decided that the time had come to abandon pride, convention & all the rest of it. I am glad I did.' In responding to Vera's dilemma over George Brett Winifred says that giving in to physical passion may get it out of her system. 'Only sometimes that means getting it *into* the system. Physical fascination can be powerfully increased by a really adequate lover. I don't know. I have no advice to give or wisdom to share.'[25] It is difficult to interpret what Winifred means here. Was Harry an adequate lover? Or was the crisis of a different kind that she would transform in *South Riding* into Carne's inability to make love to Sarah because of his heart attack? Vera was so preoccupied with her own situation that as far as the letters are concerned she didn't probe Winifred's remarks, and her subsequent writings about Winifred offer no information on the sexual nature of her relationship with Harry. Margaret Ballard assumed that Harry was homosexual but this was based rather more on conjecture than evidence. The tolerance of different kinds of sexuality in *South Riding* perhaps suggests that Winifred would not have wanted Harry to be labelled so categorically; it is the variety and variability of sex, from lusty Mr Huggins to repressed, probably homosexual Councillor Snaith, which constitute its interesting and mysterious nature. As she would write at the end of *Women*, 'We do not even know – though we theorise and penalise with ferocious confidence – whether the "normal" sexual relationship is homo- or bi- or hetero-sexual.' Even more pertinently, she wrote in 1935, in a review for *Good Housekeeping* of a book on Christina of Sweden, that 'like most adults [Christina] was capable of both homosexual and heterosexual relationships'.

Whatever happened in Withernsea in the spring of 1934, by the autumn of the year Harry was once again distant from her: 'I fear I have bullied him out of love into positive dislike. Ah well, we must follow our natures, & if he had liked me better, he would have enjoyed the bullying.'[26] When they did meet, he was in a 'lethargy of complete hopelessness. I seem to beat with all my energy against a barrier of despair. He is so sweet, so generous, so gentle, so anxious to cause no trouble, & so impossible to help or comfort. It is like loving the dead to love someone you can't touch or help.'[27] His attitude made her envious of those who could help their lovers, even if this meant sadness: 'Joan Temple's man, St John Lucas, has died. He has been the centre of her life for years. Yet lucky Joan. She could do something for him.'[28]

But by the spring of 1935, the relationship had revived again, possibly on less demanding terms from Winifred. In March Harry invited himself to Hornsea: 'I never asked him. I want him & don't want him. I want to WORK,' Winifred wrote. She took herself vigorously in hand, she said, '& decided that if I could not have what I wanted, I would want what I could have. It is undignified and ridiculous to regret or complain, & I am damned if I won't enjoy everything.' She had been watching planes at bombing practice over the North Sea, and this seemed to her like a rehearsal for pandemonium. 'Life is so short,' she wrote. 'The menace of horror is over us all so completely; that to waste time on self-pity seems extremely unintelligent.' As his visit drew near, she wrote to Vera, 'I have written across my heart, "I will not be dismayed." And the curious result is that, at the moment, I am not. After all, it is loving and not being loved, which is the vitalising experience. I will give him anything that he is prepared to take, though I think that this is very little, & be thankful that at least I have known what it is to love.'[29] As it turned out the visit was a success, she told Vera three days later: 'Harry really was so sweet that he made everything easy. It was by chance the one really warm & glorious spring day. We walked 11 miles & sat & smoked on a rifle range & watched aeroplanes bombing a target in the sea. It was curiously like being back in the war.' As a postscript to these pleasant times, Winifred wrote to Vera, still miserable about George Brett:

My long & often painful experience has taught me this –

that passion can become friendship. I don't say without
heartache – yes, & physical ache. But then one never
expects it to be without heartache, & I personally have
never known it to be without some humiliation. That is a
quality you have rarely had occasion to experience; but I
assure you that one need allow it only to affect a very small
area of one's consciousness, & need not affect the relationship to the person involved at all.[30]

When Winifred wrote this in April 1935 she had only five months
to live. During the late spring and summer of the year she came
back to London and continued her normal life as best she could:
journalism, finishing her novel, being involved in Vera's family
and their problems, collecting funds for her African enterprise.
When she became too ill to remain at home, and was taken into a
nursing home for the last nineteen days of her life, Vera
telegraphed Harry when it became obvious that Winifred was crit-
ically ill and unlikely to recover. She had asked for him. He came
the next day, 24 September, in a brown tweed suit, 'blue-eyed,
bronzed & handsome like an Army Major'.

What is known of the final days of the relationship between
Winifred and Harry is dependent almost entirely on Vera's account,
in particular the diary she kept during this period. Vera's wishes for
Winifred, her desire to write a happy ending to this uncertain and
unsatisfactory love story, undoubtedly influenced her record and
make it difficult to be sure how willing a participant Winifred was
in the narrative Vera constructed for her. It is, however, easy to be
sure that Harry was an unwilling participant. This is not to say that
his affection for Winifred would not have brought him voluntarily
to her bedside. But the pledges he was persuaded to make were
contrary to his characteristic habits and behaviour, and it is overwhelmingly likely that if he made them he did so only because by
now everyone was sure that Winifred was dying.

According to Vera, then, who would give the title of 'Since

journeys end . . .' to the penultimate chapter of *Testament of Friendship*, Winifred was 'in rapture' because Harry had come. He sat by her bed holding her hand, and seemed to be the person she wanted to sit with her during the night, which he did. The next day, 26 September, she told Vera of the happiness it had given her to have Harry with her, adding that Vera was not to think she loved him more than her but 'quite differently'. He sat with her again the next night. During the following day, in talking to Vera, Winifred wondered if Harry might be willing to look after her, if she recovered, even if he might be willing to marry her. This conversation, two days before Winifred died, convinced Vera that the one thing Winifred still wanted to make her life complete was an assurance of Harry's love and for them to become engaged: 'Harry must be persuaded to play his part before it was too late.'[31] The person who persuaded Harry to play his part was Gordon, Vera's husband, who, according to Margaret Ballard, offered Harry money to do this deed. Harry told Gordon at the dinner they had together to discuss the proposition, that 'without ever having been violently attracted to Winifred sexually (he prefers temporary diversions with the venal, apparently) he had always thought he would marry her in the end – when he would mind the contrast between their positions less. Gordon said how important it was for W.'s happiness that Harry should speak to her now . . . Harry agreed.'[32] After Harry's proposal visit on 28 September, Vera received a message from Winifred: 'Yes, all through,' which Vera interpreted as meaning that Harry had loved her always. She did not see Winifred in a conscious state again, the doctor having administered morphia during the early afternoon. The only person whom Winifred saw before she became unconscious was her mother, who apparently told Vera that Winifred had ecstatically told her that Harry wanted to marry her: 'It's just an understanding between us – no engagement,' she had said.

The diary entries Vera made during Winifred's last days formed the basis of her account in *Testament of Friendship*, with slight

embellishments. In *Testament of Friendship*, Winifred is reported as
saying to her mother, 'Mummie, when I'm better, [Harry] and I are
going to get married. It's just an understanding between us – not
really an engagement.' After Mrs Holtby had assured her how
delighted she was, Winifred apparently 'repeated happily, "Not an
engagement — just an understanding," as the doctor came into the
room.' The diary entry doesn't give the repetition, and it also
expresses a regret that the information was not given to Vera direct,
in other words that it was reported, like the 'Yes, all through' message that Vera had earlier received: 'When I heard she'd been given
the morphia already, something died in me. I realised then how
deeply I'd been counting on seeing her conscious and herself once
more & hearing about Harry from her own lips. It was pure selfishness, of course; but I just wanted to feel that I'd been the
instrument of bringing her the one happiness she had wanted all
her life and never had.'[33] In *Testament of Friendship*, any doubts
about the substance of Winifred's last words are omitted and
Winifred dies 'in the belief that the elusive happiness which had so
often mocked her was to be hers at last'.

There are apparently no other remaining, detailed accounts of
Winifred's death than these by Vera. If Harry ever wrote one, or
Alice Holtby, nothing of them seems to have survived. Vera's
intense desire to write a love story for Winifred has therefore led
to a definitive version which imposes a romantic ending on
Winifred's life, but also depicts her as deluded in her final hours
and dying in a kind of sanctification which is difficult to believe
she would have approved of: 'She died in her sleep just as dawn
was breaking over London. It was the last Sunday in September
and a gentle, radiant morning.' Against this must be placed an
account by Lady Rhondda which restores to Winifred the interests
and preoccupations which dominated her life and which dominated even the clouded and sightless hours of her last days. When
Margaret Rhondda had visited her in the nursing home, about a
week before she died, when 'her mind was near the border-land of

vagueness', Winifred had said 'there was something she particularly wanted to say to me' about an employee in a certain big firm 'who had given her reason to believe that the conditions were wrong and unjust. Would I have the thing fairly investigated and, if it were true, see that it was shown up in *Time and Tide*.'[34] When Margaret Rhondda reviewed *Testament of Friendship* for *Time and Tide* in 1940, she made two comments concerning the relation between Winifred and Harry: that she remembered sitting on Winifred's bed, on the last morning of her life, feeding her with tea, and discussing marriage with Harry; and that she disagreed with Vera's interpretation of the relationship in *Testament of Friendship*, that she didn't believe Harry counted for as much or as continuously as Vera thought.[35]

There is no doubt that what Winifred described as her 'long & often painful experience' with Harry Pearson was important to her. Other men found her likeable and may have wanted to marry her: James Anderson, for example, the widower of Stella Benson, began a mild courtship of her in 1934 but although she found him interesting and was flattered by his interest in her, 'I don't find him a quarter so physically attractive as Harry, no one I have yet met is so, to me.'[36] The evidence suggests that, however briefly and unsatisfactorily, they were sexual lovers, and that this intensified the bond between them for Winifred. But perhaps more important to her than this was that Harry was the lover of her youth, belonging to her childhood, to Rudston, to her father's farm and her mother's household. In August 1932, the year before her father's death, she and her parents had a 'curious *pre-war* evening' when they visited Rudston after a gap for Winifred of many years. They met some of her father's old employees, and everything seemed the same, 'so familiar that part of me seems to fit into [the] hills and hollows as one does into a familiar and well-hollowed bed'. As they drove along in the twilight on the road where she used to meet the Pearson boys, 'we saw a familiar figure striding along' and it was Harry, newly back from India, like a ghost, it must have seemed, from the days of her youth and the time of her strength and unclouded optimism. Such old ties mattered to her; rootedness and long familiarity were a counterbalance to her otherwise adventurous and modern life, and in her dying days, her mind often dimmed by pain and drugs, she wanted near to her those whom she'd known longest, however disappointing and exacting they may sometimes have been: her mother, Harry, Vera. The unsuitability of a match between her and Harry had never escaped her; as she said as early as 1920, when Harry had become engaged to another woman, she would have made him a poor wife, being more like a 'rather patronising & superior friend' but one who nevertheless 'harbours a secret desire for all the romantic trimmings of life'. As he became more cynical and disaffected, his political opinions and his whole attitude to life diverged more and more from hers: 'Harry calls all Negroes "niggers," & all little music hall chorus girls "pretty little tarts," & thinks another war might give him a job. Well . . . As I say, it's educative,' she told Vera in March 1934.

At Winifred's memorial service at St Martin-in-the-Fields on 1 October 1935, Harry came with the Holtby family and sat at the end of the pew nearest the altar, with Vera at the end of the pew opposite, across the aisle. When the coffin, with its long cross of violets, came to rest for the service, it did so between Harry and Vera, the two people, Vera wrote, 'whom I think she loved best'. Harry joined her and Gordon for tea but it doesn't seem that he travelled with them that evening to Cottingham, in readiness for the journey to Rudston the next day for the burial service. A letter remains from him to Alice Holtby after Winifred's death, undated but from the time of the publication of *Letters to a Friend* in 1937: 'I am reading W's letters from the end of the book, backwards. Which is, I feel, the way to read them. Success that is mere success (and there was none of that, thank God, in Winifred) may go fresh-field-conquering in all its glory. I (& I feel that W. did too) follow the music of a different drum, to fields less hard, less rolled,

less dusty. I read her letters backwards, because after all Life is a journey back to our beginnings, to the only field that is at the last, the green pasture of the waters of comfort. God bless you. Harry.'
He also at some point wrote a poem, 'To Winifred':

> Somewhere among those lovely sleeping hills
> You dwell;
> And if I wander to the highest rills,
> And call you by the name we loved so well,
> From hill to hill your voice would ring as clear
> As though were here . . .
>
> But not till daylight trembles into dusk,
> And earth and sky are knit in harmony,
> And stillness like soft rain descends,
> And time is lost in beauty's heart;
> Not till then,
> I see you as a part
> Of sunset and the vast silence of the stars.[37]

It is difficult not to believe that, at least at the height of her powers, Winifred would have reacted with some scepticism to the romantic and religiose sentiments of the letter and the poem. Did he understand her life so little that he could describe it in the bland, pastoral terms of the letter or the vague pantheism of the poem?

After Winifred's death Harry helped Gordon Catlin fight (and lose) a parliamentary election in Sunderland in November 1935, then he did some work for Storm Jameson, and by 1940 was back in the Air Force. His response to the copy of *Testament of Friendship* Vera sent him was typically irreverent and cryptic: 'And God who guards our liberty and livers / Forgive us our gifts as we forgive our givers . . . But it seems you have played God – so I think you should play Good Angel & send me Three Ways of Thought in Ancient China and/or The Apes of Man by way of penance!! Ever heard of the dumb blonde who thought the Yankee Clipper was an American Rabbi? A dios H.'[38]

After the war Harry moved to London, taking a job as cinema commissionaire during the early 1950s, becoming preoccupied with religious matters. As Winifred's friend Hilda Reid, who knew Harry well during these years, said, he was always a God-haunted man. He told his interviewer in 1958, 'Nowadays religion is my chief interest – only damn it, I can't bring myself to accept the creed.' At one point, according to Margaret Ballard, he thought of becoming a Roman Catholic priest. He never gave up hoping his verses and prose pieces would be published, and though some of them were, it was never in more exalted outlets than the *Driffield Times*. His final days were spent in Stockwell, in the 'luxurious boredom' of an old people's home. When Hilda Reid visited him he would inveigh against the Common Market and against capitalism, against money altogether: 'he was *that* kind of Yorkshire man, the dissident kind'. He died on 1 February 1976, after a stroke, leaving with Hilda a few last poems: 'Thoughts on Reforming the Common Market', 'Old Man's Prayer', 'Obvious', and the one Hilda liked best, 'Zero:' 'Sitting in a silence / Staring into space – The flesh-self and the soul / Sit face to face.'[39] Hilda thought him the 'kindest, most amusing and most faithful of friends' but even she recognised his unwillingness to commit himself. It was she, his most loyal and loving of friends, who said he was 'as wary as a bird in a bush'.

Hilda also thought that a small portrait of Harry had surfaced in *South Riding*, when Nancy Mitchell, the desperately poor, pregnant, would-be middle-class wife of an unemployed clerk, meets an ex-officer near the camp where she lives. He is cheerful and friendly but he exasperates her because 'he was a gentleman yet lived like a tramp. . . . She could have hit his scarred amiable face. Men who had no responsibilities, men who had no children to provide for, they could be casual and philosophical. She hated them. She hated all carefree and unburdened people.' Nancy's situation wasn't Winifred's, Harry's scars were psychological rather more than physical, yet the exasperation at a man who wastes his privileges and education, using the war as an excuse for irresponsibility, was surely part of her response to Harry. But *South Riding* is a response to Harry in more ways than in this small incident; its elegiac acceptance of change, of a failed love affair, of the need to carry on in single usefulness, and to find triumph in duty and work – these find their emotional roots in all the lessons of love that Harry had taught her. The novel more fittingly summarises her relation to him than the romanticised conclusion Vera procured in the nursing home in the last days of September 1935.

CHAPTER 3

Celia and Rosalind: Jean McWilliam

In June 1916 Winifred was eighteen. Earlier that year she had taken and passed the entrance examination for Somerville College, Oxford. She did so well that she could have gained a scholarship or an exhibition but the financial need for this had never arisen to prompt her or her parents to seek to gain one. No doubt she could have taken up the place at Somerville immediately, starting in the October of that year. It isn't quite clear whether she decided to delay entrance until 1917 because the opportunity arose to nurse for a year or whether she undertook the nursing to fill the vacancy of a year she and her parents had decided on in any event. She told Vera Brittain that she was one of the very few women who 'went to Oxford because their mothers wished it' and whose parents had been wise enough, and unconventional enough, 'to accept the fact that their younger daughter was a "sport" of the most unexpected variety, and to act without criticism on the advice of teachers who predicted a distinguished career'.[1] Perhaps her parents wished to keep this talented but very youthful eighteen-year-old at home a little longer but this does not tally with Alice Holtby's willingness to allow Winifred to work in a nursing home in London, albeit one run by a family acquaintance. Evelyne White's explanation, that the 'sensitive, imaginative girl was deeply moved by what was happening in France. . . . Thus she did some work [for] a year in a London Nursing Home in order to release an experienced nurse for foreign service',[2] is augmented by Vera's account of the apparently accidental way in which Winifred came to do this work. Grace had been asked for but was already working in a military hospital in Darlington and Winifred 'pleaded urgently' to be allowed to go instead. Winifred's own and her mother's sense of duty, and the likely safety and propriety of a private nursing home, combined to make this an ideal 'year out'. A short letter to her mother from Netley House, 11 Upper Woburn Place, suggests Winifred's immaturity and lack of sophistication at this time, as well as her affectionate rapport with her mother: 'Mother of my heart, This is just a tiny birthday note to send you your baby's love and all best wishes for the best of years to come. I am not going to write a long letter, because I shall probably answer your own dear one, which arrived last night, tomorrow . . . I hope you will have a very happy birthday, and every blessing afterwards. A kiss from your baby who loves you more & more each year. Love from the Babe.'[3]

Years later Winifred described her experience as 'a probationer in a non-recognised nursing-home, earning eighteen pounds [a year], "uniform money" and bus fares, by cleaning sterilisers and doing any job I was told to, from holding limbs for operations to disposing of unwelcome visitors'.[4] A brief fictionalised account is also given in *The Land of Green Ginger* in the experiences of the heroine, Joanna, at the South Park Nursing Home, Kingsport (Winifred's name for Hull) as assistant secretary at 25 shillings a week, a position and a salary grander than Winifred's. Joanna's work consists of doing accounts (sometimes incorrectly), sorting linen, preparing dressings, and sitting with patients, one of whom haemorrhages whilst she is with him. In Winifred's London nursing home Sir Herbert Beerbohm Tree was the patient who died suddenly in her arms; in Joanna's case the dying patient is a Mr Crowle whose desperate plight evokes both horror and pity: ' "Oh don't . . . don't let him touch me. I can't bear it". The shadows jeered at her. "You've got to bear it. . . . You can't escape from pity. Pity will pursue you always. If you run away from here, it is out in the streets, it is on the battlefields. It is in your private room, everywhere. It has marked you down. You can't escape, ever." '

On the whole, though, Winifred's year of nursing was enjoyable and liberating and Somerville College after the cosmopolitan freedom of London seemed restrictive and parochial. Many years later, in 1934, in an article entitled 'Should we abolish Oxford and Cambridge?', Winifred would advise these universities to modernise, especially as they were now in competition with an increasing number of new universities; Oxford and Cambridge 'could profitably borrow a few pages from the book of their younger successors: a greater restriction upon personal expenditure, a more natural relationship between the men and women . . . and a more realistic concern for the life of the contemporary world would not in any way destroy the unique gifts which these ancient places of learning still offer to posterity – the beauty of their architecture, the high tradition of their scholarship, the noble heritage of their intellectual integrity.'[5]

Winifred later told Vera that her first year at Somerville was one of 'anguished indecision'

in which my *desire* was to join the army, & my *duty*, as presented to me by all the people I respected, the Oxford authorities, my school authorities, Miss Fowler, everyone, was to stay at college. It always seemed to me then that I yielded to desire to join the Waac, a desire which my poorer contemporaries, who had to hurry through with their preparations to earn livings, could not afford to indulge in. And I felt very tentative about my own choice, & a little ashamed of flaunting it, as though it were a liberty bought by my parents' money. I had been so infinitely happier both nursing & in the Waac than I had been in that ghastly year at Oxford in 1917.[6]

The Principal of Somerville in 1917 was Emily Penrose, 'the Pen', as she was known to students, and the first woman head of an Oxford college to be a scholar in her own right rather than a relative of a distinguished man. She inaugurated a rigorous intellectual regime in which no student was admitted who would not take the degree course. Somerville was to be no finishing school for young ladies waiting on marriage but the training ground for the professions and academia, and for a life of service and thought. Non-denominational in its foundation, the 'rare combination of intellectual integrity and spiritual independence'[7] which had given rise to its foundation flourished under her ambitions to gain for women educational opportunities fully equal to men. Not until 1921 would women be able to graduate even though they were permitted to study and be examined for degrees. Emily Penrose, correctly, believed that to prove her women students' capabilities by increasing the number of first-class 'degrees' they attained, would be a powerful argument in winning the case for formal acceptance. So Somerville College was a hard-working and intellectually stimulating place when Winifred joined it, though its physical conditions were austere in the extreme: poor food, cold rooms, inadequate bathing facilities and little medical attention when students were ill, the very conditions Virginia Woolf was to describe so eloquently ten years later in A Room of One's Own. There were also the conventions and rituals to be observed: 'the social distinctions between first, second, and third years, the proper position at high table, the amount of deference due to cliques, seniors, college officials . . . we addressed each other as "Miss So and So" until one by one our more intimate seniors "propped" us. "May I prop?" meant "May I propose to call you by your Christian name? in which case you

may do the same to me." To "Prop" a senior was one of the un-
forgivable sins.'[8]

But in 1917 Somerville was also a college in wartime. In 1915
its buildings had been requisitioned by the War Office for use as a
military hospital and the college had migrated to St Mary Hall,
Oriel, where it remained until 1919. Rooms were found for forty-
eight students and others lived in lodgings nearby. For the first few
months, before moving to St Mary Hall, Winifred lived in one of
the college houses at Holywell, the one 'at the right-hand corner
looking up Mansfield Road'. Hilda Reid, who arrived at college as
the same time as Winifred, recalled her as 'standing out among her
contemporaries, a tall girl, beautifully built, with pale golden hair
and an eager profile'. She was exuberant and resourceful, and
Hilda remembers her flinging a slipper up to a tutor's room to
arouse her because someone was ill, and hopping around in the
cold, 'torn between dismay and laughter' because the slipper had
lodged on the sill.[9] By her own accounts she led a strenuous life,
tearing about Oxford streets on a very rusty cycle, flying from lectures, tea-parties, concerts, lacrosse matches, 'and all the thousand
and one other things that insist on taking place at the very farthest
point from my headquarters'. Some of the feverish and anxious
behaviour of women undergraduates during this period is registered by the student Judith in Rosamond Lehmann's *Dusty Answer*:
'From early morning till late at night the desperate meek untidy
heads of girls were bowed over tables in the library. . . . Pages rus-
tled; pencils whispered; squeaking shoes tiptoed in and out.
Somebody tapped out a dreary tune on her teeth; somebody had a
running cold; somebody giggled beneath her breath; somebody
sighed and sighed.' Hearing the girls after an examination breath-
lessly discussing their papers, Judith thinks, 'Girls really should be
trained to be less obviously female students. It only needed a little
discipline.'[10] The artificiality and otherworldliness of Oxford
would come to irritate Winifred in later years, even the unfash-
ionable appearance of its academic women: 'But their hair! Dear

Lord, Bless all Learned Women and help them to be beautiful, for the sake of Eugenics and the future. Amen. But will He answer? I doubt it.'[11] But in 1917 she seems to have been very obviously a female student: enthusiastic, energetic, naive.

Hilda Reid became one of the enduring friends Winifred made at Oxford at this time. She too left Oxford for a year, for medical reasons, returning at the same time as Winifred and Vera in 1919. Her father was a retired Indian judge, 'a beautiful, stately old man', Winifred described him[12] and the family lived at Pamphill Manor House, in Wimborne, Dorset. Winifred visited there for the first time in the autumn of 1920, finding the gracious but frugal customs of the household enchanting and slightly intimidating – 'but I enjoyed myself more than I have done for years'. Hilda was exceptionally fond of her father, writing at the time of his death in 1930 that though it was inevitable an old man of eighty should die, 'it happened I loved him better than any-one in the world and liked his company better than any-one's'.[13] This made her especially sympathetic to Winifred when her father died in 1933: 'You must find a little cave or island in yourself and hide there till its all over. I admit I rather overdid the hiding myself – buried myself so successfully that I was no good to man or beast for a year or more. . . . Tell me when you come back and have any time to play with me.'[14]

Winifred recognised the elusive, fluctuating quality of Hilda's friendship: 'My fugitive Hilda was to have stayed here last month – but she is like a fairy. Unless she decides to appear, she will not. She left no word of why she never came on the appointed day, but I conclude that she is helping her mother to "move house." She is charming & strange & difficult and fine. I love her pride and fastidiousness. I am saddened by the fatal diffidence which always prevents her from finishing anything. Perhaps she really is a sort of fairy.'[15] But though Hilda was an undemanding friend, particularly after Winifred and Vera became friends, her affectionate and even passionate feeling for Winifred is captured in a poem, probably of 1931, called 'A Garland for Winifred' in which their green and golden student days, during Winifred's first stay at Somerville, before she met Vera, are remembered. They used to cycle to the river, passing a row of poplar trees, 'tall like you', Hilda wrote: 'Through their twigs the sky was blue / Like your eyes. The young leaves were / Gilt with sunshine like your hair.' But it is Winifred's mind that is most like the poplar: 'From every side she takes the light / To give it back in sparkles bright . . . /Shivers with the breath of rain: / Moved by every far distress, / Rooted in steadfast-ness. . . .' The 'garland' of the title records, in the poem's ending, her witness 'That I have a friend and she / Is lovelier than the poplar tree.'[16] But though these were happy times, they were over-shadowed by the war. Another of Hilda's poems, 'The Picnic', published in 1934 but again looking back to student days, recalls the uneasiness of their first year in wartime Oxford:

> . . . Still unseeing as we sat,
> Where the heather shrills and hums,
> – Wind for fife and bees for drums –
> Right across our talk there came
> A breath of rage, a sudden flame.
> What ghost alighted that?[17]

Unlike Winifred and Vera, Hilda Reid spent much of her time after Oxford in her parents' home, though she taught for brief periods and worked in the Publications Department of the Ministry of Home Security from 1942 to 1945, followed by work on an official history of the war. She was also a respected novelist and poet although she never made what she later humorously called her Break Through into fame and financial success. Her novels, *Phillida*, 1928, and *Two Soldiers and a Lady*, 1932, were well-researched historical romances of Cavaliers and Roundheads, full of exciting action and exotic locations, the later one featuring a female hero, as capable of honour and bravery as any of the men. Winifred reviewed a third novel, *Emily*, on its publication in 1933:

this time a modern story in which a 'placid, friendly and courageous' girl from Hinton Tankerville finds herself involved in European espionage. The incongruities of the two worlds create 'a delightfully inconsequent and exciting entertainment'.[18] Like many women novelists of this period – Naomi Mitchison, for instance, or Phyllis Bentley – Hilda Reid found in the historical and the thriller novel scope for her expertise and sense of adventure. One of a first generation to read History at university she also, like Vera Brittain, wanted to use the past to explore the present and safeguard the future: 'Perhaps the careful study of man's past will explain to me much that seems inexplicable in his disconcerting present. Perhaps the means of salvation are already there, implicit in history, only awaiting rediscovery,' Vera wrote,[19] in explaining her own decision to read History rather than English.

The Oxford that Winifred and Hilda knew in 1917 had been drastically changed by war. Physically it changed, with green spaces given over to drill squares, bugles competing with bells, and buildings converted to hospitals. Spiritually it changed too and became a ghost town haunted by the young men fighting, or dead, who should have been its students. By the end of 1917 only 350 remained where there had been 3,000. 'Everywhere their invisible presence was inescapable,' as Vera described it. Many women students continued with their hard-won education, from desire or financial necessity, but a few, and these included Winifred, 'found safety intolerable while their unfulfilled male contemporaries were dying. In ones and twos these left their work at Oxford temporarily or permanently unfinished, and went off to serve at home or overseas.'[20] Even at this late stage of the war there was still plenty of unofficial pressure for women to volunteer: an advertisement in the *Hull Times* in 1918, for example, was asking for women orderlies to work in field hospitals in France, at a rate of pay of £26 a year, plus board and lodging.

According to her discharge papers, Winifred enrolled in the Women's Army Auxiliary Corps (WAAC) in London on 27 July

1918 and was discharged in London on 6 September 1919. Her work during this period was 'excellent' and so was her character. The first two months of her service were spent as a forewoman, equivalent to a non-commissioned officer in the army, in the New Zealand Officers' Club, 35 Hill Street, off Berkeley Square, a large private house 'of dim gold and pale grey and green, with carpets that reflect the latest comer's footmark, and many mirrors and lifts and large sofas in £1.10.0 chintz'. There were up to twenty-one officers resident there at any one time, and a staff of fourteen WAACs who were doing the domestic work of the club, supervised by an officer, Miss Stuart, an NCO and Winifred. Winifred's duties, as she eagerly told her sister, were to inspect the domestics' work, sort linen, help with meals and washing up, oversee the eating arrangements for the domestics, and take roll calls and registers. Her day was from 6 a.m. to 10 p.m. with time off most afternoons and a half day on Tuesdays. Winifred's letters to her family are full of enthusiasm for her new job and for the social life that went with it. 'Perhaps washing dishes and counting linen is very uninspiring work', she wrote, 'but when you are in the Women's Army there is always a chance that you may suddenly be taken away from your sink or your linen-cupboard, or your dustpan into something big and noble and beautiful, that takes the little bothering things right away, and gives one strength from its vastness and beauty.' The event that inspired this comment was 'a memorial service at St Martin's for all the women belonging to the London Area QMAAC. . . . It was one of the most wonderful things I ever saw or heard in my life. There were fifteen thousand of us there, all in khaki . . . many of the girls were sobbing.' At the same time she was meeting friends – Cicely Williams, whom she'd known at Oxford – going to lectures – Maude Royden preaching at the City Temple – shopping, going to the theatre, taking tea. It was a good time, 'I'm awfully happy here,' she wrote.

In September she was posted abroad to become a hostel forewoman at a signals unit at Huchenneville, near Abbeville in

France. In a letter to *Time and Tide* in May 1930, written to try to correct the impression given by a recently published book which depicted WAACs and VADs as 'sex-maddened girls' who indulged in orgies at their French bases, she described the highly disciplined life at the New Zealand Officers' Club, where conversation with the officers except on matters of duty was forbidden, and then her brief period at the depot at Folkestone registering the girls returning from France on leave or discharged. 'During this time I saw many hundreds of forms, and so far as I can remember, met only one girl who was being sent back to England and discharged as pregnant.' She then recalls being sent to the small camp at Huchenneville 'consisting of signallers, clerks, and domestic workers'. The camp was surrounded by an Australian Remount Depot and was isolated among fields, orchards and woods. Expecting discipline to be even stricter she found that the camp administrator had made the WAACs' recreation room a centre for 'homely companionship for both men and women when off duty'. Again, there was only one pregnancy, and on visits to other bases 'I saw nothing that could possibly be described as the mildest form of orgy. We were all worked much too hard; our hours off duty were too short; our supervision too strict, our mobility too circumscribed, even after the Armistice, to give us much opportunity for further activities.'

The enlightened administrator was Jean Fergusson McWilliam, Scottish, strikingly tall, 'Diana-like with her uncontrollable coppertinted hair.'[21] She was born in 1881 and was therefore seven years older than Winifred. She had been a student at Somerville, having taken degree examinations in 1906, gaining marks of a third-class standard in English. From 1907 to 1914 she was a teacher in Liverpool, then an English lecturer in the Training Department of Bedford College before becoming Assistant Deputy Chief Controller in QMAAC. At some point she taught at the Oxford High School, probably before going to Liverpool, and in 1924 she took a Diploma in Education.

The Huchenneville unit had twenty-five telegraphists, eight tele-phonists, five office staff and twelve domestic workers. Most of the staff were in tents under apple-trees until German prisoners of war built huts for them. Jean McWilliam had a room in a gar-dener's cottage in which Winifred had a loft without doors or windows. Sanitation was primitive and lighting was by candle. Jean recalled first meeting Winifred, 'a tall, pale, tired-looking girl' who saluted smartly when asked if she was Holtby and replied 'Yes, ma'am.' It would be a gesture repeated when Jean said goodbye to Winifred – 'beautiful and glowing' – on the last occasion of their meeting in February 1935.[22]

Winifred was, according to Jean, a 'wonderful forewoman but inclined to do things herself instead of making others do them'. Her job was to supervise the WAAC orderlies who looked after the Deputy Assistant Director of Railway Transport, who lived with a small staff of officers in the chateau at Huchenneville. When there were dinner parties extra waitresses had to be provided and Winifred, always sociable and avid for experience, liked to be amongst these. But her habit of writing stories of her experiences put an end to this. One story in particular, 'By Might of Pen', which tells of a writer's satiric talents influencing a military deci-sion, seems to have upset the colonel.

Winifred's Huchenneville stories, 'written by candlelight sitting at the kitchen table completely absorbed while cooks and general domestics and Australians and other WAAC moved in and out and about', were her first attempt at writing a full-length book. With the title 'The Forest Unit', they comprised a sequence based loosely on *As You Like It* in which, Jean wrote, 'she imagined us all in the Forest of Arden, wistful but happy exiles like the duke and his followers.' Many of Winifred's companions were described as the play's characters, with the colonel as the duke, and Jean's bat-woman as Phoebe. Jean and Winifred were, of course, Rosalind and Celia, and remained so in their correspondence to each other ever afterwards. This was the closest friendship Winifred had with another woman to this point and, at least in its early days, it had some of the fondness and intimacy of the two girls in Shakespeare's play – 'dearer than the natural bond of sisters' – and also some of the intensity and romance that would characterise Winifred's later relationship with Vera Brittain. But Jean – 'Mac o' my heart', as Winifred sometimes called her – was very different from Vera, older, more experienced, less physically vulnerable in appearance, and probably less needy in other respects, and she was, of course, Winifred's superior in the army. There seems to have been no suggestion that they should make a life together and although when Vera married in 1925, Winifred turned to this old friend to lessen the loss, it was as a visitor to South Africa where Jean now worked rather than in the expectation of anything closer.

When Winifred stayed with Jean in Pretoria in 1926 she said that 'The Forest Unit' was 'sentimental and, therefore, bad', and it is true that most of the stories are fanciful and whimsical, aspects Winifred seems to have been aware of even at the time in her excuse of them as a 'dream night's day'. The twelve chapters which comprise 'The Forest Unit' recount WAAC anecdotes and also events concerning the French villagers. They do, however, indicate how happy Winifred was at this time, partly due to her ebullience of character and partly because the war's impact on the Huchenneville unit was indirect. The war had only two months to run when Winifred went to France and although the Marne and Western Front offensives had taken place only days before she was posted, and the Allies were to make bitter progress through occupied France during October, the nature of the work in the Huchenneville unit – arranging which trains the British might run on the southern part of the French railway lines – meant that no wounded came there. Even the Australian unit lodged nearby had come to recuperate after ten months in the line, their wounded having been taken elsewhere. Winifred's war service was almost like a student's experience of living abroad, which even poor living conditions and sparse resources cannot quite deprive of excitement. She was on the fringes of the war and its enormity would strike her only on reflection, to prompt her, for example, even as late as 1931 to write one of her best poems, 'Trains in France', recalling her time in Huchenneville, and the military acts she had, in however a minor way, helped to promote: '. . . And I,/ Who thought I had forgotten all the War,/ Remember now a night in Camiers,/ When, through the darkness, as I wakeful lay,/ I heard the trains,/ The savage, shrieking trains,/ Call to each other their fierce hunting-cry,/ Ruthless, inevitable, as the beasts/ After their prey.'

One of the sources of Winifred's enjoyment of the Huchenneville unit was the presence of the Australian soldiers in the nearby remount depot. 'The Forest Unit' tells of some of the comings and goings between the Australians and the WAAC and one sergeant in particular, 'one of the nicest men I ever knew', she wrote later, attached himself to Winifred, taking her riding and even, it seems, arranging his leave to coincide with hers. 'Ken is waiting to get leave till I do if possible, so we may land home together.'[23] Apparently he did visit Cottingham, probably as a friend and not as a boyfriend. The splendidly handsome Australian friend in Winifred's short story, 'When Brenda Came Home', is based on him. Ken remained in Winifred's memory as a benign figure and particularly as an advocate of self-defence for women; asked how the women in the camp could be protected against predatory men, he and his men taught the women jujitsu, and 'how to ride and run and wrestle. They taught us leg-throws and arm-throws. And that was the last we heard of helpless women in that camp.'[24]

In January 1920, after demobilisation, Jean McWilliam went to Rhodes University College, Grahamstown, in South Africa, as a lecturer in English. By that time Winifred had returned to Somerville and had begun the correspondence with Jean that, in a selected form, became *Letters to a Friend*, published in 1937, edited by Jean and Alice Holtby. During the early 1920s Winifred and Jean wrote – or at least aimed to write – to each other weekly. By Winifred's death the letters had become infrequent and it is clear that the correspondence had become little more than an occasional duty, and the friendship that sustained them a memory rather than a living force. 'Darling Rosalind', Winifred wrote in April 1934, 'I was so pleased to have your letter – so glad to hear from you – so glad you liked my book [perhaps *Mandoa, Mandoa!*, her African novel, or the satire *The Astonishing Island*, also published in 1933]. I feel so ashamed that I write to you so little. I often think of you. But oh, how weary my hand gets with the actual exercise of writing.' The next year she wrote: 'Darling Rosalind, I think of you so often and with much love though I never write.' And her final letter, a brief note concerning an attempt to get an acquaintance's novel published, ends: 'Always rushing, but *so* much better, and enjoying life and finishing my novel. Dear, dear love to you, Winifred.'

According to Winifred, her family liked Jean 'best of all my friends'[25] and *Letters to a Friend* was intended by Alice as a counterbalance to Vera Brittain's control of Winifred's posthumously unpublished work, most obviously *South Riding*, and as a pre-emptive strike against her forthcoming biography of Winifred. Alice seems to have determined not only to add other dimensions and other friendships to Winifred's life but also to let Winifred's own voice be heard. Jean McWilliam's motive in this was probably similar, and *Letters to a Friend* was exceptionally self-effacing on Jean's part in that only Winifred's letters are present. Nevertheless, Winifred's voice is not fully heard because the letters were heavily edited; how much so is suggested by two surviving letters from Alice Holtby to Vera Brittain of February 1936 in which she describes how she is going through the letters, cutting out much and crossing out some passages on which she asks Vera's opinion. She and Jean also probably changed the sequence of the letters sometimes, since she mentions Jean having written asking to 'put Nov.11 one out of 25 into 26.'[26] Jean did persist, however, against

Alice's wishes, in retaining the letters about the disagreement she and Winifred had in 1925[27] on the eve of Winifred's visit to South Africa 'because they explain the dedication of her life to Service'. Alice found the willingness to confess such things puzzling: 'Is she blinded by friendship,' she wrote, 'or is she right in thinking [the letters] the greatest and holiest ever written?' What Alice and Jean feared was that someone would be hurt because of the letters or would try to take legal action against them. Perhaps also Alice was fearful for her own reputation, already under threat, as she believed, from *South Riding*. But for all her care in censoring the letters there was a scare when a woman recognised herself in Winifred's description of a 'sad little adventure' of a visit from a woman, a stranger, who had identified with the spinster heroine in *The Crowded Street* and 'being singularly friendless, she came to me'.[28] After reading *Letters to a Friend* she had felt betrayed and tried to sue Collins, the publisher, for libel. The action was never brought.

In the Preface[29] to *Letters to a Friend* Jean recalled how she and Winifred met, and how Winifred wrote 'The Forest Unit' in Huchenneville. As a conclusion, and also as a memorial to the lost time of their early friendship, Jean placed at the end of the letters a poem Winifred sent her in 1926, written presumably after her return from South Africa and itself something of a goodbye to a friendship that she had by now outgrown:

> . . . Rosalind, sometimes do you
> Leave the twisted, dry Karoo,
> Leave the aloe spears aflame,
> Leave the kopje's tortured shame,
> Seek another, greener hill,
> Through the woods of Huchenneville? . . .
> Rosalind, when next you go,
> Call to me, and I shall know –
> Call, and I will run apace

To our secret trysting place –
Rosalind, where you and I
Walked beneath an April sky.

Jean's desire to idealise their early friendship led her to comment in the Preface that the letters 'are haunted by an Arcadian atmosphere'. But this is born more of wishful thinking than accuracy, for Winifred's letters are rarely nostalgic for the Huchenneville days but brimming with plans and opinions. They are youthful and rather self-conscious, sometimes seeming to be exercises in which she practised her style in descriptions of landscape, people, books and political activities. She kept Jean's letters, at least for a time, with the possible intention of a volume of correspondence: 'your letters are wonderfully interesting. I keep them all. One day we may edit them together and let the world see them.' She knew that Jean was hoarding her letters and told her not to return them: 'I doubt whether I shall ever want to write my own diary. The things that happen to my friends are the only things worth recording.'[30] The letters also served a kind of mail-order function with Winifred buying clothes on Jean's behalf; and they mention trying to place Jean's stories and articles in London periodicals, or they offer her advice about what she should write: 'Rosalind, you must write a series of little articles . . . I'll get them typed and send them to *Time and Tide* . . . sketches of South African life, of the underworld of "low whites", of the Dutch women with their hair down, nursing their babies in the stations, of Stellenbosch University, if that's allowable – these I am sure I could place.'[31] But Jean seems to have preferred writing either what Winifred called 'party stuff'[32] or reminiscences about WAAC life, such as *Three Primroses and Two Violets* which Winifred tactfully described as having a 'gracious wistfulness quite of its own [but] editors don't seem to want things about Waacs now'.[33]

Jean was unsettled during her first years in South Africa, trying to move from Rhodes University in 1920, the same year she arrived in South Africa, and applying, unsuccessfully, for several schoolteaching jobs, including a headship in Johannesburg in 1922. In 1923 she was worrying about taking a degree; in order to claim her degrees, she needed to have taken all the university's examinations and residence requirements. Like many early students, she had not taken qualifying examinations such as Responsions and would have to take them now if she wished to claim the degree. Winifred undertook to explore the possibility of examination papers being sent out to Jean in South Africa but 'the authorities are ridiculously red-tapeishly adamant and . . . all attempts to induce them to send their papers out are useless.'[34] There is no evidence that Jean took Responsions but in any case, by the end of the year she was thinking of going to Australia, 'without even the prospect of a job', which alarmed Winifred even though she could sympathise with Jean's restlessness and ambition. 'My chief fear is that you should, for stupid financial reasons, have to seek a second-rate job. Are you going to be very short?' Winifred offered to lend her £100: 'I am selling out some stock to pay the premium for our flat. . . . So I could without inconveniencing myself in the least.'[35] As it turned out Winifred's offer was unnecessary because, having gone so far as to book her passage to Australia, Jean applied for and was offered the post of headmistress at Pretoria High School for Girls, to start in January 1924. She was to stay in this post until 1938.[36]

Pretoria High School for Girls had been founded in 1902 with 106 children aged from kindergarten to fifteen. It was non-denominational, with a strong academic tradition and with the aim of reconciling the Dutch and English communities in the aftermath of the Anglo-Boer war. Its first headmistress was Edith Aitken, who had been educated at the pioneering North London Collegiate School for Girls and then at London University, graduating with a double first in science. She was a highly successful product of nineteenth-century idealism towards the education of girls and women and her credo for the school reflects her serious commitment to the creation of 'women citizens', based on an English model, for the new colony: 'The school was opened with the earnest hope that here girls of different races and different denominations might meet in that commonwealth of letters which gave Erasmus and Shakespeare to the world; to acquire there, in accordance with the ideals of Christian duty, the healthy physique, the trained mind and the disciplined character which should fit each to live worthily in that state of life into which it should please God to call her.' The 'different races' did not, of course, include black girls, an exclusion which would strike Winifred forcibly when she visited in 1926.[37]

By 1924, when Jean became its head, Pretoria High School for Girls had moved into new premises in Park Street, with good accommodation for her in the school house. The number of pupils had increased, and would continue to do so to around 500 by 1930. Both Dutch and English were taught nationally in all schools when she first arrived, with Assembly being taken alternately in English and High Dutch, but in 1924 Dutch was replaced by Afrikaans and since there was an Afrikaans High School in Pretoria Jean's school became wholly English-speaking. Jean thus presided over a period of expansion and change in the school's history and the evidence suggests that she was a successful and efficient head-mistress. She was not always a happy one.

The main problem was loneliness and Jean's visits to England, still thought of as 'home', and visits from Winifred to South Africa, were always being planned. When she came to England, Jean thought, she could sleep on the sofa in Winifred and Vera's Doughty Street flat when in London, because money was short, or she could stay for some of the time with Winifred's family in Yorkshire. Jean proposed living on £8 a month whilst in England, which wasn't much, Winifred commented, but 'I think you could do it'.[38] In August 1923 Winifred and Vera were plotting if they could afford to visit Jean, Vera commenting that the trio of them together would provoke the *Punch* joke, 'Gee! there ain't much

ham in that sandwich'. This was accompanied by a drawing by
Winifred of two large women with a small one between them. The
thought of the three together prompted some nervousness on
Winifred's behalf, no doubt increased by Vera's recently published
novel *The Dark Tide*, which Winifred had sent Jean and which
gives an unflattering and unkind portrait of Winifred. In preparing
Jean for the meeting Winifred wrote perceptively about Vera,
revealing also her own loving protectiveness towards this exacting
and difficult friend who clearly was now of pre-eminent importance in Winifred's life:

> She is a person whom life has battered, and who has been
> given by circumstances and heredity such a temperament
> that every blow and every snub, even every casual coldness
> makes a wound and a scar, where many people would
> hardly know that they had been touched. The War has left
> her with a real sickness of apprehension . . . but never for a
> moment does she give way, nor lose her sweetness, nor her
> tenderness for suffering, nor an imagination which is con-
> stantly trying to devise ways for protecting other people
> from the sorrow she has known.

'I want you to like her', Winifred wrote anxiously, 'for when you
come home we will go together to theatres and big shops and
good concerts, and we'll buy materials and make clothes if you
like. And we'll look at the newest books and Vera shall play the
piano (we'll have one by that time) and we'll talk and talk and talk.
It will be lovely.'[39]

But it wasn't lovely. Jean's visit in late 1923 was, she explained,
a last-minute arrangement springing from a need to be reassured
by friends that she had been wise to accept the appointment of
Headmistress of the Pretoria High School for Girls. She left Cape
Town in late November and this gave her seventeen days in
England. She stayed at a boarding-house in Earl's Court where the

South African novelist Ethelreda Lewis lodged and she visited Winifred and Vera several times, 'sitting on the fender seat beside the hearth with her long thin hands clasped behind her head as she talked. The four of us [Mrs Lewis was there too] discussed South Africa, inspiring Winifred with a determination to see the country as soon as she could.'[40] Winifred's first letter after Jean's visit begins apologetically for not having written sooner and hints at the awkwardness of these fireside conversations which must, perhaps inevitably, have been a disappointment to Jean. There had been much shyness during the visit, and some misunderstandings. Vera had said, 'The person who appointed you to Pretoria must have had a sense of humour.' It was, commented Winifred, 'one of the prettiest compliments that were ever paid you, and you won't see it'.[41] Soon afterwards Jean complained percipiently that she feared that her 'bodily presence may have been bad for friendship' and yet, wishing to test the friendship again, pressed Winifred to visit her, fearing that if Winifred delayed her visit to South Africa, she would never come, to which Winifred replied, 'if I live, I will. All things in their time.'[42] Perhaps that time may never have come had it not been for Vera's forthcoming marriage and the question 'How shall I live?' that it forced on Winifred. Her resolution not to 'fall into the common error of circumstantial victimisation' sharpened plans to visit South Africa and by January 1925 she had determined to go the following January, not September as previously planned: 'I want to be here for the autumn. There is so much doing and I can make money for my passage.'[43]

How she would spend her time in South Africa and how her visit would be financed caused some disagreement. She didn't intend to take a job because that would tie her to one place whereas she wanted to travel widely in the country 'and learn things', particularly learn things about how South Africa could effectively co-operate with the League of Nations and about the colour question 'because that is going to be immensely important too'. The best way to do this would be to travel about Africa lecturing for the League of Nations Union, paid if possible but she would still do it if not, and was earning money as hard as she could during 1925 to pay for the trip. Jean was angry at this, wanting Winifred to use her savings (most of which Winifred had given to pay for an apprentice's premium for someone invalided out of the war) to stay with her all the time on a protracted holiday, complaining of Winifred's obsession with questions of the day, of her losing the common touch and growing arrogant and intolerant of ordinary concerns, of her rushed and frantic lifestyle, and, tellingly, of putting 'causes in front of friendship – some friendship at least'. In some respects Jean's complaints resembled Alice Holtby's and Winifred again needed to defend her course of action against the criticism of someone who wanted to control her. This time she could be more outspoken: 'I do not need a holiday,' she wrote to Jean. 'I am strong, eager, at the height of my capacity for learning and working . . . I've got to fly where no woman flew before . . . you can't shake my purpose; you'll only shake the joy from it.' The letter ends, 'Oh Rosalind, love me if you can. If not, don't be grieved. Just give me up as one of those who went their own way . . . in the belief that – for them – it was the only way possible.'[44] Winifred's responses throughout the correspondence of 1925 were a mixture of stubbornness, even defiance, followed, characteristically, by compunction at the dissension between them:

> This letter is not a good one. It conveys so little of the love, remorse, and longing that I feel for you. I want to come and to put my head on your knee like I once did at Huchenneville, and say 'I am so sorry'. . . . Dear, beautiful Rosalind. I love you. I do not really think that anything except my stupidity and my tendency to write down the mood of the moment lies between us. Forgive me. The fault is all mine. Celia.[45]

Nevertheless, Winifred persisted in her plan of making her lecture tour to Cape Town, Kimberley, Durban, Stellenbosch, Bloemfontein, Johannesburg and elsewhere before going to Pretoria, to arrive there in March or April, and 'then, I imagine, and if you will have me, I will stay for a little'. Her intention was to visit others she knew in South Africa, like the novelists Ethelreda Lewis and Sarah Gertrud Millin, and those to whom she had an introduction, like the socialist Mabel Palmer. As it turned out, because of a seamen's strike – England was moving inexorably towards the industrial crisis of the General Strike of 1926 – Winifred could not get a sailing until 14 January, on the SS *Grantully Castle*, later than she wanted and not the shipping line she would have preferred. As the time grew near she became increasingly excited about the visit and also more generous about the time she would spend with Jean; having established her independent concerns in South Africa she could afford to be spontaneously affectionate: 'Darling, I want to come lots to Pretoria if I may. May I run up between being at Durban and Johannesburg? . . . Then I'm going to your Prize Day and coming for Easter. I am looking forward frightfully to that.'[46] In the next letter, however, written on board ship on 7 February within sight of Table Mountain, she again made clear her intention to be free to pursue her own concerns, 'to use you as headquarters while I am in the Transvaal'. Her plans, after a hectic schedule of meetings and lectures, including setting up a branch of the League of Nations Union in Ladysmith, would bring her to Jean on 6 March for a weekend visit before moving to Johannesburg two days later for further lectures and meetings: 'I had no idea people would want me to do so much. Things down here seem just to be moving, and I am an excuse to push them further – especially with the Dutch.'

The weekend visit was a success: 'I have seen Jean McWilliam again', she wrote to Vera, '& very happily smoothed away the irritations of our correspondence last year.' Winifred also was with Jean for the prize day where she gave the prize-giving speech. Like all such speakers she stressed the value of education, complimented the school on its progress and achievements, and added a characteristic pledge to the 'realisation of the adventure of work' in which not just the 'successful manufacture of shorthand typists' was aimed for but a more complete fulfilment of each individual girl according to her aptitudes: 'Agriculture and medicine, domestic work and industry have all their special possibilities, their special service to the community.' This occasion was followed by a pleasant motoring trip with Jean over Easter, brought to a sudden end by the news that the well-loved school secretary, Mr A.E. Barrow, had been taken ill. When they returned, by train because of rain storms and flooded roads, they found he had died. Towards the end of Winifred's visit to South Africa she caught influenza and this brought a spell of 'doing absolutely nothing', being looked after in Jean's house for more than a week, waiting also for news of her return boat, the SS *Barrabool*, delayed in Durban. She later described her enjoyment of this journey home, by third-class ticket on a part-cargo boat to Tilbury rather than the expensive Mailboat because she had only 30 shillings left, with its liberating freedom from luxury and its interesting assortment of passengers: 'You cannot really see the world unless you sacrifice your comfort. Blessed are the poor in pocket, for they shall see life.'[47]

In spite of frustration with the social snobbery affecting the organisation of LNU branches, particularly in Johannesburg, the 'whirl of more or less useless activity' overwhelming her, and her horror at the racism of white South African society – 'I heard women in lovely clothes holding up their hands in dismay, because one of them had talked to "niggers" '[48] – Winifred's visit to South Africa was stimulating and enriching. Vera believed that it matured her and that she went to South Africa 'an eager, uncritical girl, full of enthusiasms, a little sentimental; she returned a young woman, balanced, experienced, confident, mature'.[49] In the experience of racism it also provided her with the cause that would dominate the rest of her life. In relation to Jean the euphoria of the visit seems to have continued for the rest of 1926 and into the early months of 1927, with Winifred promising future meetings, and sending presents of clothes, shoes and money.[50] After this, the letters begin to tail off. The return of Vera from America and the birth in 1927 of her son, John Edward, no doubt contributed to the decline, but perhaps more than anything else, Winifred's increasingly busy life, particularly her involvement with *Time and Tide* and eventually her South African work, and her growing success as a journalist, claimed her. 'I saw Lady Rhondda in London', she wrote to Jean on 27 July 1926. 'She was very kind and is giving me lots of work. The *Manchester Guardian* is publishing my Eulogy on Railway Trains – South African railway trains – and the *Yorkshire Post* has written to ask me for articles. I have three short stories on the *tapis*, and my *Land of Green Ginger*.'[51] In the midst of all this, the visit to Jean, along with their friendship, began to recede into the safety of memory. 'Oh, I did love that time', she wrote in recalling 'the wild rides' they had taken together round Jean's home: 'Wasn't it fun? . . . It's something to remember always, to live over again, to build into a world as real and vivid as this other world of immediate circumstance.'[52] They intended to take holidays together – 'But what shall we do when you come home? Would you like to do a Balkan with me? Or shall we go to Florence and Sienna?' – and they did go to Paris in March 1927, to stay in a hotel recommended by Lady Rhondda. They went again to Paris at Easter 1929, with Lady Rhondda of the party too, and Theodora Bosanquet and Dot McCalman: 'Jean & I had an argument in the train about Happy Endings. I said that they could always be obtained – all you had to do was to keep silence after one point of time. Any story is happy sometime, though all really end with death', Winifred wrote to Vera, and included in her letter a poem she wrote after the argument, which ends: 'What if estrangements follow greetings? / What if our lovely loves grow cold? / Since journeys end in lovers' meetings / Keep silence now; this tale is told.'[53] The holiday had been 'more enjoyable but possibly less useful than I hoped . . . I have spent most of the time in the Rue de Rivoli & Restaurants,' Winifred told Gordon, Vera's husband. She intended, incidentally, to smuggle D.H. Lawrence's *Lady Chatterley's Lover* into England on her way home, 'so if I am in prison when you next hear about me, you will know why'.

The strains in a friendship now growing cold surfaced in Winifred's article in 1929 for the *Manchester Guardian* called 'External Memories' where the irritating absent-mindedness of a 'friend of mine who is head mistress of one of the largest girls' schools in the Dominions' is blamed on her having left behind all the office apparatus necessary to an efficient administrator. Worse still is the fuss this has caused, with Jean furious with herself, indignant with her memory, certain that something odd must hang in the London atmosphere which deprives efficient headmistresses of their customary caution and sobriety.[54] Jean was coming under pressure from her work in the school, and this would filter through into the few letters of hers to Winifred that remain. In March 1934 she wrote complainingly that conditions at her school were very difficult: 'I am often inclined to give up the unequal struggle. I am allowed twenty mistresses including myself for 490 girls. . . . It ruins all good methods of teaching. There are times when I long to be ill & get invalided out . . . [working in the Transvaal] gives one such fear of bureaucracy that I can never now believe in Socialism or the Soviet. It is the tyranny of the inefficient.'[55] Jean apparently visited England later in the year on leave after an operation. 'I want to see her,' Winifred wrote to Vera, who was lecturing on *Testament of Youth* in America, 'yet as usual I don't want her to be here, & to feel the drag of conscience for all the hospitality she gave me & which life is too full at the moment to return.'[56] Winifred's life was indeed full at this time; she was looking after Vera's children, and also visiting Vera's father in a nursing home and helping Vera's mother move house. Her health maintained a fragile stability and she managed a steady, although by her standards, modest flow of engagements: 'I have been speaking a little lately & shall be doing so almost daily till after Armistice,' she wrote to Vera; 'I find I can manage a half-hour's lecture if I rest before & after – but that's my limit. Alas! no American tour for me, I can see. Well, I can do it vicariously through you.'[57] There is no further mention of Jean's visit during this last autumn of Winifred's life, nor of any further visit, except for the one mentioned by Jean in the Preface to *Letters to a Friend*, when she said goodbye to Winifred in February 1935: 'as my train moved, with a radiant smile she gave me the WAAC salute'. Their last encounter in Jean's account mirrored their first, the Celia–Rosalind friendship restored in memory even if in life it had lost its radiance. For Winifred, too, towards the end of her life, it was the memory of the Forest Unit, an idyllic episode amidst the dereliction of war, that was the lasting aspect of their friendship. She never revisited Huchenneville, although in 1931 she flew in a plane over it 'in *driving* rain', and the following year two of the staff of *Time and Tide* visited and brought back photographs of the orchard which she sent to Jean: 'Do you recognise it?'[58]

When Winifred became absorbed in the unionisation of black workers in South Africa, and spent much of her financial and emotional resources in promoting this cause, she seems not to have included Jean in her concern. There is only one mention of Ballinger, the trade union organiser she helped to sponsor, in *Letters to a Friend* and he is referred to in such a way as to suggest that she has told Jean little about his activities since 1928 when he went out to South Africa: 'He's a fine man. He has stuck out for six years on uncertain pay, against terrific discouragement and with hostility and misunderstanding all around him.'[59] Perhaps this was one of Winifred's activities that Jean did not approve of; more likely it was simply that the relationship had become so remote that Winifred no longer cared to share her most passionate political commitment with her erstwhile friend.

Jean lingers in Winifred's writing as Rachel, Joanna's lecturer friend in *The Land of Green Ginger* whom she sets out to visit in

South Africa at the end of the novel and whose disappointed expectations of their friendship she has perhaps partially in mind when she says, 'Everyone has to find his own security. The awful thing about life is that we really are alone in it. We can't live for anyone else. I wanted to. I tried to. I tried to.' But more painfully behind this remark is her own bereft state after Vera had married. After all, friendship, like romance, cannot be fully relied on; it grows cold or is interrupted by the demands of others. It is work which remains the constant factor, a conclusion reached in *South Riding* by Sarah Burton, whose red hair and enlightened competence as a headmistress are reminiscent of Jean, though aspects of Miss Fowler, Winifred's headmistress at Queen Margaret's, are there too, along with some of the physical attributes and fiery disposition of MP Ellen Wilkinson. Sarah is a composite portrait of the new professional woman of the inter-war years and Jean must to some extent have identified with the character and been heartened and comforted by this posthumous tribute.

CHAPTER 4

'Very small, very dear love': Vera

Winifred returned to Oxford for the beginning of the Michaelmas term in 1919 to a warm welcome. She had been away for only a year and was affectionately remembered whereas Vera Brittain, after an absence of four years, was forgotten. This was one of many differences between them prompting towards hostility rather than friendship. Physically and temperamentally they were opposites: large, fair, exuberant, easy-going Winifred and small, dark, introspective, difficult Vera. Their college contemporary, Hilda Reid, remembered that Winifred was humorous and 'very good company' and Vera was 'a very little creature with wet brown eyes', melancholic, frightened of thunder and mice.[1] Vera had had to face parental opposition in order to go to Oxford, and the war for her had been personally tragic with the loss of her brother, fiancé, and two other close male friends. She had also had nursing experience as a VAD and had seen the horrors and indignities of war for herself. This background had intensified the nervousness of her disposition and also given her a sense of superiority towards those who had not suffered similarly.

The Somerville College they returned to had been used by the army as a hospital during the war. Recalling it years later Vera remembered the 'long process of cleaning and redecoration' necessary to rid the place of 'the squalor which descends upon all habitation occupied for several years by military units'.[2] Oxford had become grim and desolate during the war's final years, and its reaction after the Armistice was, in Vera's words, to become 'abnormally normal'. The return of normality brought back rowing to the Thames, garden parties to the college lawns and men to the lecture theatres and libraries. Newly abnormal was the number of war veterans who came to study alongside eighteen-year-olds, and, most revolutionary of all, was the increase in the number of women students. Women's progress towards full membership of the university was drawing towards a successful conclusion and the 'Women's Statute', whereby women 'may be matriculated and admitted to Degrees in the University', would be accepted in May 1920 and come into force in October of the same year. None of the famous women of Oxford prior to that time, including the five women principals, had a degree from the university and a first duty following the Statute was to admit them to MA status. The first degree-giving ceremony in which women took part was held on 14 October 1920; '[i]nside the Sheldonian Theatre, its atmosphere tense with the consciousness of a dream fulfilled, younger and older spectators looked down, moved and entranced' as the first women Masters of Arts received their degrees, followed by nearly 5,000 undergraduates, 549 of them women. As Vera tartly pointed out, magnificent as the occasion was, it established a precedent whereby 'all the men were admitted to degrees, however minor, before all the women, however impressive'.

To return to Oxford in 1919 was, then, to return at a time of decisive change for women in the university. But to Vera it was, at least at first, a bleak and hurtful time, unrecompensed by any sense of a dream fulfilled, either for herself or for women in general. With Winifred it was quite different. Immediately she set about enjoying this second experience of Oxford and her letters to Jean McWilliam are full of accounts of the beauty of the countryside around Oxford, of poetry readings, the Oxford University Dramatic Society productions she was involved in, the agreeable nature of her lodging-room in Bevington Road with its sloping roof and a view over gardens, and of societies she had joined and people she had met, particularly those whom she and Jean had known in France. It was a more relaxed Oxford as far as relations between the sexes were concerned and Winifred told of walks with young men, although she also wrote of a visit from Grace as being 'invaluable by shopping, chaperoning river parties, and making dresses for the Going Down Play'. Grace would be twenty-four by that time and old enough to act as a chaperone, at least for the younger women undergraduates. The immediate time before the passing of the Statute was a sensitive one as far as decorum was concerned and the Principal of Somerville, Emily Penrose, had to balance the right to freedom of mature students like Winifred and Vera with a need to ensure propriety amongst eighteen-year-old girls to whom she was in *loco parentis*.

After she left it, Winifred was to say that she sometimes hated Oxford, with its attitude of 'magnificent inconsiderateness to anything that does not come immediately within its own exalted sphere . . . reclin[ing] gracefully upon the centuries like a lady on a sofa, and let[ting] the charwomen scrub about on their knees . . . completely complacent, and absorbed in its own affairs – a lovely, intense, secluded life, detached from the world outside'.[3] But Oxford's self-assurance and its comparative disregard of convention were very congenial to Winifred's expansive personality. She was popular, successful and ambitious, interested in politics and literature, people and clothes: the new woman undergraduate confidently seizing the fruits of knowledge and independence as her birthright. Where Vera was to campaign 'with partisan fury' in the months before the awarding of degrees to women in October 1920, and years later to recall the occasion with emotion as 'the visible signs of a profound revolution',[4] Winifred's account in a letter to Jean McWilliam is matter-of-fact, carefree, and rushes on in the same paragraph to say that 'Oxford journalism is as wild and youthful as ever. I am trying my hand at bits of it and writing verses for the *Chronicle* and stories for the *Outlook*.'[5] These were the journals in which Vera published her fiercely feminist pieces, hoping they would be read in London clubs and Oxford Common Rooms. As Vera was frequently to point out, Winifred's upbringing had been so free of the restraints that normally beset middle-class girls and young women that her feminism was slow to emerge and more relaxed in its approach.

The meeting between Winifred and Vera was written about three times by Vera, in her novel *The Dark Tide* (1923), in *Testament of Youth* (1933), and, briefly, in *Testament of Friendship* (1940). The facts of the meeting were that Vera had returned to Somerville in April 1919 and Winifred not until September when she joined Vera for coaching with the Dean of Hertford, Mr Cruttwell. They were both reading History, Winifred specialising in the Medieval period, in particular the reign of Richard II. Vera's six-month start over Winifred had served to assure her of her own intellectual gifts and had made her bitter at the crass insensitivity of both staff and students at Somerville towards her maturity and her war experience. When the eager, boisterous and apparently unscathed northerner burst into Cruttwell's study, Vera felt nothing but resentment and contempt towards someone 'whose vitality smote with the effect of a blow upon my jaded nerves. . . . Obstinately disregarding the strong-featured, sensitive face and the eager, shining blue eyes, I felt quite triumphant because – having returned from France less than a month before – she didn't appear to have read any of the books which the Dean had suggested as indispensable introductions to our Period.'[6] Winifred's essays also left much to be desired: 'voluminous, discursive, undigested . . . not easy reading', as Hilda Reid described them.

In *Testament of Youth*, published fourteen years after the meeting

of Vera and Winifred in Mr Cruttwell's study, the account follows
with the incident of a Somerville debate on the motion, proposed
by Vera on the suggestion of Winifred as secretary of the debating
society, that 'four years' travel are a better education than four years
at a university'. Winifred opposed the motion with a 'witty indict-
ment' of Vera's superiority towards those who had not shared her
experiences. When Vera was defeated she was deeply humiliated
and hurt. Her account in *Testament of Youth* admits to the humour-
lessness of her reaction but the bitterness she felt is vividly recalled
as she describes the 'series of pictures' of war horror and grief
which came to her as she reeled under what she felt to be the post-
war generation's betrayal of her and of those who had died. She
confronted Winifred soon after the debate, finding her 'puzzled and
a little perturbed', and only too willing to arrange for an official
apology to be sent from the president of the debating society.

The Dark Tide, published ten years earlier in 1923 and written
during the period immediately after graduating, when she and
Winifred had become friends and living companions, had also featured these incidents, but with far greater anger and desire to
punish. Virginia, unmistakably the Vera figure, is small, pale, elegant, attractive to men, and her essays are 'monotonously
excellent'; she has also suffered much in the war. The novel's other
protagonist, Daphne, is equally unmistakably modelled on
Winifred. Although Vera would later say that both Virginia and
Daphne represented aspects of her own personality, she did not
hesitate to use descriptions of Daphne in *The Dark Tide* as descriptions of Winifred in *Testament of Youth*. In the coachings, for
instance, Daphne writhes under criticisms 'which proclaimed her
style laborious, her sentences involved, her subject matter confused, and her spelling abominable', and this comment is
reproduced exactly in *Testament of Youth*. In the novel the character of Daphne—Winifred lurches between buffoonery – she is
gauche, masculine, clumsy, dresses badly, is always late, and is
unfortunate in her dealings with men – and pathos as she becomes

the mother of a disabled child and the abandoned wife of the tutor who has all along loved Virginia. In *The Dark Tide* the quarrel after the debate is healed by Virginia's intervention; in *Testament of Youth* it is Winifred who some months later came to Vera's sick room with a bunch of grapes, and returned the next day, thus beginning, as Vera described it in 1933, 'an association that in thirteen years has never been broken and never spoilt, and today remains as intimate as ever'. It was an association, however, which surely ran a great risk in its early days of being spoilt by Vera's ruthless lack of tact in recognisably using her friend to settle old scores in the public arena of fiction. The portrait of Daphne is a cruel one, both in how she is depicted and in what happens to her, and it is difficult to imagine how a friendship could have survived it. The fact that she revisited the incident in *Testament of Youth* suggests how deep the wound, how thin-skinned and unforgiving Vera was, and how enduring and resilient the friendship had become. The debate seems to have haunted Winifred too, for she mentioned it on her deathbed, apparently with remorse, because Vera answered, 'But just think – if the debate hadn't happened I should never have come to you afterwards – and think what I should have missed.' To which, of course, Winifred replied, 'And what *I* should have missed.'[7] At the time of the publication of *The Dark Tide*, Winifred wrote to Vera, somewhat obscurely, that she was prevented from refuting charges in the papers that the debate was not true to life, because it 'very nearly' was, and secondly, because if she did, 'the papers might say that this was evidently a common occurrence in a women's college – which it isn't.'[8]

When the forthcoming publication of *Testament of Youth* caused friends like Phyllis Bentley and Hilda Reid to protest at the portrait of Winifred, Winifred wrote from Cottingham to Vera explaining once again her motives in arranging the debate. The letter reveals something of the early stages of their relationship: that the coachings were humiliating for Winifred, that she had intended to teach Vera a lesson, that Vera was arrogant towards her fellow students.

The letter also implies that Vera is perhaps making too much of the episode, though as usual she explains this not on her own account but for its effects on others. In 1923 Somerville College had only too easily been able to identify characters in the novel as the dons and Principal, and Winifred thinks a resurgence of outrage should be avoided:

> I believe that I really am true in saying that the thought of holding you up in the pillory in revenge for the coachings never for a second did enter my head. . . . I had meant the whole thing to be a 'rag' – as we Waacs had instituted rags in the Army – dozens of rough & tumble (& no doubt coarse, clumsy & vulgar) teasings – to rub off what seemed to me something of your superiority towards all my fellow-students who had not been to the war . . . to my mind, the Debate episode is so dramatic, so typical of the misunderstandings caused by insensitiveness of perception (which my performance was), that I was all for including it in the Testament. . . . But perhaps it might revive the feelings which I know affected Somerville at the time of *The Dark Tide*, that you had taken revenge on the debate by holding me up to public ridicule, not just before college, but before the world, that you had better tone it down.[9]

In *Testament of Friendship*, with Winifred five years dead, the painful episode becomes the merest prelude – one of the 'trivial hurts and temporary resentments' of Vera's miserable first year back in Oxford – to their happy times together, walks to Tubney Hollow to see primroses or on Boar's Hill to visit the 'minor poets [who] live on goat's milk and cheese and bread from the co-operative stores'.[10] For Vera by this time, it had become the fruitful misunderstanding which initiated the romance of their friendship.

As far as Winifred was concerned the incident put her deeply into Vera's debt. It added to Vera's feminist endeavours to enter university, and her tragic and courageous history of wartime loss, another reason why Winifred would feel especially protective and obligated towards her. The friendship began with guilt on Winifred's part and it would continue with a sense of needing always to be careful of Vera's feelings, never repeating that first unkindness, perhaps excessively supporting Vera in all she did and wanted to do. Some of the gratitude Winifred felt towards Vera featured in her second novel, *The Crowded Street*, where Vera is the model for Delia, the feminist, new woman citizen of the war and post-war years whose example and encouragement inspires the heroine, Muriel, to cast aside the role of stay-at-home spinster for a more public 'idea of service'. In Delia's forcefulness of manner and her developed political attitudes, a tribute is paid to what Winifred believed Vera brought to the friendship. She would acknowledge this on her deathbed: 'I'm intensely grateful to you – you're the person who's made me.'[11]

By the summer of 1920, Winifred and Vera, each in their parents' home for the vacation, were corresponding with familiar affection, and by Christmas 1921 a pattern of letter-writing, political, chatty and encouraging, had developed. Winifred's early letters were garrulous – 'I write like a leaking tap' – and often sententious and overwrought and her praise of Vera was vehement and fulsome. It was the kind of admiration that Vera badly needed to restore her confidence and vitality. From the beginning Winifred mothered Vera, worrying about her health, proud of her beauty, encouraging of her talents, with something of a mother's indulgence towards Vera's waywardness and self-absorption. Vera's physical fragility – letters from this time stress the smallness, even childishness, of her body, and sometimes bid farewell with comments like 'I love you, my blessed little child' – thoroughly aroused Winifred's protectiveness, a wish to shield her from criticism, even when this might have been valuable. But although Vera was vulnerable, she was also heroic; she had endured much without descending into cynicism or triviality: 'there's something in you,'

Winifred wrote to her, '– burning fiery furnace or whatever you please to call it – stronger than any circumstances that ever arose yet.'[12] She had pronounced and fiercely held opinions and her feminism and her passion for peace were the kind of moral and political goals that could provide direction and focus for Winifred's diffuse benevolence and sense of responsibility. Like many good friendships, it was based on complementarity and by the time Winifred and Vera came to take their final examinations they were sure enough of it to agree to live together in London after graduating. As Vera described it, 'We both pictured a vague but wholly alluring existence of novel-writing and journalism, financially sustained by the barest minimum of part-time teaching, and varied with occasional excursions into lecturing and political speaking.'[13]

After graduating, both, disappointingly, with second-class degrees, they spent the summer with their parents until a holiday together in Italy and France in September and October. For both women, this holiday abroad was a decisive time in their relationship. It reconciled them to each other's different pasts, it proved that, in spite of Vera's moodiness, they could live together, and it was a pledge to the future. Vera described it in *Testament of Friendship* as 'the most perfect holiday of all my experience and, I believe, of Winifred's', and this to a large extent was also Winifred's verdict at the time. She wrote to Vera on her return to Cottingham: 'It has been a wonderful time, dearest. But you know, the best thing of all was finding out from day to day how dear you are. . . . Thank you, thank you, thank you, for being so completely satisfactory, you most sweet woman. And we will go again. There are heaps of lovely places to see, and things to do. Never doubt I want to see them and do them, and that I ask no better travelling companion than you.'[14] Yet though this letter begins more affectionately than any previous one – 'My dear little heart' – Winifred does not claim their friendship as exclusive; her letter continues: 'though sometime, I daresay, I may have to take someone else along, a Dot [McCalman], or a Miss Crichton; but then

you shall go with a Clare [Leighton], & we will smile at each other
sometimes.' Vera omits this passage in both *Testament of Friendship*
and *Selected Letters*, perhaps unwilling in retrospect to admit to this
element of caution in Winifred's response.

The intention initially was that Clare Leighton[15] should be
included in the flat they would share but finally it was just
Winifred and Vera who moved into 52 Doughty Street in late
December 1921, and set about earning a living. Testimonials from
Emily Penrose and from other tutors at Somerville, including
Maud Clarke and Dr Cruttwell, had praised Winifred's extensive
knowledge and lively personality and Maud Clarke mentioned
that she was considered for a First. All of them recommended her
for teaching.[16] Teaching was to be the means by which she and
Vera would earn independence but it was not the goal of their
ambitions, which was to be writers. Around the time of the Italian
holiday both women were busy writing their first novels, *Anderby
Wold* in Winifred's case, and *The Dark Tide* in Vera's. The plot of
Anlaby Wold (as it was first called) was in place by August 1921. 'It
gives me unbelievable joy and pain', Winifred wrote to Jean: 'when
one's sentences trundle clumsily across the stage, and the scenes
one meant to write with such dramatic constraint become merely
rather tiresome melodrama, it's a little difficult to keep one's faith
entire.'[17]

For all her trundling sentences, Winifred kept faith with her
novel and it was finished and with a publisher by early 1922, and
actually published, by John Lane, in April 1923. For a new author,
the process had been relatively painless and done without fuss.
This was not so with *The Dark Tide* which not only had difficulty
in finding a publisher but its composition had required constant
encouragement from Winifred. Winifred's letters during the
summer of 1921 are full of references to 'Daphne', as she and Vera
called the novel, and to the actual character of Daphne to whom
Winifred, not without self-mockery, humorously compared herself:
'To make Daphne have to entertain large quantities of young men,

& be desperately anxious to please, & yet suddenly become completely tongue tied, & flounder helplessly in a morass of platitudes,
wringing her hands and gasping like a fish! That's what would
have happened to me yesterday when Mother was in Whitby,
Grace in Hull, & six men from the "Carysfort" descended to play
tennis – only Captain Carpenter V.C. . . . . came to the rescue.'[18]
When Vera doubted her abilities as a novelist, Winifred was all too
reassuring. 'My dear,' she wrote in November 1921, 'you absolutely
are forbidden by your friend & guardian critic, to talk about your
"petty, provincial" talent. I simply will not hear a good thing
abused.' The letter continues rapturously about Vera's clarity of
vision due to suffering: 'you have broken through the mists and
have scaled the peak. You have trodden with bleeding feet the
sharp stones of the valley.' Years later, in preparing *Selected Letters*,
Vera, who did not include this letter, wrote at the top of it:
'Heavens what a letter all about nothing.' The 'nothing' that
prompted the letter seems to have been Vera's anguish at not yet, at
twenty-seven, having established a writing career. The need to do
so, the importance of her novel to her sense of this destiny,
intensely and obsessively preoccupied her, and Winifred colluded
with this self-centredness. When *Anderby Wold* was accepted for
publication, Winifred wrote to Jean: 'The really awful thing has
happened. I took [*The Dark Tide*] to John Lane and made them
interested in it and her, but they won't publish it. They returned it
yesterday. I've got the MS. She doesn't know yet. It's a horrid thing,
for her book's miles away better than mine, only Yorkshire stories
just happen to be in fashion and college ones aren't.' Such denial of
the value of her own work seems disingenuous, and her acting as
broker on Vera's behalf a kind of condescension. As the letter continues the need to behave like this is explained: 'It's the case of the
"haves" and the "have nots" again. At present I'm a "have", I suppose . . . I seem unable to give my friends any of my having,
though I'd so infinitely rather they had it. . . . If you're a "have," all
that you get seems to be somebody else's and the joy of having

them goes, or goes at intervals. . . . Always is the desire to share
them at the back of one's mind, and the ache of impotence, and the
anger of knowing that other people could use your chances
better.'[19]

Vera's shocked response to the success of *Anderby Wold* was a
sour martyrdom: 'I shall be really glad to know someone intimately who succeeds – just because all my best friends so far have
either died before they could achieve anything, or else are held up
for lack of funds.'[20] As she acknowledged, 'Somehow the whole
world seems subtly changed by your book getting taken. . . .
Almost I think of you as if you were a stranger; we are not equals
any more.' *The Dark Tide* was finally published in July 1923 and
doubtless the equality between them restored. But as Paul Berry
and Mark Bostridge have shown, there was more than emotional
cost to Winifred because Grant Richards, whom Winifred had
solicited on Vera's behalf, accepted *The Dark Tide* only on condition
of a £50 subsidy from the author, a sum paid by Winifred.[21] It is
not clear whether this was a loan or a gift. Whatever the case, and
perhaps also because of Winifred's unstinting support and praise of
Vera, their friendship survived another crisis, this time of professional rivalry, and perhaps even was strengthened by it.

By the time *Anderby Wold* was published Winifred and Vera had
been living together for more than a year, in 52 Doughty Street for
nine months followed by a move to 58 Doughty Street to a
roomier attic flat, with its 'blue and mauve and fuchsia covers and
shot blue and mauve cushions [and] blue delft plates to put on
the dark oak dresser',[22] a 'paradise' except for the mice and 'lots of
stairs'. Inconvenient though the flat was, it had – still has – a
sense of freedom and aspiration and to these two young women,
from a rural and a provincial background respectively, it represented all that was modern and emancipated. Winifred had one
paid commitment in these early days, lecturing on 'Italian people
in the Middle Ages' at St Monica's School in Kingswood in Surrey
where Vera's aunt, Florence Bervon, was the headmistress. An

almost indecipherable tape-recording remains of these lectures, Winifred's high, emphatic, un-Yorkshire voice ('like the Mem Sahib addressing the poor natives', Winifred herself later described it) floating with lofty formality across the years. 'I love lecturing', Winifred told Jean, and the girls were well-behaved and the classes easy to manage. Otherwise, she read in the British Museum in the mornings, went walking in the afternoons, corrected her novel after tea, and learned German after supper. In October 1922 she got a job as a coach to an American girl who wanted to go to college: 'I am to read with her, and criticise her essays and try and put some political economy and history into her pretty head . . . I hope she pays me well.'[23] There were also the unpaid lectures that both she and Vera gave, mainly for the Six Point Group and the League of Nations Union. Sometimes this involved open-air speaking in Hyde Park or on one occasion outside Hampstead Tube Station. 'That was killing', Winifred wrote, 'because I had to collect my own crowd. I stood on the pavement at the street corner and shouted to the empty air, two workmen, a motor-van, the policeman at the cross-roads, and a dog catching fleas on the curb. . . . I got a nice crowd in the end.'[24]

This was also the time when she was working for Percy Harris, a London County Councillor who wished to stand for parliament as Liberal MP for Bethnal Green, 'the roughest district to canvass in London'. He was also a keen supporter of the League of Nations Union. Through the connection with him Winifred became a school manager for two schools and helped to run a welfare clinic in the area. Such experience brought her into contact with the urban poor, the women overwhelmed with frequent pregnancies and the struggle to make ends meet, and the children always ill and absent from school: 'They are ill because they are sleeping regularly in the same room as three brothers, the new baby, their mother and father and the cat. . . . The mother is suspected of tuberculosis. The father is out of work. He is out of work because his cabinet-making master has failed. And the master has failed because trade is bad, because our markets are curtailed, because in Poland and Russia and Germany thousands of people are starving instead of fulfilling their destined economic function as purchasers of British and Indian goods.'[25]

Though useful experience to a budding journalist, such work brought no immediate financial return. The new life in London, for all its independence and promise, could not be paid for on the fees from St Monica's and until Winifred was established as lecturer and writer, her father, like Vera's, contributed around £200 a year to the upkeep of this independent lifestyle. It cost Winifred 'about £12' a month to live and this didn't include trips abroad nor the buying and making of the clothes she and Vera enjoyed so much. Jobs were scarce at this time – the LCC had 500 teachers on its waiting list – and though Winifred thought 'all the nice people of the world seem poor' she recognised too that there was always the security of her home in Yorkshire if the experimental lifestyle failed. But it didn't fail, and what started as an experiment soon became the norm, and any idea of a permanent return to the parental home for either woman no longer an option.

Beyond the mutual desire to earn a living through writing, what gave their life together structure and stability were the shared ideals of pacifism and feminism. In both cases, Winifred was initiated into active support by Vera. Before their Italian holiday in 1921 Vera had offered her services as a speaker for the League of Nations Union and, after a slow start, she was used regularly by the Union, sometimes as often as four times a week, undertaking 'long hot journeys in trains, or long cold journeys in trams', to make speeches or lead discussions on the League 'in almost every London suburb and in numerous small towns and villages all over the South of England and the Midlands',[26] thus carrying out the resolution she had made on her return to Oxford in 1919 to get in touch with some organisation which thought and tried to act collectively, as 'part of the surge and swell of great economic and political movements'. The League of Nations, formed under pressure from Woodrow Wilson at the Paris Peace Conference of 1919, seemed to be just such an organisation. With a covenant of principles which included collective security, arbitration of international disputes, reduction of armaments and open diplomacy, in its early days in the 1920s the League was a focus of hope, though the exclusion of Germany from membership and the refusal of the United States to ratify its covenant meant that it was flawed from the beginning. The League of Nations Union, which had come into being in 1918 with the amalgamation of the League of Nations Society and the League of Nations Association, was formed in the hope, according to Leonard Woolf, that just such 'some sort of international authority – a League of Nations, as it soon began to be called – should be established after the war in order to settle international disputes, promote the growth of a system of international law, and so help to keep the peace'.[27] The League of Nations Union was, therefore, a promotional organisation on behalf of the League of Nations. It relied on subscriptions and donations and, for the most part, used unpaid speakers. Winifred's readiness to join such an organisation – by June 1922 she was lecturing for it – rose from intellectual conviction – 'I believe that a co-operative institution like the League of Nations, although imperfect, is better than armed neutralities or balances of power,'[28] she wrote enthusiastically to Jean – and this was given emotional impetus by her sympathy for Vera's grief. On their Italian holiday, they had visited together the grave of Vera's brother and then the grave of Roland Leighton in France. As Vera later recorded, Winifred was the ideal, perhaps the only, person to share this pilgrimage with her: '[she] identified herself so closely in imagination with Edward and Roland that they almost seemed to be her dead as well as my own'.[29]

The early months of 1922 saw Winifred rehearsing her pacifist opinions to Jean McWilliam. As a historian she thought that the development of the nation state, with its extension into imperialism, had been necessary to civilisation but was now becoming obsolete and dangerous: 'The day of imperialism is passed. I heard its curfew sound when the guns startled the pigeons in Huchenneville orchard on Armistice day. Imperialism is really nothing more than dynamic and aggressive nationality. . . . What we want now is the transition to a still wider sphere of international co-operation, where empires don't matter, and patriotism becomes parochial, and the service of mankind becomes the only consideration.'[30] This was her message when she lectured for the Union, usually without pay and often at open-air meetings. The work was 'sorry, funny, exciting, wearying, interesting'. Frequently she had to raise her own crowd, and sometimes she was moved on by the police, 'like the Pied Piper with my crowd at my heels'. She learned to speak at length and in spite of heckling. She also learned how intransigent public opinion could be, and how bigoted. Speaking on LNU business to 'the most intolerant and intolerable set of women . . . wives of judges or diplomats' in May 1923, she found their xenophobia, anti-semitism and imperialism a 'pitiable example of the mentality of our erstwhile ruling classes', in contrast to the school children, town councillors, trade unionists, unemployed, and the Six Point Group she had addressed the day before.

In September 1923 she and Vera went for the first time to Geneva to a meeting of the Assembly of the League. 'I'm watching history made,' she wrote. In particular, she watched the League trying to solve the Greco-Italian crisis.[31] The following year they went from Geneva for three months to Central Europe to lecture for the Union, a sobering and maturing experience for Winifred. Vaguely idealistic, they saw themselves as 'British peace-makers who wanted to meet and mix with their former enemies', but Germany in 1924 was a tragic land, 'the population sullen and depressed from shame, poverty and malnutrition'.[32] With hindsight they both came to see the humiliation of Germany as a cause of the rise of Hitler and the inevitability of the Second World War but at the time they did little more than register what they saw, and were, if anything, confused about their role in setting the world right. 'Oh world, how blind, how suffering! I don't know where I am or what I believe,' Winifred wrote. 'I wish that I could be a Socialist, heart and soul. Or a pacifist, and die in prison. I know that . . . the only hope for peace is to keep a mind open to the possibilities of human nature. . . . If only people would not hate one another.'[33]

Her manuscript diary entries[34] of this visit in the autumn of 1924 are cautious, conscientious, non-judgemental accounts of people she and Vera met, the meetings they addressed, the state of the cities they visited, and the effectiveness of the work of the League of Nations Union. The diaries contain synopses of the speeches she gave, many of them to women's groups. Their import is of the necessity of support for the League and a promise that the LNU should seek to rectify the mistakes of the Treaty of Versailles, particularly to alleviate the sufferings of the defeated and displaced. Some of her speeches tentatively suggest a link between feminism and anti-militarism, urging resolution of the tensions between men and women, and between old and young, as necessary to the creation of a peaceful society. This was a theme she would develop more vehemently later in the 1920s: 'Women do not make war. Hitherto they have not had the authority and never have they had the desire. They know too well the value of human life, the cost at which it is brought into the world. . . . But it is not enough for women to refrain from making war; they must make peace.'[35] The causes of war, she wrote in 1928, grow from the intimate and familial structures of society, broadening from 'the individual to the family, from family to tribe, tribe to city, state, and empire and great alliance'.[36]

By 1923, Winifred and Vera had outgrown their cramped and inconvenient rooms in Doughty Street, and when their charlady resigned, incensed at the questionable lifestyle of two young women who 'dressed themselves up and went out at five o'clock at night and only came in at ten and eleven and twelve', Winifred 'went out and acquired a flat'. This was at 117 Wymering

Mansions, Wymering Road, Maida Vale, W9, to which they moved in November. Even with a Mrs Willett 'coming to housekeep' they could live more cheaply in this less fashionable, and indeed slightly sleazy, area, in spite of having to buy furniture for the new flat and 'heavenly cretonnes at Heals'. They had, said Winifred, 'been spending too much time washing dishes, when we should be writing. We are settling down.' The move confirmed both their commitment to a life together and their confident sense of creating an establishment, one with three bedrooms and a housekeeper. When the housekeeper left, Winifred arranged for her old nurse from Rudston to come to look after them. 'Nursie,' she wrote to Vera from Cottingham, was 'over the moon at the idea of London and Life. She says that she's never been really on her own. Now she's going to live. . . . She says that you shall have breakfast in bed every day if you like.'[37]

Winifred's second novel, *The Crowded Street*, at one time called *The Wallflower*, was accepted by John Lane in March 1924, for publication in September the same year. Immediately she was finished with it she began to write a fourteenth-century romance, originally called *The Princess*, then *The Runners*. Destined never to be published, this historical fiction, 'with Wycliff as the leading figure', filled her with enthusiasm; it brought together all her young ideals and used her expertise as a history graduate and lecturer. It was also, at least in its early stages, to be something of a *jeu d'esprit*:

> A pox upon your niggardly realism! For three years I have laboured to be sober, to be vigilant as a novelist, never to transgress by one epithet the constraint and prudishness of *les vies de provinces*. I'll write a romance, high tragedy, real galloping stuff, or die for it. (And what tripe it will be, to be sure, after all these brave words.)[38]

Wycliff was to feature as 'a man torn by intellectual doubts, physical cowardice, moral cowardice, and the brilliant clarity of his own mind – who leads the people up to a revolution and then denounces it'. There was also to be everything in it that was relevant to Winifred's own historical and social concerns: 'an execution or two, a democratic movement, ex-service men, the germs of English elementary education . . . an apple orchard in the sunlight, with a slim dreaming girl like [the actress] Gwen Françgon Davis, and Katherine Swynford, one of the first of the "modern women".'[39] It was also a crucial text in relation to Winifred's personal life at this time because in the relationship between Wycliff and Alice Fielde can be seen a re-enactment of Winifred's with Vera, and a casting of Winifred in a male role, a role she had sometimes assumed in college plays. Wycliff is described as a 'tall young Yorkshireman' whom people trust and like: 'because he was gauche, he must be honest . . . and misled by a certain simplicity of nature, [they] rarely credited him with subtlety of mind. Nor did they dream that [he] understood perfectly their attitude and made use of it for the fulfilment of his purpose.' Alice Fielde, the woman he loves in vain, is in the Vera mould, with 'proud, compassionate eyes that gave the lie to her bitter mouth and caustic tongue'. She is small and dark, 'with hair as soft as a bird's feathers, and a dear face that he had seen all red and wet with tears', Alice has turned to Wycliff 'as to a brother, for her true love had been slain in the French wars'. On their one moment of intimacy he addresses her as 'my very little love', words reminiscent of the manner in which Winifred was by this time signing all her letters to Vera: v.s.v.d.l. – very small, very dear love. But Wycliff cannot marry Alice because of his calling and also because she is betrothed to her cousin. His romantic and erotic love for her finds sublimation in working for his oppressed and illiterate people, aided eventually by the dead Alice's son who seems also to be Wycliff's spiritual son. Wycliff's destiny echoes the commitment Winifred herself voiced during the writing of the book: 'I am fierce for work. Without work I am nothing – I do nothing, am nothing except in so far as I may work.'[40]

The typescript of *The Runners* is accompanied by a letter from Andrew H. Dakers, Winifred's literary agent at this time, dated February 1927, in which he lists the nine publishers who had declined it. 'Two years' writing wasted,' she commented, '– or possibly not wasted . . . I may have gained experience even if it never sees daylight.'[41] The experience may have taught her the wisdom of staying with the contemporary *vies de provinces* in her fiction; it also undoubtedly helped as an emotional outlet for her during the years of Vera's engagement and eventual marriage to the political scientist George Edward Gordon Catlin.[42]

Gordon Catlin, who held a lecturing post at Cornell University in the United States, had written to Vera after the publication of *The Dark Tide*, expressing his admiration for the book and particularly the character of Virginia. An increasingly intense correspondence developed between them during the autumn and winter of 1923 and the spring of 1924. Winifred had watched Vera become flirtatiously involved with three men during their years together and regarded with some scepticism her expressed wish not to marry. Vera was now thirty and naively believed this would prevent men from finding her attractive. 'My dear,' Winifred wrote to her at Christmas 1923, 'how often have I warned you not to put your trust in being thirty? I never could think where you got hold of your absurd idea that thirty years constituted an invincible armour against sex-attraction. Forty won't with you. I should still walk cannily at fifty.' The letter continues more seriously, and also with a sense of the seriousness of the impending relationship with Catlin:

Dear child, I also hope you are not going to allow another male to prove himself devastating after this period of peace. I cannot help thinking that you can yourself prevent them being devastating, though I admit that you cannot help their being difficult. Mr Catlin sounds more than a little interesting. Perhaps it is a pity that you have not seen

him. He may be fat and greasy. I sometimes wish you were!
Anyway, he is still in America, so I don't think that there is
any need to worry, and it is a relief to hear of somebody
intelligent and interesting. . . . As for the personal side –
he does seem to be a good deal intrigued, but then it's all
rather from a distance, & he's probably quite safe. . . . My
dear love, I'll be your bulwark for as long as you want
me. . . . I regret that I have no Syren charms to entice away
embarrassing suitors – wouldn't it be a good thing if I
had?[43]

The letter concludes: 'I love you, my blessed little child. I love your
stories. I *do* think they can be good. Bless you, my little lovely one.'
By April 1924, with Vera becoming ever more deeply involved
with Catlin, Winifred was resignedly writing to her that 'one must
choose between stagnation and agitation in this world' and that the
choice between the two lay with Vera herself.

Catlin returned from America to meet Vera for the first time in
June 1924, and asked her to marry him five days afterwards; by
July she had agreed to do so. Winifred's response to this rapid
courtship was to be, as ever, self-effacingly supportive, and to balance delicately the need to assure Vera of her own love for her and
yet to leave her free and unpossessed. It was a difficult adjustment
and sometimes Vera complained that Winifred was too critical and
analytic about the forthcoming marriage, about marriage in general. Winifred replied:

. . . do I seem cold to you? Oh, my dear love, I am torn
between the exacting demands of love, and my invincible
belief that no one person should lay too heavy claims upon
another. To let each one of one's beloveds feel completely
free, even the most beloved of them all, to interpose no barrier of pity or tenderness between them and their destiny,
that needs a little careful schooling. If I have taught myself

too well, – then I am sorry – & yet I would not that it were otherwise.[44]

But the careful schooling would take its toll and Winifred's letters during this time are, as she herself admitted, portentously solemn epistles, excessively anxious to discuss marriage for the modern woman in as intellectual and disinterested a way as possible: 'the more idealistic type of woman either forswears marriage, or uses it with her husband's connivance, merely as an expedient background for her real life-adventure. . . . Neither sex nor marriage as its social expression are wrong, I think. What is wrong is this collision between the institutions of domesticity & public service, and the reason for this collision is not unavoidable. It has occurred because we live during a transition period.'[45] The discussion was in the context of interwar feminist arguments on grounds of principle that marriage and children ought to be compatible with a career. In fulfilling her own desires, particularly to have children, Vera would be the living example of an ideal. This was justification enough for Vera, and for Winifred it was reason enough, in addition to her love for Vera, to behave generously over the coming marriage.

Yet the intensity of Winifred's letters of this time suggests how great a strain was imposed on her, not only to accept Vera's marriage and departure, but also to translate what could be an occasion for jealousy and foreboding into one of high moral endeavour. One such letter was written on 27 August 1924, but in *Testament of Friendship* it is rather misleadingly transposed to the earlier period of Winifred's life following Harry's engagement to Irene in the winter of 1920–1.[46] The letter certainly recalls that earlier time when Winifred experienced a crisis of faith and when, in her own heightened words, she would 'lie face downwards in searing agony, hearing in mythical church bells the call to a devotion that my intellect would no longer allow me wholly to offer'. The 1924 letter, all ten pages, is an even more frenzied expression of the will to service, not through established religion but in various practical and scientific ways. Reading G.K. Chesterton's biography of St Francis of Assisi, she concluded that though his was an exemplary life for his time, 'the saint of the twentieth century will be a man who belongs to no particular church, but who shows the way to co-operation between all churches . . . a self-conscious thinker . . . one who shows science to be divine, and leads philosophy to its high place among the stars'.

But amidst this dedication of the spirit to service, what place is there for the body? Confronted by Vera's marriage and her own loss, Winifred's anxiety is acute: 'The old love of god would be expressed by an abandonment of the body, the hair shirt, the whip of cords. [But now the] way of asceticism is barred; but the cry remains, "Lord, Lord, give us the Highest Service." This yearning is to give everything, to stand naked before the world in an ecstasy of love & abandonment. How then shall we deal with Brother Ass the body, our servant with its dark & fiery passions . . .?' Wycliff, on whom she was writing at this time and into whose characterisation she poured this conflict, had believed that the 'monstrous agony of abstinence' came between a priest and his work, and so the argument is brought round to Vera's marriage, which is justified as liberating both husband and wife for higher service, the body 'not frustrated, but forgotten'. Such balancing of body and soul will not be without torture but patience, work and humour ('the divine sanity of humour') will bring peace after agony. Winifred's own future in this scheme of things will be different: 'If you must spend yourself completely now upon a personal emotion,' she wrote to Vera, 'and I must sublimate an emotion that I may not otherwise expend, do not think that my star rises or yours sets. We have both our way to take, & they will not be similar. If life, or Gordon's God, demands that you should at this time offer your personality – that is your fragrant body as well as your lucid mind – and if he demands that I now offer for service my mind alone – what matter?'[47]

Vera's marriage was a decisive act for Winifred; it precipitated a crisis of purpose, seeming to confirm her as a single woman and threatening her with great loneliness. Her letters of this period are the most agonised of her life; never again will she write so emotionally, even during the dark days of her final illness. Vera and Winifred were not lovers but Winifred had a lover-like relation to Vera and their separation was both personal anguish to her and a loss of bearing and intention, one she expressed in a letter to Jean of October 1924: 'In June Vera will go, and I shall be on my own again. No one will ever know what I owe to her during these five years; but now comes the choice again – how shall I live? One thing I am determined on, that I will not fall into the common error of circumstantial victimisation.' The choice was between what she called 'the Assisian way of life – contact with my brothers and sisters, social service', and the 'Aristotelian "good life" . . . culture and knowledge, and beauty of art and civilisation.'[48] This will be a recurrent motif in her life, the conflict between the political and the artistic role, or between the 'reformer-sort-of-person' and the 'writer-sort-of-person'.

An ideal of marriage such as both Vera and Winifred envisaged, required, of course, a husband who would grant his wife complete freedom and support in her career and this is what Gordon promised to do. But he too needed to be schooled, and he seems to have realised this. Since for most of the courtship time he was at Cornell University in New York, the schooling would have to be undertaken by letter. He initiated a correspondence with Winifred, writing to her from Oxford, where he was staying with his father, in July 1924, just after becoming engaged to Vera: 'I am, believe me, quite genuinely concerned by the responsibility of understanding and responding as I would wish to respond if I understood to the needs, bringing myself into the accord with the feeling of this dear, dear girl; I am genuinely diffident of my own judgement and of my own ability of keeping myself for long from rasping upon her.'[49] Recognising that Winifred had not put obstacles in the way of the engagement and that she could be a powerful ally, he wrote a month later to tell her 'how deeply I am in your debt' and that no 'flux of words would express more adequately my gratitude. No one needs to be told what gratitude one feels to the person who of their tact has been no small contributory cause to ones success in winning ones wife.'[50] Rather tentatively Winifred replied to him in October 1924, thinking he might welcome news of Vera's welfare when she and Vera were on their European tour. Winifred described how in all respects Vera had been 'a most enchanting travelling companion' including being an excellent nurse during her own sea-sickness on the voyage across the Channel. They had now paused at Bâle for Vera to rest after the 'almost over-strenuous interest of international complications'. Whilst Winifred wrote Vera slept, having been persuaded to spend a day in bed. Vera's proneness to bilious attacks and chills, a legacy of her experiences in Malta during the war, made it advisable, Winifred wrote, to 'keep her in bed & give her hot water bottles & small doses of neat brandy. She is always very meek & small & good when she is not well, & terribly anxious to give no one any trouble.' The letter continues by saying how much Vera relishes Gordon's letters, how she cherishes his photograph, and how charming she looks in a 'woollen & silk knitted dress of pale mauve colour – the shade of the most luxurious kind of parma violets . . . she looks about eighteen in it'.[51] The letter thus instructs Gordon in how Vera should be cared for and at the same time fosters the romantic, even erotic, relationship between them. This would be a vein to run through Winifred's letters during the months leading up to the marriage, and, in differing ways, beyond it too.

Gordon continued the correspondence with alacrity. It gave him intimacy with Vera by proxy and it was also a way of learning what modern young women like Vera and Winifred thought, and in particular how Vera should be looked after and loved. Sometimes he asked Winifred not only for her advice but also for her intervention. In January 1925 he wrote that the last letter he received from Vera had upset him very much, on the grounds that it stressed the sacrifice that marriage would entail for her, and he asked Winifred to 'intrude' to the extent of telling him if he has the right to ask so much. In a long and detailed reply,[52] Winifred rehearsed the arguments for and against marriage. Vera's doubts about the wisdom of marrying had prompted her also to ask for Winifred's opinion, to be given in 'brutal frankness', a phrase Gordon also had used to Winifred in asking for her advice. The conclusion Winifred arrived at was that the risk of marriage was worth taking but only if Gordon was prepared to make sacrifices for Vera to continue her literary and political career; these sacrifices must be made freely and actively and offered 'voluntarily to save marriage from destruction by false tradition'. 'She must use her liberties as her right, & you, not she, must defend her action against a critical and sceptical world.' To Gordon, whose mother's fierce feminism had destroyed her marriage and saddened his childhood and young manhood,[53] these must have seemed daunting yet exciting words, a challenge to create a new order of marriage, to put his feminist principles into practice. Winifred's astonishingly outspoken letter changes tack towards the end – 'I allow a little sentiment now after being so practical' – saying how sore-hearted Vera is at having hurt Gordon, that she has ranged photographs of Gordon as a child on the mantelpiece, and that she, Winifred, 'has borrowed the most helpless, the most confiding of these children & bore him off to my room, as a warning that, should I ever feel inclined to the too-facile prejudice of the "spinster-kind", I have that confiding and absurd little face to shame me into silence.' Finally, there is the reminder of Vera's physical charms, like those in Laurence's portrait of Lady Williams, Vera's great aunt: 'One day we will dress her up for you in ringlets, and a dress sliding from her shoulders, & your mother's beautiful pearls, & you shall see what her great aunt was like.' In the meantime, Vera 'has found a new way to do her hair, in little coils each side of her neck'.[54]

Winifred's mediation here, almost one might say her brokerage, which was intended to exhort Gordon and must also certainly have inflamed him, places herself significantly in relation to the lovers. She will be the unprejudiced spinster-friend, perhaps one who will be sensitive towards children, who is prepared to be motherly towards Gordon, remembering his vulnerable boyhood. She is also the purveyor and connoisseur of Vera's charms, vicariously appreciative through what she wishes Gordon to know. Above all, she is managing to be *included* in the lovers' relationship, keeping a hold on Vera through accepting Gordon as a legitimate intruder. There is much talk in the letters of the taking of photographs, Gordon asking repeatedly for them and Winifred doing her best in spite of bad weather and inadequate talents. If the photographs of Vera turned out badly, she wouldn't send them, and if Gordon didn't like what was sent he would tear them up. Both were engaged in a kind of negotiation over Vera's image, as attractive, desirable woman and as intellectual feminist. Gordon was as ready to engage in this as Winifred, and surprisingly willing to be admonished, as Winifred herself admitted: 'your astonishing humility and no less astonishing understanding reach beyond anything that I had hitherto experienced in a man's personality'.[55] He was very much in love with Vera and desperate that the marriage should not be called off: 'If Vera breaks off the engagement it will be the greatest disaster that has ever happened to me and I do not know how I should survive it, emphatically I should not wish to survive it,' he wrote, assuring Winifred, after much discussion about money, which was not quite the point of Winifred's argument, that he would promote Vera's interests over his own if necessary: 'I prefer to accommodate myself to her because I think she will get more happiness out of success than I shall.'[56]

His willingness to be accommodating was tested to the full in another long letter Winifred sent on 3 April 1925 in which she complained that his criticism of Vera's fiction, the writing of which was dearest of all things to Vera's heart and where her potential greatness lay, was leading her to think that she couldn't marry someone whose attitude had such a destructive effect on her abilities: 'you continually criticise, analyse & suggest about her unfinished work. . . . It has prevented her from finishing any good piece of work since she knew you, & that she is being driven more & more to dread lest marriage, which she now desires because she loves you, will become that very danger which she will sacrifice anything to avoid – a danger to her work.' Winifred then advises him on what he might write to Vera about: problems, ideas, pacifism, the position of women, and to 'let her sometimes talk to you of her ideas, of the story, that it may clear herself in her head. She does this to me. I often disagree. But I have learnt from my own experience to hold my tongue.' If Gordon cannot do this, 'then don't marry her'. Winifred compares his criticism of Vera with Vera's criticism of her own work: 'knowing my very great faults as a writer, she tried to cure them by analysing & criticising my ideas before they became books. . . . It nearly drove me crazy until I had to set a complete taboo upon her discussion of my work save after it was done.' The letter concludes with the revealing statement that 'I have come from a sense of an intense unwillingness for you to marry Vera, to a sense of catastrophe if you don't, & that I feel if you cannot avoid failure here, there is small hope in the world for the marriage of any two really gifted, creative people.'[57]

Winifred later felt some compunction about this 'violent & disquieting' letter but Gordon seems either not fully to have registered its impact, or to have misunderstood it, an obtuseness that would become a bedevilling feature of his relationship with both Winifred and Vera. But at least the tone of his letters to Vera altered, to Winifred's delight, provoking a rapturous description of Vera reading his letters and trying on new shoes, 'seated on the floor in new silk stockings, surrounded by six pairs of minute, high-heeled, large-buckled, absurd little shoes, completely absorbed for the moment in your letters, & all the dimples coming out again in her cheeks like flowers after rain'.[58] Her final remaining letter to him before the marriage describes Vera trying on her wedding dress: 'she looks eighteen or less & prettier than even you may imagine. You will begin to wonder whether this child is old enough to be your wife.' And so begins a disconcerting habit that Winifred and Gordon will maintain for some years of referring to Vera, who was thirty-one at the time of her marriage, as 'the child', placing them in a quasi-parental relationship to her and in a curiously conspiratorial relation to each other.

Gordon's flux of words to Winifred continued anxiously throughout the spring of 1925 to the time of the wedding in June, as though only by Winifred's approval and help could it possibly take place. He fretted over the practical arrangements of the marriage, how the next five years would be crucial to Vera's career and therefore his should take second place, how unworthy he was to marry Vera, about his journalism and her fiction, and finally, and perhaps more significantly than he intended, he thanked Winifred for her help with the wedding: 'You were I think almost more indispensable to the wedding than the bridegroom himself since it was conceivable with a different bridegroom but could simply not have been carried through without your supervision.'[59]

Winifred had made no secret of her closeness to Vera: 'she is more than part of myself,' she wrote to Gordon, adding that she had nevertheless made up her mind that only by losing her to Gordon could Vera 'find her greatest richness of life'. This disinterested love was, she explained, 'based so deeply upon reverence that I could never regard lightly anything that touched her interest'.[60] To Jean McWilliam she wrote similarly: 'I like, respect [Gordon] – I could say, love him, and am very happy, though it means losing Vera's companionship and no one can tell what she has meant to me for these four years. But I covet for her this richer life.'[61] Her account to Jean of the wedding itself was terse: 'Vera and Gordon were married on Saturday [27 June]. All went well, and I will send you some photographs to show how beautiful we all were.' She also enclosed a copy of the notice in *The Times* which described how the bride's ornaments were 'a pearl and gold bracelet (the gift of the bridegroom), and a pearl, gold and platinum necklace (the gift of the bridesmaid)'. ('It was too little', Winifred was to say on her deathbed, seeing it as a bracelet on Vera's wrist. 'It ought to have been bigger.') After the wedding Vera wrote to Winifred that saying goodbye to her 'for even six weeks nearly made me weep. I wanted to take you with us – I *did*. . . . Darling sweet, I do love you . . . I have my suspicions that, though others are capable of being loved in ways that you are not, the something in you that I love I shall always love best.'[62] Winifred's letter two days after the wedding – 'I am rather weary, quite pleasantly so' – undertook to retrieve a number of Gordon's mislaid possessions and see to other practical matters such as the wedding fees. It concludes: 'Au revoir, sweet child, dear heart, beautiful & beloved creature . . . lover, comrade. v.s.v.d.l.' But though Winifred would miss Vera intensely, she resolved not to fall 'into the common error of victimisation'. She had assured Gordon that she wouldn't cling to Vera: 'when you return to England you will find I have effected a quite neat and painless divorce', and in this resolution there were other people very ready to help her. Her letter to Vera pointedly describes how she has been 'whirled off in a taxi to some Soho restaurant' by Lady Rhondda 'to have lunch with Cicely Hamilton [and] a select, but formal gathering chiefly of Time and Tide Publishing Co.'[63] Determined on her own account not to be the pitiful spinster left at home during the honeymoon trip, Winifred was also determined that no shadow of this spectre should fall across Vera's first days of marriage.

As it turned out, the divorce between her and Vera would not be the 'decree absolute' that Winifred promised Gordon. But in June 1925 it certainly seemed such to Winifred and at the age of twenty-seven she had to set about structuring her life without the emotional centre that Vera had provided. Other friends, work, and a visit to South Africa all played their part in this reorientation but the psychological effect of the loss of Vera was a profound one and it drained Winifred of some of the intensity and exuberance of her personality. The sense of not being the one preferred above all others, of having to take second place, had to be accepted and turned to positive ends, and emotional needs sublimated into generalised benevolence and social duty.

CHAPTER 5

'Leader . . . Editor . . . Friend': Margaret Rhondda

According to Vera, Winifred never throughout her life was made to feel a personal sense of feminine inferiority; her background in this respect contrasted with Vera's early environment with its 'complacent acceptance of female subordination'. Winifred's commitment to equality between the sexes was, Vera said, a 'cool intellectual conviction [which] dawned on her at Oxford, and . . . I was its source.'[1] This conviction was, however, a source of impatience to Winifred: 'I dislike everything that feminism implies . . . I want to be about the work in which my real interests lie, the study of inter-race relationships, the writing of novels and so forth. But while the inequality exists, while injustice is done and opportunity denied to the great majority of women, I shall have to be a feminist.'[2]

Yet however unusual her home background may have been, and dominated by a powerful and ambitious mother, the wider circumstances of her childhood in a conservative rural community and the expectations regarding the typical lifestyle of a girl from her own class of wealthy farmers cannot have left her untouched.

Though she may not have been a conscious feminist in her years before Oxford, and later claimed that the pre-war suffrage campaigns came to her only through 'the distorting mirror of caricature', the roots of Winifred's feminism, particularly as it emerged in her fiction, lay in the pre-Vera years. In *Anderby Wold*, for instance, both Mary Robson and Sarah Bannister are frustrated by the indirectness of their paths to power. Married to ineffectual men, this is nevertheless the only way they can gain access to respectability and economic stability, in contrast to the 'undowered spinsters' of the family. *The Crowded Street* depicts the life of just such a spinster whose life is dominated by the requirement of 'sex success'. Her sister who does marry, desperate for sexual recognition and satisfaction, dies of neglect in childbirth. There are family echoes in these stories – Winifred's mother, Winifred's sister Grace, various cousins, aunts and uncles, maids who worked at the house in Rudston, tennis-club acquaintances at Cottingham – but they also give a representative picture of women's predicaments in the inter-war period.

At the time Winifred published her first novel, women were in excess of men in the population by approximately one and a half million, and this figure would persist, and even slightly increase, throughout the inter-war years. The figure of the unmarried woman, the spinster, would be a controversial one during the period and would feature extensively in Winifred's journalism as well as in her fiction. The alternative to spinsterhood, marriage, also had its hazards, most obviously those of pregnancy where there was a 1 per cent chance of dying in childbirth,[3] and a 10 per cent chance of the baby dying at, or soon after, birth. As far as work was concerned, women comprised 41 per cent of a work force of nearly 14 million, a slight decline in the number of working women since the late nineteenth century due to the decrease in the number of domestic servants. Most working women in the 1920s were single; only 10 per cent of working women were married. During the war women had shown an ability to extend their range of occupations and had proved that the distinctions between men's and women's work were largely artificial, a finding that a Home Office Report of 1919 had recorded with some surprise.[4] In spite of this, after the war women were denied access to most areas of skilled employment and even where they were permitted to do the same work as men, as in teaching, they did not receive equal pay for it. For although women had achieved some measure of equality during the war, government and trade union pledges to restore men's jobs to them, and their wage differentials, ensured that women were very quickly either swept out of employment altogether or were reduced once again to work of low status and low pay, approximately 50 per cent of the male rate. The War Cabinet Committee Report on Women in Industry, set up in 1919 'to investigate and report on the relation which should be maintained between the wages of women and men having regard to the interests of both as well as to the value of their work', made little progress on the issue and was unmemorable except for a famous Minority Report by Beatrice Webb which challenged many of the assumptions on which the committee had operated, namely that 'industry is normally a function of the male, and that women . . . are only permitted to work for wages under special conditions'. Webb, who was sixty by this time, and therefore representative of an earlier generation of reformers, put forward a resounding list of recommendations which set the parameters of the debate concerning women and the family during and, indeed, after the inter-war years. These were that there should be a National Minimum Wage, which should be equal for men and women; there should be standard rates of remuneration for every occupation, which should be equal for men and women; that the principle of the 'vested interest' or prior right of the male to any occupation should be rejected; that provision from the Exchequer should be made for children; and that adult dependants, such as the infirm and the aged, should be provided for as a national obligation.

As an Appendix to *Women and a Changing Civilisation*, published in 1934[5] as a summary of her thoughts on the position of women, Winifred listed some of the laws passed in England since women obtained the vote in 1918 and also some of the campaigns conducted by women which had resulted in reformed administration. The Acts of Parliament and the campaigns that Winifred listed cluster exclusively round welfare issues, particularly the welfare of infants and children. The first three of Webb's recommendations, which relate to women in the work force rather than in the home, had met with little success. The failure of one kind of reform and the success of the other reflected a division in feminism during the 1920s which may crudely be described in class terms – the middle class versus the working class – and whether women as workers or as wives and mothers should be the primary concern of reformers.

As middle-class, university-educated women, bent on pursuing careers in writing and lecturing, it was likely that Winifred and Vera would choose a feminist alignment which would be concerned with the rights of women as workers and as citizens, and that this would be of the equal rights variety that the weekly review, *Time and Tide*, and its parallel organisation, the Six Point Group, promoted. The first issue of *Time and Tide* had appeared in 1920 and introductory copies sent to Somerville, as to other women's colleges. Vera subscribed and also began to send articles to the paper, her first accepted for publication in 1923. By this time both she and Winifred had joined the Six Point Group, had started lecturing for it – 'once or twice a week', Winifred told Jean, 'not paid, except for expenses' – and Winifred too had begun to try to get her pieces accepted by *Time and Tide*. At Six Point meetings they came into contact with the woman whom Winifred was later to refer to, in the dedication to her collection of short stories, *Truth Is Not Sober*, as 'Leader . . . Editor . . . Friend': Margaret Haig Mackworth, Viscountess Rhondda.

Winifred and Vera first met Margaret Rhondda in the spring of 1922 when they decided to attend a mass meeting of the Six Point

Group in the Queen's Hall. She had, wrote Vera,[6] 'the reputation of a harsh and pitiless feminist [but] I was astonished beyond measure at the deprecating sweetness of her expression, the mild earnestness of her hesitating voice, as she spoke rather shyly on the subject of child-assault.' But this impression would later be balanced by a very different one of a combative campaigner whose 'fighting speech', 'flushed face and indignant blue eyes' were formidable attributes in public debate. Winifred's impressions were also mixed: 'large, in black, outspoken and capable, like a cabinet minister (which she ought to be) and a successful managing director (which she is)', but she was, Winifred noted, 'desperately shy when *tête-à-tête*. . . . A nice woman, but rather a lonely one, I think. Possibly she wants to be nothing else.'[7] But Margaret Rhondda did want something else and within a couple of years a friendship and working partnership with Winifred had been formed, beginning with a lunch at Margaret Rhondda's house in February 1924, she and Winifred *tête-à-tête* but apparently anything but shy. 'We talked for nearly three hours about everything in the world: marriage, families, education, loyalty, plays, religion, socialism, fire-screens, provincial towns, Americans, Woman (and women), war, and the future of the race. I don't know what else.'[8]

Born in 1883, Margaret Rhondda was fifteen years older than Winifred and turned forty when they met, a wealthy business woman and a veteran suffrage campaigner. Her autobiography, *This Was My World*, was published in 1933, the same year as *Testament of Youth*, and could hardly have provided a greater contrast. Written with an amused detachment from the events she describes, it has none of the anxiety and anguish of Vera's account. Both women saw their lives as exemplary but unexceptional – 'to tell my own fairly typical story as truthfully as I could', in Vera's case; 'the autobiography of a normal person', wrote Margaret Rhondda – yet their experiences of the 'incomparable changes' brought about by the women's movement and by war were quite different. Whereas Vera had to fight for educational opportunities in a narrowly conventional middle-class family, Margaret had a sympathetic and unconventional family, including a mother who got herself arrested in support of the suffrage campaign and 'an amazingly modern-minded father'[9] who made Margaret, in effect, his business partner. Margaret lost no lover or friend in the war but she did nearly die herself, being torpedoed on the *Lusitania*. Her account of being sea-sick in a lifebelt, in a 'comfortable sitting position, with one's head lying rather back, as if one were in a hammock' before losing consciousness, is laconic in its avoidance of the emotional and melodramatic. Her greatest sense of loss related to her father's unfulfilled ambitions as a politician – 'in some sense tragedy' – and his death in 1918, aged sixty-two, amidst plans for the creation of a Ministry of Health. After his death, and after taking steps to have her marriage amicably dissolved, she was free, 'free as never yet in my life had I been before . . . I had a profession. I was rich. Owing to being my father's daughter I had, almost by accident and much to my own surprise, made a name. A name is a platform. Life was before me to do what I chose with.'[10]

What she chose to do was to try to change the world. Like Winifred and Vera, in the aftermath of war she wanted 'passionately, urgently, to change customs and to influence ideas [which] unless they were radically changed, mine along with the rest, of course – seemed likely to lead back . . . towards the same abyss. . . . I wanted to find, to test, and to spread the customs and the ideas that could be health-giving and life-saving.'[11] The platform she chose, and the life it created for her, was *Time and Tide*. She had been inspired by the reforming influence of the *New Statesman*, 'insensibly, subtly, gradually heading opinion towards Socialism', and came to believe that she too could found a similarly influential paper, a weekly one because that would combine a degree of topicality with opportunity for reflection. There would be uncertainties: could it be a success commercially as well as a *succès d'estime*? could it be done by a woman: 'the thing had never yet been done by a woman', did she have the knowledge to do it? 'I had first to get experience . . . an uncommonly expensive and rather painful experience, but at the end of eight or nine years I had gained it.' She later recalled in *Time and Tide* how she came by this experience when her father pledged her to write an article on the suffrage for a local newspaper, after which she went on to write three a week, 'mostly lifted bodily from leading articles in *Votes for Women*'.[12] As a merchant and a merchant's daughter she knew that 'in one coin or another all things worth having must be paid for' and she concludes her autobiography with the Spanish proverb that Winifred would quote at the front of *South Riding*: ' "Take what you want," said God. "Take it and pay for it." ' Winifred would add, through the mouth of Mrs Beddows, 'Ah. . . . But who pays?'

In a footnote in her autobiography Margaret Rhondda acknowledged that '*Time and Tide* was not, of course, founded by me alone [but] by a like-minded group of people, all of whom gave to it of their best'. Although she took over its editorship in 1926, in the beginning she was the Vice-Chairman of its directors and the first editor was Helen Archdale. The other directors, all of them women, were Mrs Chalmers Watson (the Chairman), Dame Helen Gwynne-Vaughan, Mrs H.B. Irving, Christine Maguire and Elizabeth Robins. Between them they represented the professions, business and the arts. With a capital of £20,000 the Prospectus for the paper was filed with the Registrar of Joint Stock Companies as a limited publishing company on 14 May 1920, Margaret Rhondda owning 90 per cent of the company's shares. Its first editorial advertised it as an independent paper, 'one whose attitude is not dictated by any party or personal bias but whose convictions and whose honest criticisms . . . are stated without fear or favour . . . a Press which shall aim at showing all sides of national life'. It also aimed to treat 'men and women as equally part of the great human family, working side by side ultimately for the same great objects by ways equally valuable, equally interesting; a paper which is in fact concerned neither specially with men nor specially with women, but with human beings'. Nevertheless, the group behind the paper was composed entirely of women and though men did write for the paper, women contributors predominated. Although in general terms Margaret Rhondda did not believe in separate spheres of activity for men and women, in the case of *Time and Tide* she felt that women's political emergence made them 'especially conscious of the need for an independent Press'. The journal attracted famous contributors – or they were pressed by Margaret Rhondda into writing for it: Nancy Astor, Ellen Wilkinson, Cicely Hamilton, Rebecca West, Helena Swanwick, Rose Macaulay, E.M. Delafield, George Bernard Shaw, G.K. Chesterton and Gilbert Murray all contributed and the journal quickly established itself, with a readership of between twelve and fifteen thousand readers in the early 1920s. Its success increased during the next decade so that by the 1930s it was offering serious competition to the *New Statesman* as the leading weekly review in Great Britain.[13] By the 1940s its circulation had risen to around 40,000 but its fortunes declined in the 1950s, it began to lose between £400 and £500 a week,[14] and after Margaret Rhondda's death in 1958, her personal fortune exhausted in supporting the journal,[15] it was able to survive independently for only a short while before being absorbed into *John O'London's Weekly* in 1962. In that year the Time and Tide Publishing Company went into liquidation; Winifred Holtby's two shares were sold in the proceedings.

The first number of *Time and Tide*, on Friday 14 May 1920, comprised twenty-four pages, tabloid size, and cost 4*d*. The pattern it established was of a Review of the Week in politics and public events, followed by Leading Articles (in the first issue on Housing Bonds and the Bastardy Bill), Notes from America, a 'Personality and Powers' feature (on Elizabeth Robins in this issue), book reviews, a gardening article, some poems and a small play, a music feature and one on lawn tennis. During the early years this pattern varied slightly, for example, by the inclusion of a financial section, cinema reviews (by 'Hecate') and a letter page. In the news columns the issues that attracted recurrent attention were Ireland, the League of Nations, suffrage, equal pay, the marriage bar, and social concerns like alcoholism and housing. There was also a round-up of general political news. The advertisements, which increased as the paper became successful, were for insurance, hobbies, women's clubs like the Women's International Franchise Club, charities, and books, which included books of especial interest to feminists, such as Marie Stopes's books and Arabella Kenealy's *Feminism and Sex Extinction*. There were sometimes advertisements for clothes but only rarely for beauty products. The paper was instructive and engaged and it also aimed to be wide-ranging, non-specialist and not too heavy. As its advertisements, its favourite topics and its general tenor indicate, it was, of course, middle-class in orientation. The paper's politics were liberal (or liberal democrat), favouring constitutional change through persuasion and negotiation. It was therefore unsympathetic towards the General Strike of May 1926 (during which it was published in a cyclostyled form), which it considered 'a battle to decide whether the leaders of the trade unions shall overrule the elected government of the country . . . obviously the community must fight, and go down, if needs be, fighting this attempt to substitute the rule of an unconstitutional body for the rule of constitutional government'.[16] After Margaret Rhondda took over the editorship, the paper lost some of its campaigning zeal, becoming more miscellaneous and general, and with a greater emphasis on cultural matters. Its changed cover page, which was more decorative and magazine-like than its first cover design, was indicative of a general softening in manner.

In *Testament of Friendship* Vera tells how Margaret Rhondda invited Winifred to become a director of *Time and Tide* immediately on her return from South Africa, and how delighted and surprised she was to be asked. She enjoyed going to the dinners for directors Margaret Rhondda gave at her flat, and she enjoyed the company of journalists and writers the paper provided. Endearingly for someone usually so lacking in self-importance, she had cards printed which announced:

> Miss Winifred Holtby
> Director, *Time and Tide*
> 32 Bloomsbury Street
> W.C.1

After her promotion to a directorship, her contributions to *Time and Tide* were less in the way of leading articles and more of frequent book reviewing and assistance to the editor, by this time Margaret Rhondda, in providing regular news coverage, and also commentary of a miscellaneous nature in 'Notes on the Way'. There is little doubt that Winifred became Margaret Rhondda's right-hand woman, someone she could trust to be committed and efficient and who in most respects shared her beliefs, and who, it must be assumed, colluded with the mild popularisation of the paper during the later 1920s. In the early 1930s Margaret offered the editorship to Winifred but Winifred refused; her health by then was not good and in any case, she didn't enjoy office organisation. Vera thought Margaret Rhondda should buckle down to the task herself, and 'be the real editor instead of the rich leisured woman who runs a paper as a hobby'.[17]

Journals usually come into being to promote an organisation already established. In the relation between *Time and Tide* and the Six Point Group it was the other way round. An editorial in *Time and Tide* on 19 November 1920, seven months after the journal's launch, issued a challenge to action on the part of feminists who should, the editorial suggested, use the partial franchise women had won in 1918 to agitate for a totally equal franchise and for other equalitarian reforms. The editorial may have been written by Margaret Rhondda; certainly it represented her views. In *This Was My World* she described how she answered this challenge, with 'an equality society, the Six Point Group. We joined with such bodies

as the National Union of Women Teachers and the Open Door
Council, who were doing the same kind of work. We co-operated
in the Equal Rights Committee. For seven or eight years we
worked away at all these things; at a heap of niggling little laws that
needed altering.' A fuller account of the Group's origins and policy
was given by Elizabeth Robins in the introductory number to the
Six Point Group Supplement that *Time and Tide* ran from January
to March in 1923. During that time, six numbers of the paper carried articles by various individuals, including Rebecca West, Cicely
Hamilton, George Bernard Shaw and Joseph Cohen, covering the
points the Group was particularly concerned with. Elizabeth
Robins called her introduction 'The Six Points and Their Common
Centre' and after listing the six points[18] she described how in
February 1921, 'a little group of women framed a programme of
social betterment' which would offer a non-party rallying ground
and would be a 'political instrument to hasten the ends desired, by
the only sure means, i.e. the Government measure'.[19] *Time and Tide*
was thus to be the means by which opinions would be formed and
attitudes changed and the Six Point Group would exert political
pressure through debate, meetings, lobbying and petitions, and as
a research capability would provide the information on which
Time and Tide could base its articles. The overlap in personnel
between contributors to the paper and the Group was considerable, including Rebecca West and Cicely Hamilton as well as
Elizabeth Robins, and, later on, Winifred and Vera. Margaret
Rhondda was the chairman of the Group from its inception until
April 1931.

By the time Elizabeth Robins wrote her introduction to the
Group, it had succeeded in its first aim of acting as a rallying
ground for other societies, twenty-four of them initially, in the for-
mation of a Consultative Committee of Women's Organisations
under the chairmanship of Lady Astor. The first success was in the
area of child protection, easy enough to achieve, according to
Robins, because 'women, who differ from one another on every

other count, were ready to join hands to protect the child'. The Criminal Law Amendment Bill of February 1921, a private member's bill including clauses to raise the age of consent, had been wrecked in its final stages. In the aftermath, the Consultative Committee passed a resolution, proposed by Margaret Rhondda from the Six Point Group and supported by thirty-four societies, urging the government to bring forward its own Criminal Amendment Act. After intense lobbying, a Bill amending the Criminal Law Amendment Acts of 1885 and 1912 was introduced in February 1922 raising the age of consent in regard to indecent assault from thirteen to sixteen years, abolishing 'reasonable cause to believe' as a defence, increasing penalties for brothel keepers, and repealing the secrecy clause in legal proceedings relating to incest. Vera, who with Winifred had listened throughout a hot July night in 1922 to the third reading of the Bill in the House of Commons, commented afterwards on her quite 'ferocious satisfaction [that] the plea made by a few gallant English men that our liberties would be curtailed if the opportunities for attacking female children were made more difficult had not succeeded'.[20]

Another success Elizabeth Robins recorded was the White and Black Lists, 'framed with skill and patient labour [and] of invulnerable accuracy', in which the record of parliamentary candidates and MPs on issues of equal rights was compiled and maintained by the Group. There was, Robins wrote, anger and outcry at the Black List[21] and its sponsors 'were remonstrated with by letter, denounced from platforms, and threatened with libel action. But eventually silence fell. Likewise some of the largest majorities. Even certain seats, considered safe, fell to White List candidates.' Robins noted that in all this the one great material advantage the Group had from its inception was a 'participating newspaper behind it'.

In her account Elizabeth Robins acknowledged the tactical issues confronting the Six Point Group, and, indeed, inter-war feminism in general. Though she could state the Group's belief that the reforms which were sought had a solution common to them all, which was the end of the disqualification on account of sex, she and the Group recognised that reforms would have to be achieved piecemeal with those affecting women as mothers being the easier and those concerning women as workers the more difficult. Feminists like the Six Point Group, who believed equalitarian measures were the most important and would make everything else fall into place, were at odds with those who thought that women as wives and, particularly, as mothers should receive the most urgent attention. The two groups came to be known as the Old Feminists and New Feminists, and though in practical programmes the differences were ones of emphasis and priority, there were underlying differences of principle which led to sharp exchanges in which Winifred would be a prominent debater.

An issue which illustrated the divisions was what came to be known as the Rhondda Peerage Claim in which Lady Rhondda, citing the Sex Disqualification (Removal) Act, decided to take action against the House of Lords on the grounds of its exclusion of her, a peeress in her own right. This seemed to the New Feminists to be an elitist cause on which women should not waste their efforts. But it was more than this in being a test case which would illustrate the failures of the Act, of which there were many, particularly in respect of the dismissal of women on marriage from the civil service, teaching and nursing, the refusal of Cambridge University to give women degrees, the dismissal of women from the police force, and the refusal of the London Hospital to take more women medical students. To Vera the feeble functioning of the Act sprang from 'a post-war reaction in which war neurosis had been transformed into fear – fear especially . . . of the loss of power by those in possession of it; fear, therefore, of women'.[22] Wealthy, experienced in public speaking, and with a sound and focused case, Margaret Rhondda seemed the necessary woman to take the fight into the very heart of the conservative establishment; if she won, the victory might cascade into other institutions. Her petition to the king was referred to the Committee of Privileges which heard the case in March 1922 and decided in Lady Rhondda's favour. But a rearguard action led by the Lord Chancellor, Lord Birkenhead, overturned the decision. The Act, in this as in other respects, was, in Lady Rhondda's words, 'a leaky saucepan'.[23]

There was, of course, to be more success with equalisation of the franchise, although not without delays and difficulties.[24] During the early 1920s, successive governments had procrastinated over the issue and by 1925, particularly in view of the reluctance of the newly elected Conservative Prime Minister, Stanley Baldwin, to honour his pre-election pledge to introduce an equal franchise bill, Margaret Rhondda had become active in the Equal Political Rights Campaign Committee which had the sole aim of co-ordinating the activities of a number of feminist groups in a concerted effort to gain the vote for all women over the age of twenty-one. After repeated petitions, meetings and a press campaign, a bill was announced in April 1927 to give women the vote on the same terms as men and the Franchise Acts were passed in 1928. Lady Rhondda's remark in her autobiography that this last big purely legal inequality having been removed, 'one felt free to drop the business'[25] was an indication of the limited nature of her equalitarian feminist sympathies. There was a great deal of feminist work still to be done, even in Old Feminist terms, and the 1930s would prove to be a decade of very little progress as far as women's employment rights and opportunities were concerned. As Ray Strachey would point out in *Our Freedom and its Results*, published in 1936, 'Women can earn more than they could do in 1914; but they still cannot earn what their work is worth.'[26] By the time Strachey wrote, Margaret Rhondda had begun to shape *Time and Tide* as less a feminist than a liberal and reformist paper of a general kind. This would bring her into conflict with feminists who had supported the paper in earlier days,[27] but the bond with Winifred remained unthreatened, perhaps because Margaret's staunch individualism, her very definite alignment as an Old Feminist, was not unsympathetic to Winifred's own views.

Slower than Vera to get her journalism accepted for publication, Winifred's first acceptance from *Time and Tide* was in 1924 for an article called 'The Human Factor'[28] which, drawing on her experiences in Bethnal Green, was concerned with the reduction by the London County Council in the number of teachers, particularly in infant schools in the poorer areas of London. A low wartime birth-rate had appeared to make this desirable, and where this was not so, classes could be taught by headteachers. This, Winifred argued, was a misuse of a head's time which should be spent in overall care of the school, most particularly in contact with parents. In schools in poor districts this is especially important, and she gives examples of a would-be scholarship girl, and of families confronting insanity or drunkenness or prostitution, where the headteacher should be available to deal with these human factors. The concerns of the article are, of course, those she will fictionalise in *South Riding*.

This article was followed by one in August of the same year, 'Ladies First', her first piece of feminist journalism. It describes the reinstatement of the distinction between men's and women's trades in the post-war years and attributes this to four causes: the decline in munitions manufacture, the return of men from the war to resume employment, the slump in trade and resulting increase in unemployment generally, and trade union protection of men's right to work. 'The old, deeply-rooted feeling that women ought not to be in industry at all, combined with the perfectly justifiable, but indiscriminately applied, sense of gratitude to the ex-soldier' was being used, Winifred argued, as a smoke-screen behind which men resumed a privileged relation to employment, even where competitively they were not entitled to do so. The crucial issue was that of equal pay for equal work: whilst women were paid lower wages, 'the unions must fear their competition and condone their exclusion' from employment.

Winifred's advocacy here of equal pay was one which she would return to frequently in the years that followed, part of her desire to see the end of sex-differentiation and consequent sex-antagonism, and it also related to an overarching belief in the rights of the individual irrespective of gender. Her beliefs in this respect remained unshaken during the following decade and were summarised in the conclusion to *Women and a Changing Civilisation*, written ten years later:

> We do not know how much of what we usually describe as 'feminine characteristics' are really 'masculine', and how much 'masculinity' is common to both sexes. . . . We might, perhaps, consider individuals as individuals, not primarily as members of this or that race, sex and status. . . . We might allow individual ability rather than social tradition to determine what vocation each member of our community should follow.[29]

Winifred's Old Feminist convictions brought her into heated controversy with the New Feminists during the mid 1920s. One of her chief antagonists was Eleanor Rathbone whose *The Disinherited Family*, published in 1924, had already argued that the end of the family wage and the introduction of equal pay on their own would benefit neither women nor children. In her view, in the *laissez-faire* employment system such as equal pay creates, the family must be protected: 'If society is to lend its ear to the plea that justice demands that those who do work of equal value shall receive equal pay, it must also listen to the plea that the service of parenthood has likewise its value.'[30] Rathbone's forum was the National Union of Societies for Equal Citizenship (NUSEC), a group evolved from earlier suffrage societies, of which Winifred, with her predilection for belonging to various and sometimes opposing societies, was also a member. Rathbone's presidential speech of 1925 drew up the terms of the debate between Old and New Feminists. 'At last we have done with the boring business of measuring everything that women want, or that is offered them by men's standards,' she said. 'We can demand what we want for women, not because it is what men have got, but because it is what women need to fulfil the potentialities of their natures and to adjust to the circumstances of their own lives.'[31] She carried the debate into the heart of Old Feminism in a letter to *Time and Tide* of 12 March 1926. This was in response to an article a week earlier on 'The New Feminism' which had provocatively described as a 'cleavage of opinion' a debate at the Council meeting of NUSEC between reformers and feminists on the importance of equality and self-determination in relation to welfare reforms. Eleanor Rathbone refuted the accusation that NUSEC was anti-equalitarian but she did endorse the opinion of many NUSEC members that, particularly for working-class women, political equality by itself would be an empty achievement, born of middle-class 'me-too-ism':

> the women's movement comprises a large number of
> reforms, all of which are 'feminism', but some of which are
> 'equality'. The 'equality' reforms are necessary and
> immensely important. . . . But this aim of enabling women
> to be and do their best will not have been accomplished
> even when every sex barrier has fallen. Those who think it
> will are suffering, I suggest, from a sort of 'inferiority com-
> plex' bred in them by generations of sex subjection. . . . To
> every proposal for the good of women they apply the test
> 'do men do it'. . . . We of 'the new feminism' apply a differ-
> ent test, 'Is it good in itself? Does it meet the needs of
> women's natures and women's lives? Do women want it for
> themselves?'[32]

In June of the same year, *Time and Tide* returned to the attack in relation to the refusal of the International Woman Suffrage

Alliance, a body comprising many organisations, to admit to membership the feminist National Woman's Party of America. As a result, the Six Point Group had resigned from the IWSA and, in explaining why this was necesary, Margaret Rhondda summarised the situation:

> one may divide the women in the women's movement into
> two groups; the feminists, and the reformers who are not in
> the least feminists, who do not care twopence for equality
> for itself [and who only vote for it because] the woman's
> vote would further the reforms that they had at heart;
> infant welfare; prison reform; temperance; and a dozen
> other things. Now every woman's organisation recognises
> that reformers are far more common than feminists . . . and
> are in a very big majority over the feminists in the
> IWSA. . . . [W]hen they saw [the NWPA] advancing
> towards the IWSA [they] were terrified and they rose in
> their big majority and barred the way.[33]

Because she was in South Africa at the time, Winifred did not immediately join the debate. Her comments came in July 1926 in a letter to the *Yorkshire Post*, reprinted in *Time and Tide*, stating what she saw as the fundamental difference between the two feminist positions: 'The New Feminism emphasises the importance of the "woman's point of view," the Old Feminism believes in the primary importance of the human being.' She acknowledged that sex-differentiation is important 'but its influence on human life is unlikely to be underestimated, and the Old Feminists believe that thitherto it has been allowed too wide a lordship'. 'When liberty and equality of action and status for men and women has been obtained,' she continues, 'then all other reforms, including those arrangements of domestic life, such as Family Allowances, will concern sons and husbands as well as mothers and daughters. It would be a grave mistake if they appeared to an easily misguided public as purely women's reforms, in which a few kindly and philanthropic men took a measure of gracious interest.'[34]

This letter also contains the paragraph quoted at the beginning of this chapter expressing Winifred's impatience with the need for feminism. The wish to be done with it was again expressed in an article she wrote in 1928 as a result of having attended a Promenade Concert at which Ethel Smyth conducted her own Concerto in A for violin, horn and orchestra. Not particularly musical, Winifred had been prompted to go by having read Smyth's account of her involvement in the suffrage campaign in *A Final Burning of Boats*. Winifred went to see 'Feminism at the Queen's Hall' but what she saw pleased her more. The orchestra had women in it, some of the singers were women and then came Ethel Smyth, 'accepted at last as a master of her particular art by pure virtue of merit, dominating a crowd of performers, both men and women, moulding their wills by a gesture of her arm to her own creative purpose. . . . The music alone mattered, and the desire to perform. And this, after all, is what feminism is about.' The image of an orchestra in which men and women as individuals, regardless of their sex, co-operate in the production of harmony and pattern seemed to her 'the most civilised form of society that it has ever been my fortune to observe . . . it did not matter the turn of a hair whether a man or a woman was performing, a man or a woman was conducting, or men or women listened'.[35]

These were the attitudes which underlay her approach to equal pay. A crucial profession in this respect was nursing which suffered, as it still does, from being classed as a female occupation and therefore as a 'sacred vocation', undertaken as a mixture of sacrifice and philanthropy. But this is to the advantage of neither nurses nor patients: 'it is not among highly paid, highly trained, self-respecting women, proud of their profession, that callousness or inefficiency is found, but among the over-worked and underpaid, wearied by long hours of exacting labour, weakened

by inadequate food, and handicapped . . . by a sense of grievance.'
In 'Would I Like My Daughter to Be a Nurse?'[36] Winifred listed the
long hours of duty, compounded in the first three years by having
to pass exams, the rigid discipline, the curtailment of social life, a
poor diet, a preposterous uniform with endless buttons and hooks
to be fastened, and above all, the poor pay: a trained nurse earned
between £50 and £60 a year. Her answer must be that, no, she
wouldn't advise her daughter to be a nurse. Furthermore, though
she happens to be a woman journalist protesting about women's
experience, it oughtn't to be of concern just to women. It is a
human concern to ensure that workers are paid properly, irrespective of gender.

This is the theme of an impassioned and probably unpublished
article on 'Are There Any Women's Questions?' which concludes
that there aren't any. Implicitly accusing the New Feminists of not
really being feminists at all, she holds that the world divides quite
simply into 'the people who want women to be subject to special
sex legislation and those who don't; the people who want to per-
petuate irrelevant sex distinctions and those who want to end
them'. Extrapolating into wider concerns she asks, 'Does not one of
the sharpest divisions in the world lie between those who think in
terms of categories – of niggers, servants, foreigners, women, sub-
urbans, and those who think in terms of human beings?'[37] By
1928–9, when this article was probably written, Winifred wished
to give her most serious attention to the conditions of black workers in South Africa. The fact that by all rational measures feminism
ought to be obsolete as a political cause, but remained one which
still made urgent demands on her, was a source of exasperation,
extending, even, to women themselves, particularly to those who
stayed, complacently as she thought, within the domestic sphere,
and to those women who exploited their femaleness to ignore
public responsibilities. This surfaces contemptuously in *Women
and a Changing Civilisation*: 'The consciousness of virtue derived
from well-polished furniture or rows of preserved-fruit bottles is

too lightly acquired. In too many small homes women use the domestic relation to evade responsibility for everything else.' It was a contempt echoed by Vera in her essay 'Can Women of the World Stop War' in which she too denounced the woman who restricted her interest to her own domestic affairs as 'guilty of gross irresponsible selfishness . . . I believe women could stop war if they ceased to be completely absorbed in themselves and their homes.'[38] It was an uncompromising stance in the face of changes in the lives of many women. This was the era of growth in small-home ownership and in an increase in domestic consumerism, encouraged by a plethora of housekeeping and baby-care manuals and sustained by a huge output of romantic fiction and film ('a romantic attitude towards work and a scientific attitude towards love would be a welcome change', was Winifred's comment on this output[39]). To her such middle-class comforts and palliatives seemed in danger of distracting women from their political and social responsibilities. Her unease at the decline in idealism towards female citizenship extends even to motherhood when it becomes complacent and self-absorbed:

> 'I am a private person. My job lies within four walls,'
> [women] say complacently. . . . So slums remain uncleared,
> milk is wasted, nursery schools are exceptional luxuries,
> educational reforms are delayed, while 'good wives and
> mothers' shut themselves up in the comfort of their private
> lives and earn the approval of unthinking society.

The danger of being a wife, or rather defining herself only as a wife, leads a woman into intellectual debility: 'Why does . . . general conversation so often hang, spiked upon the uncomprehending inattention of the "wives" who sit among the men and women?' This contempt is directed particularly at middle-class women but working-class women fare hardly any better. In her fiction, where they feature more frequently than in her journalism, working-class women, though deserving of compassion, are attended by waste, muddle and ineffectuality. In *South Riding*, which she was beginning to write at the same time as *Women*, the working-class Mrs Holly cannot escape a maternity as deadly in its biological progress as Lily Sawdon's cancer. To survive, the young woman of the future, Lydia Holly, who rides her bicycle 'like a boy', has to overcome her pregnant mother's fatalism about the female condition: 'It's no good looking at me like that,' says Mrs Holly. 'You'll be a woman yourself one day and know all about it.' The passivity and servility of most women's lives seemed to Winifred to be a denial of humanity and a repudiation of the rationale which won the vote.

Her sense of the responsibility of newly enfranchised women citizens to play their part in a democratic society led her to publish, in 1929, *A New Voter's Guide to Party Programmes*. This sixty-three page booklet of political dialogues between Juvenis, a young voter, canvassers from the three main parties, a feminist, a farmer, a Communist, an open conspirator, a Fascist, and a cultured stranger, was based on material which originally appeared in *Time and Tide*. Margaret Rhondda had been the instigator and had asked Winifred to write it because 'I also am a new voter, who has not yet joined any party.' She had sent off to the three chief parties for their literature for Young Voters and had augmented this with a fair amount of additional reading. The intelligent, accessible and fair-minded result is very much in keeping with Six Point Group philosophy of educated participation in social organisation. Its feminist dialogue rehearses the Group's agenda, and Winifred's own: equal pay and opportunities, protective legislation based on the nature of the work instead of the sex of the worker, maternity grants so that a woman worker can choose to stay at home if she wishes, legislation to recognise an equal moral standard, the right of married women to engage in paid work, separate taxation for married women, and international feminism leading to an Equal Rights Convention to be ratified by all member states of the League of Nations.

One of the most sensitive figures for feminism to deal with during the inter-war period was that of the spinster. Always a cause of anxiety and opprobrium, unmarried women were now not only more numerous than ever before, but also more powerful, because of their greater potential for economic independence. Fear of wage-earning women was particularly directed at the younger ones: 'pin-money girls', as they were called. 'Better pay and smart clothes for the girl typist. Unemployment and patched pants for men,' was the sort of comment that greeted campaigns for equal pay and better employment opportunities for women. As Winifred noted, announcing a mass demonstration in support of equal pay in the Central Hall, Westminster, in March 1935, it is a muddle-headed world that consigns equal pay agitation to women's organisations and then objects to their claims, because 'the real injustices of inequality affect men just as much as women' by creating a 'blackleg' class who undercut wages.[40] But if fear of the young, unmarried woman was largely economic, fear of the older spinster was compounded by assertions from popular psychology that a full sex life was essential to both physical and psychic health. As Winifred noted, during the inter-war years the terms 'spinster' and 'frustrated' went together like egg and egg-cup, and although she could joke about her status, it was enraging to encounter social censure or pity, ranging from Oswald Mosley's contempt for 'this distressing type' to Havelock Ellis's more kindly meant belief that although celibacy may not cause any serious psychosis, 'it is apt to cause minor disturbances of the physical well-being, and on the psychic side much mental worry and a constantly recurring struggle with erotic obsessions, an unwholesome sexual hyperesthesia which, especially in women, often takes the form of prudery'.[41]

Much of the stereotyping of spinsters in this way, indeed of women in general, was driven by newspaper and commercial demands for easy labels. Winifred wrote a spoof article for the *Listener* in 1933, purporting to be from a Martian visitor reviewing the 'Native Woman' on the basis of advertisements and the popular press, who concluded that the Native Woman is divided into categories – Girl, Wife, Mother, Spinster – and that her main preoccupation is Sex and that when a Girl passes over into a Spinster 'the wretched woman immediately becomes unbalanced and embittered, and frequently ends her life in a lunatic asylum suffering from hallucinations, melancholia, or homicidal mania'. In reality, the Martian visitor finds that the islanders do not quite conform to this scheme and are obviously passing through 'that transitional period of decadence always characterised by the dissolution of pure categories.' An expanded version of this satire would appear in the good-natured, whimsical, illustrated book *The Astonishing Island* of 1933, in which Robinson Lippingtree Mackintosh, the visitor to the Island, England, from Tristan da Cunha, is told by the newspaper editor of the various types of women there are: mothers, spinsters, vampires, Modern Girls, Women who get to the Top. When Robinson goes looking for them he finds all the types contradicted and is left in as much doubt as when he set out about whether a True Woman actually exists.[42]

Many of the novelists of the time, particularly the women novelists, explored and exploited the figure of the spinster. One of the more striking examples is Sylvia Townsend Warner's *Lolly Willowes* in which the spinster, quite literally, goes to the devil. Agatha Christie's Miss Marple novels used the stereotypical behaviour and appearance of the spinster – fussiness, genteel poverty, propensity to gossip – to conceal detecting acumen. Dorothy L. Sayers made ironic play with assumptions about spinsters in *Gaudy Night* in which an Oxford women's college is subjected to a rash of obscene poison-pen letters. This is just the kind of sexually obsessed behaviour that might be expected from the spinster dons yet it is a widowed mother who has sent them, resentful of the 'silly old hags' who take men's jobs and threaten her livelihood. E.M. Delafield's *Thank Heaven Fasting* tells of Monica, who, like Muriel in *The Crowded Street*, has been brought up to believe that 'a woman's success or failure in life depended on whether or not she succeeded in getting a husband.' *Thank Heaven Fasting* was published in 1932, eight years after *The Crowded Street*, and it is a measure of Winifred's strongly adventurous feelings on this subject that in her novel Muriel does not marry the only suitable man who asks her, whereas Monica does, even though she does not love him and he has 'prawn-like' eyes. Though she provided Muriel with a more or less satisfactory escape route, Winifred remained sensitive to the deprivations of spinsterhood, especially when they could not be relieved by a redirection of energies: 'No agony of loss, anxiety or over-strain can be more devastating than their prolonged and negative tragedy of frustration,' she wrote in 1933. Yet 'in spite of the spurious "psychological" nonsense fashionable to-day, the frustration of the mating instinct is less harmful in the end than the frustration of that common human instinct to be used for some end greater than one's little personal life.'[43] It was a conviction she had used as the theme of her second spinster novel, *Poor Caroline*, which daringly takes a comic, near-caricature version of the spinster – ridiculous, credulous, foolishly dressed and muddle-headed – and fully recognises the exasperating nature of such a woman but also her courage and vision. Eleanor, the young protagonist of the novel, stands by Caroline's grave and thinks of her futile yet valiant life:

> Caroline was dead, and all her dreams died with her. The school which she had tried to found had failed. Her poems and *Path* of *Valour* lay unread and unremembered. The Christian Cinema Company had apparently existed in order to provide Mr Johnson with a means of escaping his debts. Her many other plans had progressed no further than their conception in her fertile brain. . . . And yet [as] though she heard it now, she remembered Caroline's quick excited voice from the infirmary bed, crying, 'When you come to think of it, Eleanor, I've had a very remarkable life.' That

was it. That was the way to live, acknowledging no limitations, afraid of nothing.

Small, shabbily dressed, disorganised, Caroline bears little physical
relation to Winifred yet her life is what Winifred's might have
been, the unsuccessful alternative as spinster, and what Winifred in
her darkest moments must have contemplated. The autobiographical elements are carefully implanted in the novel: the
memories Caroline has of her childhood on a farm, 'squeezing
herself into the hay rack above the stalls in the cowshed, eating
cubes of raw turnip and composing poetry', and the poem she
wrote, 'Epigram on the End of Love', when an early love affair
failed to develop, is the poem Vera Brittain quotes in *Testament* of
Friendship in the context of Winifred's grief over the loss of Harry
Pearson's love.[44] Other sorrows, too, are projected onto Caroline:
the fear of being abandoned by Eleanor going to America recalls
Winifred's sadness and perhaps also her anger at Vera's departure in
1925, and Caroline's despair at a friendless, solitary old age must
have been one of Winifred's own less optimistic prospects. But
Poor Caroline is also a fighting book on behalf of spinsters. ' "These
women," ' Clifton Roderick Johnson says, ' "'Smy belief it would be
the salvation of half of 'em to be raped by the butcher's boy. . . .
Don't you see what's wrong with 'em all? Sex-starved. Sex-starved.
Must use their energy somehow. . . . Nosing round to find nice
juicy stories about child assault an' prostitutes. Rescue work.
Excuse for bishops to talk sanctimonious smut to a lot of sex-
starved spinsters. Anti-slavery. Feminism. Peace. Pshaw!" ' But he is
a bombastic fraud, served his own medicine by being trapped in a
sordid sexual liaison. And although Caroline's life and death are
hardly successful or dignified, they have a transforming gaiety and
energy which the lives of older married women do not possess:
'Their grey sagging faces drooped into slackened necks which slid
into huge, shapeless bosoms and distended stomachs. Their
swollen legs bulged out of broken shoes. Life, work, child-bearing

and poverty had torn their bodies, making hideous what had been lovely, draining their vitality and robbing them of self-respect.' Caroline, like Winifred, has, however imperfectly, served a greater end than her insignificant personal life.

The triumphant spinster in Winifred's fiction is, of course, Sarah Burton in *South Riding*: 'I was born to be a spinster, and by God, I'm going to spin.' She has known what it is to desire and be desired; her spinsterhood has come about because of death or principle, it is not a forlorn fate but one which equips her to carry out the larger service to society which teaching demands. Although after Robert Carne's death she believes she would have risked everything she had achieved to be his mistress, the novel does not end on this note but on her renewed dedication 'to finish the task before her'. The rallying of the spinster to the call of public service had been the theme of 'The Non-Combatants', an article in the *Manchester Guardian* in 1930. With typical robustness Winifred advised any spinster who is 'in danger of an inferiority complex because she has never faced the ordeal of childbirth [to] make it her business to face some other ordeal, possibly more dangerous. And far more to the point, let spinsters do their utmost to make maternity safe. If it is true that 45 per cent of the deaths investigated by the Committee [for the Midwives Report] were preventable, then let us make it our business to prevent them. . . . There is plenty of work for [spinsters] to do and the sooner they tackle it the better.'

Winifred's endorsement of spinsterhood was not at the expense of marriage as such. A good marriage was the best arrangement possible but this did not mean that a poor marriage was better than none at all. As Eleanor in *Poor Caroline* says, 'A perfect marriage is a splendid thing, but that does not mean that the second best thing is an imperfect marriage.' It was the emphasis on marriage as an exclusive career for a woman that was limiting. In describing a medical student of her acquaintance she rejoices that this particular woman was pursuing a career but with no assumption that she

would not be able to marry. The marriage of such a woman would
be more rather than less successful: 'I have seen a fair number of
happy marriages. . . . But so far as I can tell not one of them was
the "one divine event to which the whole creation" of the wife
had moved.'[45] This, of course, was very much Vera's opinion too,
and the principle on which she conducted her own marriage with
Gordon. It is their marriage which provides the model for that
envisaged between Eleanor and Roger in *Poor Caroline*: 'I couldn't
endure a wife who was prepared to "give it all up" for me,' he says.
'I can't imagine a more humiliating situation. Think of the strain it
would impose upon the husband, having to live up to some sort of
ideal of value which would compensate to his wife for everything
she had missed. . . . The ideal thing, I suppose, would be some sort
of arrangement whereby neither husband nor wife need sacrifice
their own work. And I believe it could be done.' And as Eleanor
thinks to herself, 'Why, after all, should she remain celibate just
because she intended to have a public career. . . . "The present generation of feminists must marry. . . . And if we fail, we can always
separate. There's nothing final in this world but death."'

Winifred's sense of the necessity for women to grasp all opportunities for fulfilment reached into even the relatively trivial matter
of clothes. Both she and Vera were passionately interested in
clothes and believed they shouldn't have to sacrifice this interest in
order to be taken seriously. In the *Manchester Guardian* in 1928 she
complained that there is no need for feminists, nor socially active
women, to be dowdy and frumpish. It stems from a pernicious
belief that '"we can't have the best of both worlds." Under the
tyranny of that dilemma women have been told that they cannot
marry and have a career outside the home, that they cannot preserve both domestic and professional efficiency, that they cannot
sustain a decorous and exquisite standard of taste in their own
appearance and in their possessions, and at the same time perform
useful service to the public. And only a few of the very wise or the
very brave have yet replied to the proposers of the alternatives, "We

will have both." We want the best of both worlds, and we believe
that we can and ought to have it.' Her very trenchant tone in these
articles of the late 1920s, as though in her asperity of approach she
wished to prove how sensible and down-to-earth a spinster such as
herself could be, is most apparent in an article on the double standard in sexual matters. She attacked confused establishment
thinking exemplified by the Chief Constable of Edinburgh who
had told the Home Office Committee on Street Offences that 'if the
common prostitute were removed from the streets, "you remove
one of the main safeguards of the virtuous woman." But if the
prostitute is indeed the protector of virtue, why is she not hon-
oured for her necessary and noble work? . . . if the healthy
prostitute is a desirable member of society, we are foolish to
oppose. . . . State toleration of vice, the establishment of licensed
brothels, and the compulsory inspection and medical treatment of
prostitutes.'[46]

After the equalising of the franchise in 1928, and during the
economic decline and high unemployment of the early 1930s, it
seemed to Winifred and to many other feminists that the spirit had
gone out of the movement, perhaps even that it had failed, and that
the very women 'who should to-day be showing signs of readiness
to take the place of pioneers in public life . . . do not seem to be
anxious to carry on the work.' It was easy to understand why this
was happening:

> To inherit democratic citizenship just when democracy is
> losing its prestige, to inherit a claim to 'equal economic
> opportunity' at a time when fathers, brothers and lovers are
> losing their jobs, to inherit a responsibility for public affairs
> at a time when the whole world is in disorder, and the most
> optimistic theorists are throwing up their hands in
> despair – this is really a harder ordeal in many ways than a
> straightforward fight for freedom which confronted the pre-
> war suffrage workers.[47]

Her pessimism focused on what seemed to be an intensification of antagonism between the sexes: 'It seems a set-back . . . a tragic thing. The ideal should be a human ideal – "neither Jew nor Gentile, male nor female, bond nor free."' In trying to understand the causes of division between the sexes, she looked back to primitive societies where the non-fighter was not respected and women were feared for their biological powers and their 'uncleanness' associated with pregnancy. In such societies there may have been economic advantage in sex divisions but no longer in modern society.[48] Such old instincts die hard, however, and to them must be added 'the post-war slump, the economic distress, the revolt against reason affecting intellectuals, politicians, sociologists and artists alike, the political philosophies of Fascism and nationalism, the long bred inferiority complex of being the "weaker sex" – all these give impetus to the backward-swinging pendulum. It is never easy to be free; it demands effort to be responsible and independent. Equality is not a frivolous assertion. During twenty-five years doors have been opened; it is not yet certain whether the coming generation will choose to enter its hard-won heritage.'[49]

This was Ray Strachey's disappointed conclusion in *Our Freedom and its Results* of 1936 where she blames the stalling of feminism on 'modern young women [who] know amazingly little of what life was like before the war and show a strong hostility to the word feminism, and all which they imagine it to connote.'[50] More bitterly, Storm Jameson accused feminists, particularly of the Old variety, of having become 'the spirited and insensitive imitators of men. . . . In the end, the world is not yet a rap better because women have been let loose in it. Our effect on its major evils – war, poverty, and what belongs to them – is nothing, our achievement of independence nothing. . . . If civilisation as we know it ends in poison gas, the fault will be ours because we have taken a hand in the game only as following and competing with men.'[51]

A major cause of this kind of pessimism in the 1930s was, of course, the rise of Fascism. Its ominous militarism was of concern to Winifred as a pacifist but its domestic ideology was no less disturbing to her as a feminist and a humanist. In a review of 1933 she had commented on worryingly reactionary movements in Europe which sought to subordinate human individuality to 'mystical conception[s] of status [of] the "Aryan," the "German," the "Fascist,". . . the "Jew," the "Alien," – and the Woman'. It is 'an anti-democratic craze for "status" rather than individual contract [which] is bringing back the whole question of women's position in society once more into the fighting-ring of controversy.'[52] That thousands of German women were prepared to abandon paid employment on Hitler's suggestion that if they did so their homes would be furnished free when they got married was followed by news that 'thousands are prepared to surrender their parliamentary vote and "reserve their energies for higher things." '[53] Hysteria was sweeping through Germany in which individuality, liberty and happiness were to be sacrificed for the sake of the 'dark spirit of the German soul'.[54] Those who were not part of this, she wrote presciently – the non-Germans, the Jews, the Poles, or the unrecognised Germans, the Socialists and the Pacifists – were to be exiled, beaten, or imprisoned in concentration camps. Women are valued in this philosophy as mothers and little more. In the extreme philosophy of Fascism, a woman 'who tries to be "human" as well as womanly gives an impression that her womanliness is inadequate.' Her business is to be the breeder of heroes and the recreation of the tired warrior.

Out of curiosity and to assess the strength of the movement, Winifred attended a number of meetings of the British Union of Fascists. Mosley had sprung into prominence during 1931 and 1932, offering his followers, as Winifred herself admitted, a programme of discipline, action and order which contrasted attractively with the National Government's indecision and powerlessness in the face of nearly three million unemployed. In a *News Chronicle* article of May 1934, 'Shall I Order a Black Blouse?', she commented that the Blackshirts were 'too closely related to nationalism to be comfortable' and the civilisation they promised too imbued with 'the austere satisfactions of intolerance . . . the civilisation of the concentration camp'. Mosley's essentialist views on sexual relations were particularly abhorrent to her: 'At present I feel and think as a citizen and an individual; if the Blackshirts were victorious, I should be expected to think only as a woman. Mosley has written that *"We want men who are men and women who are women"*. The italics are his. They are characteristic of a creed which wherever practised has resulted in an attempt at sex-segregation.'

Her most probing analysis of the relation between feminism and fascism came, however, in the play she wrote not long before she died, called first of all *Dictator*, then *I Give You Back Your Freedom*, then *Hope of Thousands*, and finally, in a version edited by Norman Ginsbury after her death, *Take Back Your Freedom*. The play was not produced in Winifred's lifetime.[55] Its principal male character, Arnold Clayton, is a gifted academic who has become tired of the expediency and lack of vision of the National-type government of the day and has formed his own party, the British Planning Party. Clayton has the good looks, strong personality and leadership qualities of Mosley and he also is moulding his organisation into a dictatorship. The most interesting feature of the play, however, is the relationship between Clayton and his widowed mother. She is the victim of the policies against which Winifred and the Old Feminists had campaigned, those of allowing women no exercise of their talents except as wives and mothers. On marriage she has had to give up professional work and as a result her considerable energies have been directed towards her son and his career. His urge to power, along with his homosexuality, is seen as the result of the uncritical adulation she has given him, and recognising that she has produced a tyrant, she kills him. In the final line of the manuscript she says, 'I shot him. He asked me to set him free.' The play's theatrical crudity – the psychology of its characters is not particularly convincing and its scenes frequently veer towards melodrama – should not disguise the radical nature of its thinking at the time it was written. The play points to later writing on this theme, such as Katherine Burdekin's dystopia, *Swastika Night* (1937), in which men and women in a futuristic fascist state are totally segregated, with women reduced to the condition of breeding animals and men to fighting monsters. Woolf's *Three Guineas*, of course, adumbrates the theme, as does her late essay, 'Thoughts on Peace in an Air-Raid', and her last novel, *Between the Acts*. How difficult it was to persuade even quite progressive thinkers to make the connection is suggested by Woolf's comment in a letter of January 1941: 'I don't see what's [to] be done about war. Its manliness; and manliness breeds womanliness – both so hateful. I tried to put this to our local labour party: but was scowled at as at a prostitute.'[56]

Though Winifred's ideas in *Take Back Your Freedom* were consistent with Six Point Group thinking, by the time she wrote it her relation to Margaret Rhondda had ceased to be a formative one. Winifred reviewed Margaret's autobiography, *This Was My World*, in March 1933, and pointed out that not only was its title in the past tense but that the greater part of the book itself was devoted to pre-war times. The implication is that Margaret Rhondda's achievements were by now complete and her future as a feminist without purpose. Although the autobiography is informative and readable, Winifred argues, it reveals very little about Margaret herself who remains, according to the title of the review, 'the unknown Lady Rhondda'. This reticence was something Winifred felt even after getting to know her: 'I find it strange to know some one so well and so little!'[57] This was still during the time when the friendship included Vera and the three lunched frequently with Margaret Rhondda at her elegant London flat. Once Vera married and left for America the relationship between Winifred and Margaret developed more intimately. Late in October 1925 Winifred spent the first of many weekends at Stonepitts, Margaret Rhondda's house in Kent, a fifteenth-century barn-like house with oast houses in the garden. 'There is a field in front,' Winifred told Jean McWilliam, 'and a view right across a brown, autumn valley to the Downs. We motored through country so tame and pretty that it looked like stage scenery specially set down for an act.'[58] Thereafter there are frequent records of Winifred and Margaret on holiday together, in Brittany, Paris, and, in July of the last year of Winifred's life, at the Malvern Festival. Margaret Rhondda's last surviving letter to Winifred, sent to Wimereux, was written on 25 August 1935 from the Scilly Isles where she was once again on holiday. She returned to London in time to visit Winifred in the nursing home before she died.

In April 1936, six months after Winifred's death, for four weeks *Time and Tide* printed pieces by Margaret Rhondda entitled 'Some Letters From Winifred Holtby'. These were excerpts from Winifred's letters to Margaret with accompanying comments. There were enough letters, apparently, 'for a big book' and the selection Margaret Rhondda made was 'in the nature of a lucky dip', though avoiding the indiscreet and the ephemeral. Some unpublished letters from Margaret Rhondda to Winifred also survive.[59] Athough tantalisingly incomplete, the correspondence affords glimpses of the relationship between the two women.

The lengthiest extract Margaret printed was Winifred's reply to her criticisms of *Poor Caroline*. The two women disagreed about the value of novels, of novel-writing altogether and Winifred's in particular, although, with ironic pathos in view of its posthumous publication, Margaret did acknowledge that *South Riding* was not only a good book but 'a new departure', marking the end of Winifred's apprenticeship as a novelist. Perhaps defensive about her own life as a single woman, Margaret had been particularly incensed by *Poor Caroline* which she said was 'dull & confused as though written in extreme fatigue',[60] was not only lifeless in its characterisation but represented everything that Winifred was frightened of and guilty towards, showing a 'dead-sea-apple feeling and fear underneath your balanced surface'.[61] Winifred staunchly replied that she disagreed with Margaret in almost every criticism but particularly in her belief that Caroline was 'a symbol of me' and that such a life was depressing where she had intended to give the impression of someone 'silly but vital, directly futile but indirectly triumphant'. She then continues in characteristic strain that rather than being fearful of life she is in love with it: 'I love my work. I love London. I love the multifarious activities which go to make the kind of life I lead.' She writes so vehemently, she says, because 'I cannot bear that you should feel otherwise about me . . . I cannot bear you to think that anyone who has worked as intimately with you, as I have worked since 1926, should feel the world dead-sea-applish. I don't. I don't. I don't.'[62] Margaret was duly chastened by this and by Winifred's good nature over her 'grumbles and jealousies'.[63] But later the same year she was once more trying to manage Winifred's life: 'I am not at all satisfied about your present way of life – You are quite deliberately over-working all your time & living on your capital of nervous energy & vitality,' and this concern continues throughout the remaining letters. It is possible that by emphasising Winifred's unsatisfactory lifestyle Margaret may have been, even unconsciously, trying to advance her own friendship with Winifred. She could provide Winifred with material comforts sufficient to save her from overwork. Yet if this was a kind of courtship it was not a very considerate one, and Margaret's relation with Winifred in some respects replicates Alice Holtby's with Winifred. Both very managerial women, Margaret and Alice expected service from Winifred, often, ironically in view of Winifred's own declining health, making use of illness to impose duties on her. In Alice Holtby's case it was notions of 'family' which Winifred had to serve, in Margaret's it was *Time and Tide*. Margaret's own real or imagined ill-health frequently led her to ask Winifred to undertake extra work: 'My dear, I know this weekend [at Monks Risborough, where Winifred had gone to rest] is going to be a difficult emotional one for you [but] could you do a 200 word note on some light subject (anything you fancy) . . . and post it up to me

Winifred and Grace
Holtby, aged about
eleven and thirteen.

Rudston House, in the
1970s.

David Holtby, around
1930. Photograph in the
possession of Margaret
Ballard.

Alice and Winifred Holtby, 1934.

'Bainesse', the Holtbys' home after 1919.

Winifred at Queen Margaret's School; she is last right on the second row.

Somerville students, November 1917. Winifred is last right on the first row. Photograph in the possession of Paul Berry.

Winifred (and Dorothy Clark) at a fancy dress party at Somerville College. Photograph taken by Hilda Reid, now in the possession of Paul Berry.

Jean McWilliam. Photograph in the possession of Margaret Ballard.

Harry Pearson, probably taken during the 1940s.

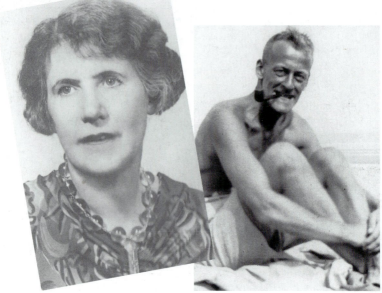

A Victory Luncheon to celebrate votes for all women over twenty-one, Hotel Cecil, 24 October, 1928. Margaret Rhondda is standing on the right at the top table. Others present included Dame Millicent Fawcett, Emmeline Pethwick-Lawrence and H N Brailsford.

Winifred, probably taken in the garden at Cottingham.

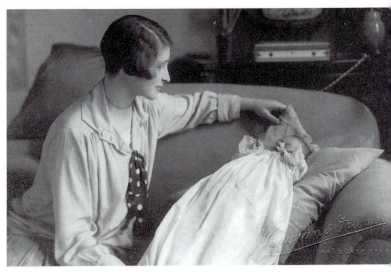

Vera Brittain with John Edward. Photograph taken by Hilda Reid, now in the possession of Paul Berry.

Clements Kadalie, with permission of the Africana Museum, Johannesburg.

William Ballinger.

Winifred with George Bernard Shaw and Margaret Rhondda, at the Malvern Festival, July 1935.

Hilda Reid, Winifred and Edith de Coundouroff in Wimereux, probably August 1935. Photograph in the possession of Margaret Ballard.

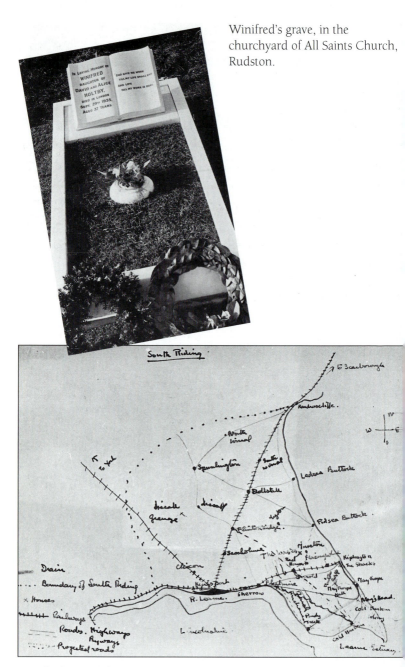

Winifred's grave, in the
churchyard of All Saints Church,
Rudston.

Winifred's map of the South Riding.

at the office.' There is genuine anxiety over Winifred but also a driving need to keep *Time and Tide* running as efficiently as possible. The letters are full of affection – 'Dearest Winifred . . . don't waste your precious golden substance – you who are so fine & made of such rare stuff'[64] but the next year, 1933, Margaret went to Greece, Palestine and Egypt for five months for her health's sake, leaving *Time and Tide* to be run by the Assistant Editor, Phoebe Fenwick Gaye, with Winifred as 'the obvious person to turn to' if there were crises, as there inevitably were. Winifred reported frequently to Margaret about the paper, about difficulties with Ellis Roberts (the literary editor), Phoebe Gaye's illness, contacts with numerous people, including Ellen Wilkinson, Cicely Hamilton and Sean O'Casey, Blackshirt meetings, reviews and leaders. There is no doubt she enjoyed all this – 'Oh Margaret, life is so inordinately Rich' – but her appetite for life, or at least her cheerful expression of how ready, even delighted, she was to undertake any tasks, left her vulnerable to exploitation. This extended in Margaret's case to asking Winifred to find a house for her and Theodora Bosanquet on their return from holiday: 'My dear I'm *terribly* thrilled about the house! and I do think its so clever of you to have chosen one that still leaves me free to get out of it quite easily . . . if by any chance I don't like it.'[65] She wanted the house to be ready immediately, and if this was not possible then she would rent an extra room next to her flat for six months: 'In fact I suppose the truth is I hate living alone & don't want to do it for a whole 6 months more.'

After the death of her father, the most important emotional relationships in Margaret Rhondda's life were with women.[66] Vera was probably right in believing that Margaret's relationship with Winifred was not a sexual one, although Margaret may have wished it to be so. But they were certainly close, particularly during the time after Vera's marriage when Winifred was contemplating the question she put to Jean, 'How shall I live?' and Margaret was becoming estranged from her friend Helen Archdale, the first

editor of *Time and Tide*, with whom she had shared her London flat
and her house in Kent. But of course Vera was to come back into
Winifred's life within months of her marriage, and in due course
Margaret established an intimate relationship with Theodora
Bosanquet, on a Mediterranean cruise in 1933, and they agreed to
live together, remaining together until Margaret's death. It seems
unlikely that Winifred ever seriously contemplated moving in with
Margaret; to have done so would have been a surrender to a personality and a lifestyle which would have inhibited her work and
her independence, almost like going to live at home again. As she
told Vera, 'I couldn't live with Margaret, much as I love her.'[67]
With Margaret it was different and she may have wished for and
perhaps even proposed living together during the late 1920s and
early 1930s when, to judge by the frequency of her nervous illnesses, she was especially unhappy and lonely, needing not only
companionship but also somebody on whom to expend her emotional energies. She told Vera and Winifred how much she would
like to have had a child and this slightly forlorn childlessness was
something Virginia Woolf noticed when she had dinner with her in
April 1933: 'I felt her a disappointed woman. Should have had 10
children perhaps. She was sitting alone, shawled dowdy in an old
Hampstead half [?] flat with a garden with great trees. She is what
they call, I expect, "inhibited" – something tentative furtive.
Discussed Time & Tide &c. She lives for T. & T. but is a little
under the thumb of Mr Ellis Roberts.'[68]

As for Winifred, she was certainly fond of Margaret and talked
and wrote to her confidentially and, apparently, uninhibitedly.
Though the identity of the people mentioned in her letters in *Time
and Tide* has been concealed, and the letters themselves heavily
edited, they still retain the sense of gossip exchanged and enjoyed,
of indiscretions, scandals and bawdiness, of the 'racy tongue [and]
fund of not too-vulgar-tales'[69] that had first attracted Margaret to
her. And in her 'outpouring' about *Poor Caroline* there is more self-
revelation than in most of her letters to Vera, towards whom she

was always reticent about her work. With Margaret Rhondda there was apparently more honesty, indignation, humour and self-regard, and there are glimpses of a close, almost conspiratorial friendship; describing how she has sold a story to Curtis Brown about a Russian restaurant in Paris, Winifred adds, in brackets, '(not *absolutely* our restaurant. I've altered some of the details pur-posely . . .).' Winifred obviously talked to her about Harry, whom Margaret Rhondda liked, 'except that I was just a shade frightened of him – he was apt to be very scornful'. She dreamed that Winifred was getting married to him, 'tall & broad-shouldered & very goodlooking with lovely large blue eyes & long lashes . . . & I said to myself "Its all right – she really did know what he was like when she described him, she wasn't blinded by being in love"'.[70] Whatever the desires expressed in this dream, it indicates how confiding their relationship had been. Yet there were obstacles, not least the antagonism between Vera and Margaret. Reading *This Was My World*, 'and *loving* it, and thinking what a really charming and honest and honourable person emerged from it,' Vera won-dered why she'd never liked Lady Rhondda, 'and she's never liked me . . . we have almost everything in common except, perhaps, my faculty as an artist and her business experience'.[71] Perhaps the dis-like of 'trade' implicit in Vera's comment contributed to the coolness, but each was jealous of the other as far as Winifred was concerned. Each thought the other exploitative, and in November 1931 this provoked a quarrel which was never completely healed and seems to have been over the amount of work that Winifred did for *Time and Tide*. Margaret had acknowledged to Winifred in January 1931 that the chances of *Time and Tide* 'getting through depend *enormously* on your continued health and work. You are one of its main props – I don't know what we should do if you failed us.'[72] Margaret certainly didn't think this of Vera whose con-tributions to *Time and Tide* petered out, or perhaps were frozen out, during the 1930s. After Winifred's death, when reading Winifred's letters in preparation to write *Testament of Friendship*,

Vera came to the conclusion, in discussion with Edith de Coundouroff, that 'Lady R. was really W.'s evil genius – used her time, health & energy, & gave little in return for all that she took . . . even in the appalling days of work & correspondence after her father's death she was apparently still expected to write Notes for *T & T*.'[73]

But this was to ignore the great pride Winifred took in being a director of *Time and Tide*, and the entry into the world of journalism and politics which friendship with Margaret Rhondda brought her. Margaret also lived in unmarried and childless luxury and to visit her or to go on holiday with her was an enjoyable contrast to the domestic complexities of Glebe Place. Margaret, though certainly demanding of Winifred, was also a friend whose sensitivities did not have to be watched as carefully as Vera's and with whom Winifred could be more assertive and professional. Perhaps above all, Margaret's feminism, forged in suffrage militancy, and retaining the character of those optimistic and egalitarian days, was an inspiration to Winifred and embodied principles of reason and humanism which she never forsook.

Women and a Changing Civilisation was dedicated to Ethel Smyth and Cicely Hamilton, both of whom Winifred had met through *Time and Tide*. She was aware how much it expressed Six Point ideas, and how much it owed to Margaret. Writing to her about it, Winifred said: 'Only a text book, you observe, and very much a compilation of stuff which is older than the hills to you.'[74] But it was, as Winifred was also aware, controversial, at least she hoped it would be: 'I've gone all out for abortion, just to give it a fillip.'[75] To Vera she wrote that she was 'extremely touched' because the book was given 'an extraordinary welcome . . . by all those old suffrage societies. Apparently they have decided to favour it. They had a stall filled with it, of autographed copies.'[76] Indeed, *Women* restates the case for equality before the law and in employment opportunities in a manner which harks back to the suffrage times, and into the writings of John Stuart Mill and the heart of the middle-class women's movement of the nineteenth century. In this respect it was an old-fashioned book, and this was gently pointed out by Naomi Mitchison in the *Left Review*. After praising its 'rapid and interesting' sketch of the past and its wide-ranging survey of the position of women in other countries, Mitchison then has some misgivings over the book's too exclusive standpoint from 'the professional, middle-class woman'. 'I wish there had been more about the working woman, and especially about the working woman's concept of home. She has not, for instance, considered what it is like to be a miner's wife, not only in relation to one's family and economic position, but also in relation to one's man.'[77] In other words, Mitchison believes that *Women* does not take sufficient account of the class dimension and how women may have loyalties and desires which conflict with issues of sexual equality. As the reformer-sort-of-person who wrote *Women*, Winifred did believe that equality must come first, above considerations of class, on grounds of the rights of the human individual. But the writer-sort-of-person was only too acutely aware, as *South Riding* would show, that women were complexly involved with men, did have separate spheres of responsibility and suffering, and were humanly incapable of holding to an abstract ideal or a single course of action. The conflict between a self-evident good and the wayward behaviour of human beings in relation to that good would strike her particularly forcefully in the cause which came to take precedence over feminism during the last years of her life, the rights of black workers in South Africa.

CHAPTER 6

'The goal of all men's longing': South Africa and William Ballinger

'South Africa haunts me,' Winifred said, and Joanna, the heroine of *The Land of Green Ginger*, who has many of Winifred's characteristics, describes the country as 'the goal of all men's longing'. This was the novel Winifred wrote during and immediately after her visit to South Africa in 1926, and its ecstatic ending captures some of her own passion for Africa and her sense that her voyage there would be 'the culminating experience of her youth', as indeed it was. Her interest dated from her childhood; one of her forebears had been a governor in Africa and 'my mother told me stories of him when I was a child on my father's farm'. Queen Margaret's School had connections with educational and charitable institutions in Grahamstown as well as contact with South Africa through its headmistress from 1913, Miss Fowler. When Jean McWilliam went to South Africa in 1920 it was inevitable that Winifred would visit her there. 'I want to see you and Africa,' Winifred wrote to her, but before that could happen came a visitor to London in 1923 who would have a significant influence on Winifred's involvement with South Africa. This was the novelist Ethelreda Lewis, who arrived with an introduction from Jean McWilliam and with the intention of finding a publisher for her novel *The Harp*. Winifred was impressed by *The Harp* and by Mrs Lewis herself, and she wrote to her enthusiastically during the next two years, occasionally saying how lucky she was in her own circumstances – loving and understanding parents, good education, friends, sufficient income – with characteristic comments on how she might repay the debt: 'the remedy lies simply, I believe, in work. Work which will probably be political in its nature. . . . Probably it is upon committees, upon schoolboards and widows pensions and bastardy bills, & upon lecture platforms for the League of Nations Union, that by using the educated mind that fortune has given me, I may repay my debt.'[1] On the basis of such comments, as well as having met her, Mrs Lewis would not be slow to recognise in Winifred a potential recruit for the kind of work she saw as essential for the good of South Africa.

The mid-1920s were crucial years for South African race relations. Black unrest was increasing as a result of recent legislation consolidating the supremacy of white labour, and the intensification of segregationist policies were driving black workers further into poverty and degradation. The Industrial Consolidation Act of 1924 had rendered the term 'employee' inapplicable to black workers and thereby barred them from, amongst other benefits, trade union membership. The Mines and Works Act (known as the Colour Bar Act) of 1926 specifically excluded Africans and Coloureds from obtaining certificates of competency which meant that they could hold only unskilled, low-paid employment. General Herzog's Smithfield speech of October 1925 outlining future segregationist policy, later to be enshrined in the Four Native Bills, had tacitly admitted that high white wages (the highest in the world) could only be paid for by the sweated labour of black workers. This was a policy which the South African Trade Unions and Labour Party endorsed, and, as Lord Olivier pointed out, even insisted on. An industrial colour bar, already applied in practice, was now formalised 'in legislation at the demand of the South African Labour Party which combined with the mine-owner and the farmer in exploiting the native African on the basis of an industrial economy and a theory of social relations derived direct from slavery.'[2] Winifred's visit in 1926 was, therefore, at a highly charged, even explosive time, in which white liberals, like Mrs Lewis, were fearful on two related counts: that there would be violent racial conflict and that the black population would turn to Communism. How strongly fear of Communism influenced her was shrewdly guessed by Fenner Brockway, editor of the *New Leader* and very active in the Independent Labour Party (ILP), in a letter to her and her husband in April 1929; whilst agreeing that 'to urge the negroes to follow Communist policy is criminally stupid inviting violence and bloodshed in which the natives would be butchered and crushed,' he was nevertheless alarmed that 'the main concern of Dr Lewis and your self is rather anti-Communist than pro-native unionism.'[3] At least in the early stages of their acquaintance she communicated this fear to Winifred: 'Now Communism with Bertrand Russell means one thing,' Winifred wrote to Vera in 1926, 'but this particular brand of Communism, undiluted, and superimposed upon a peculiar ignorance of history or economics, is quite another thing, and there is sufficient unrest among the native workers about the Colour Bar Bill to cause real trouble.'[4] Later, her attitude became more relaxed towards Communism than that of both Mrs Lewis and liberal thinkers in England: 'For the life of me,' she wrote in 1933, 'I cannot see why lateral committees which happen to have communist members among others should be banned by the Labour party.'[5]

Mrs Lewis, who as a Christian had been heavily influenced by the paternalistic missionary tradition in South Africa, was a member of the Johannesburg Joint Council of Europeans and Africans. She and the Council hoped the Communist threat could be averted by support from white liberals like herself for black trade unionism on a British model. In particular she wished to promote and influence the black Industrial and Commercial Workers' Union (ICU) and its leader, Clements Kadalie. The ICU had been formed in 1919 from the amalgamation of two unions involved the year before in a dock strike which Kadalie had helped to organise. The success of the ICU during its first five years was astonishing; more than a trade union in the British sense, the ICU was a social, political, religious and educational force which served to unite black people from different kinds of employment and different areas. Its membership, drawn as much from the rural districts as the urban, increased from nearly 40,000 in 1925 to 80,000 by 1927 with an income of around £12,000 a year.[6] It was particularly active in Natal and the Transvaal where the status of native workers was, according to a pamphlet the ICU published in 1927,[7] inferior to that in the Cape.

Its early success was largely due to Kadalie's leadership. The son of a Nyasaland chief, he was a man of great charm, energy and organising ability and an impassioned speaker; he was also, as Winifred would describe him, 'suspicious, sensitive, vain', and easily swayed. He would provide Winifred with ideas for the character of Safi Talal in *Mandoa, Mandoa!* – 'a prepossessing person [with a] nut-brown skin, fine features and black-pointed beard'. Kadalie was a man able to attract followers but less suited to the patient task of holding together a large, heterogeneous and scattered organisation like the ICU. Kadalie's failings, however, were only a particular symptom of general weaknesses in the ICU which became more obvious as its size increased: poor financial and administrative management, a hostile political context, divided loyalties amongst its officials, inexperience in trade union organisation, and lack of support from fraternal organisations. It was to remedy the last two of these weaknesses that Mrs Lewis believed she could be most effective, and which she felt were the most urgent. All along Kadalie had been interested in co-operation with white labour, both in South Africa and internationally. But the white unions wished neither to admit black workers as

members nor to assist them in independent organisation. The
Communists, however, were eager to help and by 1925 had infil-
trated the ICU to the extent that there were four CP members on
the ICU's national council. It was this that Mrs Lewis feared, particularly the influence of one C.F. Glass, an impassioned speaker
with considerable influence over Kadalie, and his wife, 'a Russian
Jewess with a scarlet dress and a BA degree', who was teaching the
natives to read and write whilst 'slyly expounding "red"
principles'.[8]

Winifred described herself as a 'passionate imperialist by
instinct'. As Leonard Woolf pointed out,[9] to liberals during the
inter-war years 'imperialism' and 'colonialism' were not the dirty
words they afterwards became and it was perfectly possible to be,
as he was himself, a socialist and also an imperialist, at least in the
sense of believing in Britain's parental responsibility towards the
territories she had acquired, which would include a programme of
gradual and educative devolution of power towards equal citizenship and self-government. Winifred would have agreed with
Woolf's verdict on the urgency and seriousness of the imperial
problem: 'It seemed to me certain that the revolt of the subject peoples . . . would spread through Asia and would soon reach Africa.
In the modern world this was one of the most menacing political
problems, and the world's peace and prosperity in the future
depended upon accelerating the transfer of power from the imperialist states to their subject peoples.' In Winifred's view this
transfer of power should involve the granting of dominion status to
those countries capable of sustaining it, and a mandate system on
a trustee principle for countries insufficiently developed to be self-
regulating. In each case, the franchise should be extended on a
cultural rather than a racial basis, by which she appears to have
had in mind (although she gives few details) some kind of qualifying test which increased educational opportunities would
eventually place within the capabilities of the whole population.
Implicit in her programme, as it was in Woolf's, was a belief in the

superiority of European culture but this did not mean that she believed in an inherent inferiority in the black races; the difference lay in the rate of development and in technological achievement. Unlike many of her contemporaries she did not believe that Western 'progress' in technology and social organisation could or should be withheld from the black races to keep them either in a state of uncorrupted primitivism or as a source of cheap, unskilled labour. Bill, in *Mandoa, Mandoa!*, surveys the 'muddled dirty confusion' and the 'ferocious conservatism' of the fictional African society he chooses to live in and knows that technology will not result in happiness any more than it has for the Europeans who have already acquired it. But its coming is inevitable: 'By God, we will build it better,' Talal tells him. 'Elevators and factories and electric cars. We will make it a great city.' It was an issue over which Winifred would disagree with Mrs Lewis whose novel *Wild Deer* celebrated a romantic and child-like primitivism for black peoples: 'you seem to despise machinery & modern ways, not only for Africans but for themselves – as though there were no virtue in them. I can't accept that. I am glad of the complexity of life; I do not find it hopeless . . . I do not think that the heart of man is hurt by machinery – only by its ridiculously unintelligent use.'[10] Mrs Lewis was very condescending towards blacks, speaking of them as 'our dark countrymen clamouring like children at the skirts of the white man . . . the infant race whose playground the white man burst into three centuries ago.'[11] The whole question of responsibility towards black people, particularly the danger of assumed superiority, exercised Winifred increasingly over the years. It was inherent in imperialism and created a cultural insensitivity of a kind she attacked in a spirited review of the film of *Cavalcade* for *Time and Tide* in March 1933. If *Cavalcade* itself heinously divided its characters into tragic and noble upper class and comical and vulgar lower class, this was as nothing compared with an educational film called *Round the Empire* which preceded it. In this everything of value and interest in other lands was due to English influence, and it was a matter of regret where this was not so: '"Africa is, even now," continues that cultured voice regretfully, "predominantly native." How sad! Just think of that, after all these years of British rule. In Australia and Canada our virile race succeeded admirably in reducing Red Indians or aborigines to quite insignificant proportions, but the tiresome Africans continue to increase and multiply.'[12]

During the five months of her stay in South Africa, Winifred visited Kimberley (in the middle of a February heat-wave in which 'the karoo lay like a vast red solidified flame'), Cape Town, Durban (where she met Mabel Palmer, a lecturer in the Technical College, an ex-Fabian with pro-black sympathies), Pretoria, the Transvaal, Lovedale, Johannesburg, Bloemfontein, Grahamstown and Wellington. She went out in trepidation at 'the likelihood of my making a fool of myself and the absurdity of undertaking to give lectures there'[13] and she found the experience exhausting, exhilarating, and profoundly affecting. The natural beauty of the country was a vivid background to its extremes of wealth and poverty. Johannesburg made a particularly strong impression on her of a divided and unstable society in which a rich white minority existed alongside a black 'underworld' of deprivation, corruption and degradation. Winifred's letters to Vera register moral outrage and also attempt to analyse the faults and perils of South African society:

> The stupidity and selfishness of the average South African
> in the face of the colour danger is amazing. . . . The
> patience of the Bantu is equally amazing. . . . Labour here is
> simply a white workers protection agency with all the
> autocracy of trade unionism & little of its compensating
> security. Labour, afraid of unequal competition, allied with
> a Nationalist party imbued with the Dutch notion of the
> serf-native makes an unholy combination. . . . Some people
> say that a native rising would be the only thing to shock

people awake to the true situation. I don't believe that good can come from violence.[14]

By the time of Winifred's visit Mrs Lewis had mobilised white liberals in Johannesburg to support Kadalie. She had had some success; as Kadalie recounted, her advice and that of her friends, 'led me to adopt a middle course'[15] away from Communist extremism. But Mrs Lewis recognised that effective help must eventually come from similar organisations and must have some professional help. It must also involve men; the involvement of only European women did not inspire confidence, and even roused suspicion as to why 'Kadalie has always women to help him?'[16] Such support, a 'settlement' as she came to call it, might be solicited from British sympathisers, and it was in this that Winifred could be instrumental: 'Mrs Lewis had a happy idea,' Winifred wrote. 'She is getting together a small body of really expert & able men [Oliver Schreiner (Olive Schreiner's nephew), Professor W.M. MacMillan of the University of Witwatersrand, and Gertrude Millin's husband] to . . . try & find points of contact, with the natives taking the initiative. She herself has got into close contact with Kadalie & my job is to keep the I.L.P. and the New Leader informed. A curious little sideline; but really, the situation here is quite terrible.'[17] It was, of course, to be much more than a sideline; it was to be the cause that Winifred had been searching for in order to pay her debt to life, and the fact that it was a difficult, even imposssible, cause would be in no way a deterrent. According to Hilda Reid, Winifred's friendship with a Eurasian nurse during her year as a wardmaid in London had awoken her to 'the existence of race discrimination' and 'both her intellect and her instincts rebelled' when she met it on a large scale in South Africa.[18]

Her first action in London was to insert an appeal in the *New Leader* on behalf of the ICU libraries in Johannesburg and Durban. She pointed out that 75 per cent of the industrial sector of its membership had become detribalised, 'accustomed to urban conditions and completely cut off from their old pastoral life. It is too late now to expect them to return to primitive simplicity. . . . The ICU is endeavouring to act, not only as a trades union in the ordinary sense, but as an education centre [and] there is the greatest need for up-to-date books.'[19] The response was good and Kadalie acknowledged receipt of parcels of books in a letter of 10 September in which he also asked for advice on whether the ICU should apply for affiliation to the ILP or the Labour Party. He urged Winifred to make contact with the Imperialism Committee of the ILP[20] in the belief that 'African workers can obtain more help from British Labour if our position is impartially laid before them.' When she had met Kadalie in South Africa Winifred had suggested that he make contact with British politicians and intellectuals (including Gordon, Vera's husband) and so this letter was simply following up what had been previously mooted. By this time Winifred had become a member of the ILP and had also had an interview with H.N. Brailsford of the *New Leader* about the ICU. He too suggested she get in touch with the Imperialism Committee. She was also contacted by Arthur Creech Jones, General Secretary of the Transport and General Workers Union and a member of the Industrial Advisory Committee of the ILP, who had been primed on the ICU by Mabel Palmer during her visit to England earlier in the year. In October 1926 Kadalie himself, at the prompting of Mabel Palmer, wrote to Creech Jones urging action upon him; it was time, Kadalie said, 'that the British Labour Movement should interest itself in the position of South African Native workers'.[21] The belief was that the ILP would be the most likely, if not the only, organised body to be sympathetic to the ICU, and certainly more willing to offer support than the main Labour Party which was reluctant to offend white trade unionists in South Africa.[22] The ILP was not, however, the most powerful of parties at the time; its quarrels with the Labour government in 1929 and 1930 absorbed much of its energy and also helped to fracture the labour movement in general. There would be little spare energy, funds or motivation to devote to the plight of black workers in South Africa.

It seemed to Winifred necessary to have the support of an experienced trade unionist to give authority to her efforts, and the obvious man in this respect was Arthur Creech Jones.[23] His initial response was to think of creating an informal committee 'to prepare the way for more official action', and he aimed to get together people like Harold Laski, Helena Swanwick, Lowes Dickinson and Professor Hobhouse, 'and he has asked me to join them', Winifred wrote to Mabel Palmer.[24] It is not clear that this informal committee ever met; what is certain is that Winifred and Creech Jones met the Imperialism Committee, which had a quite different membership from that of Creech Jones's informal committee, in January 1927.

In this way Winifred and Creech Jones began a campaigning partnership, cordial and even affectionate, on behalf of the ICU and, beyond that, in pursuit of the probably contradictory – at least in the short term – ideals of the advancement of the black races and racial harmony. Their campaign was to go much further than the collection of books but never quite far enough, primarily because of the unwillingness of the labour movement in Britain to commit itself officially and wholeheartedly to the cause of black labour. Reluctance to offend their South African counterparts and to interfere in what they considered a domestic matter, were to inhibit Labour Party and TUC leaders from publicising the issue and from pressuring the South African Labour Party (SALP) and the South African Trade Union Congress (SATUC) to resolve matters in favour of the ICU: 'the difficulty', Winifred wrote, 'seems to be fear of disapproval among the unions.' Although the ILP was more helpful and relaxed in its response, it was also cautious and limited in the help it could give, agreeing to act in an advisory capacity to the ICU but unable to raise funds for it. The situation was complicated by an almost paranoid fear of Communism amongst many labour leaders so that not only was co-operation with any organisation tainted by Communism out of the question but restraining their influence seemed at least as important as helping black workers. The essentially liberal Leonard Woolf believed that Communism was 'in some ways worse than nazism and fascism. *Corruptio optimi pessima* – the greatest evil is the good corrupted. The Hitlers and Mussolinis are just thugs or psychopaths. . . . But communism has its roots in some of the finest of human political motives and its corruption is repulsive.'[25] These anxieties were shared by Creech Jones who wrote to Kadalie in September 1927:

> The real test of the [ICU] both by the state, your own members and the public, will be the capacity of the Union to cater for the industrial needs of the natives. It is therefore important that whatever is done in the political field is done with caution so that no one can suggest the Union is unconstitutional, or behaving in an unconstitutional manner, or that it is stirring up racial feeling, or that its main interest is politics to the prejudice of the white Government. . . . The Union should not be side-tracked by Communism [and] should not embarrass itself by affiliation to the League Against Imperialism. . . . If it can endorse the objects of the South African Labour Party, then the Union should apply for affiliation [but] if affiliation is refused, then there is a case for the LSI [Labour and Socialist International] but at least the South African Labour Party should not be affronted by a direct application to the LSI.[26]

How seriously Kadalie took this advice is suggested by the ICU's 'constitution', which Winifred seems to have been involved in drafting,[27] which states that the union 'shall not foster or encourage antagonism towards other established bodies, political or otherwise, of African peoples, or of organised workers.'

Winifred's and Creech Jones's tentative and unrewarding

approaches to various groupings within the British Labour movement, and their personal efforts at fund-raising (for instance, the donations from Winifred and her friends to keep the ICU newspaper, the *Workers' Herald*, in publication), were given urgency by a visit to Europe by Kadalie in 1927. Under pressure from Mrs Lewis, Kadalie had been trying to sever his union's ties with the Communists and this visit to England was seen by them both as an attempt to 'get in touch with the *best side* of a movement of which [he has] only been in touch with the dregs'. Kadalie was proving worrying to the white liberals in South Africa: 'he has been very disappointing at the Durban conference: a good deal of wild language which has set everyone by the ears and alienated a good many people whom I have been carefully nursing up to believe in his recent moderating of principles',[28] Mrs Lewis wrote to Winifred, adding in a later letter that it really was a good thing that he was going away because the 'communist crowd' was trying to get round him again, seducing his followers and making him ill with the strain of withstanding their pressures.

Kadalie arrived at Southampton on 30 May 1927, noting with delight that the dockers at Southampton were white, the train to London was not segregated, that a white porter carried his luggage, and the surprise of white South Africans at Waterloo when they saw 'the tall young Englishwoman rush up and shake hands with the black man whom they had all barred on the voyage, and see her drive off with him in a taxi!'[29] There had been welcome noises from the ILP but it seems to have been Winifred's responsibility to look after Kadalie for the one day he spent in London before leaving for the International Labour Conference in Geneva. When he returned in August, before his next continental visit to Paris to the International Trade Union Council, it was to undertake a lecture tour throughout Scotland and England arranged for him by the ILP's Imperialism Committee with help from Winifred, Creech Jones and Fenner Brockway, secretary of the ILP. One of the places he visited was Hull where he was taken, of course, to Wilberforce

House, to pay homage 'at the shrine of the great saint and [where he] wished for the rise of another Wilberforce in Africa . . . to denounce the modern slavery as he did the old.' The purpose of the tour was to publicise the ICU and to protest about the South African government's Native Administration Bill. The tour was encouraging and flattering to Kadalie but it barely offered him the kind of tangible help he must have wanted. Very little money was forthcoming and when he wished to attend the Annual Conference of the British TUC as a fraternal delegate there were objections. According to Kadalie, Margaret Bondfield wrote to Fenner Brockway, secretary of the ILP, that 'Congress must be careful not to do things through sheer sentiment which will in the long run antagonise or upset other sections of the trade union movement. . . . Kadalie's union is not affiliated to the South African Trade Unions.'[30] Kadalie did attend the conference but unofficially, not as a delegate.

There is no doubt that Kadalie's visit to England increased Winifred's commitment to the ICU. She liked him, though well aware of his weaknesses, and, characteristically, she began to feel responsible for him and his union since he obviously trusted and needed her. She also believed that he was the right man, perhaps the only man, to bring about the success of black trade unionism through non-violent, constitutional means. She wrote to Fenner Brockway in August 1927 saying that, like Creech Jones, she was advising Kadalie against affiliation to the League Against Imperialism (which Brockway had been praising in the *New Leader*) because it would jeopardise Kadalie's chance for co-operation: 'I do most sincerely believe that the first necessity now in South Africa is that there should be a native trade union movement, that it should be allowed to develop [and] that its hope lies in association with the white labour movement there . . . I am sure Kadalie is going on the right lines when he works for this. The gulf between black and white labour must ultimately be fatal for South Africa.'[31] And in a letter to the *Daily Herald* of 20 October 1927 she wrote that she was convinced by his policy of moderation, 'and his desire for co-operation with the white peoples of his country. He hopes that his visit to Europe would better enable him to promote that common understanding between black and white labour in South Africa which he realises to be essential to the welfare both of his own people and the country at large.' When he returned from Geneva his 'moderation' seemed confirmed by his good behaviour during the six weeks he spent in London. 'I personally have been delighted by his behaviour,' Winifred wrote; 'certainly his manner to me, for instance, is an absolute contradiction of the saying in South Africa that if you treat a native man like a human being he takes advantage.'[32]

What now seemed to Winifred and Kadalie's other British sympathisers to be the ICU's most urgent need was effective organisation, and during or shortly after Kadalie's visit, and with his approval, the idea took root that 'an experienced trade union organiser from England should visit South Africa, for the purpose of giving technical advice, making suggestions, and helping to build up the ICU on its administrative side. . . . All members of the [ILP Imperialism] committee felt strongly that the idea was a good one and would not only be of technical service but might strengthen the position of the ICU with regard to white labour in South Africa.'[33] Winifred and Creech Jones were given the task of finding a suitable candidate and arranging the means by which the man would be paid. After several months of unsuccessful canvassing, Winifred was approached in February 1928, through contacts in the WEA and in the Union of Democratic Control, of which she was a member, by William George Ballinger from Motherwell whose introductory letter[34] made clear his willingness to do the work, his idealism with regard to racial harmony, his credentials as a trade union and local government activist, and his readiness, 'if necessary, to make it my life's work'. He impressed the ILP Imperialism Committee as moderate (that is, without Communist leanings) and free from racialism, and Creech Jones, although with some misgivings about Ballinger's relative lack of industrial experience, found him acceptable also and recommended him to Kadalie who persuaded the ICU Executive Council to approve the appointment. In fact, the circumstances of the ICU, as Mrs Lewis's letters of this time make clear, were by now such that it seemed even more a matter of urgency for someone to be sent out. During Kadalie's absence in Europe, financial chaos, corruption and dissension had spread, and Kadalie's leadership was threatened, particularly since his application for affiliation to SATUC (which Creech Jones had advised) had been refused. Panicked and angered by these events he appeared to be about to turn to the Communists again: 'I fear Mr Creech Jones' man will come too late to save a serious retrograde step,' Mrs Lewis wrote to Winifred, '. . . this man Glass [whom Kadalie now proposed to appoint as Assistant General Secretary] is the one Communist here who has had the sense not to quarrel with Kadalie when he defied the Communists. . . . Now he has his reward for always being on the spot and saving the ICU from financial scandals.'[35]

Mrs Lewis welcomed Ballinger's coming as that of a Daniel, 'with five smooth stones in his suitcase to slay the giant with two heads, capitalism and communism',[36] but the task of rescuing the ICU, let alone any grander undertaking, probably lay beyond the capabilities of any individual. Even so, Ballinger was not the most suitable man for the job, however well-intentioned, idealistic and industrious he may have been. Winifred liked him when they met in the spring of 1928 and he admired and respected her, indeed he may possibly have wanted to marry her at some later date in their acquaintance.[37] But in her fictionalised portrait of him as the Scots trade unionist Joe Astell in *South Riding* she recognised the unsympathetic qualities as well as the excellences in his personality: 'a fighter, driven by faith, shrinking from no hardship . . . an awkward, priggish man, with a harsh voice and a tactless manner.' One of her last letters, written in August 1935, was to him and takes many words to explain patiently, even wearily, as to someone easily affronted, how difficult it is to place the articles he sent her and how his style is not best suited to journalism: 'And now my dear William, please let me as a friend & a most profound and affectionate admirer, implore you not to take offence at criticisms & suggestions.' Just because his reports have to be edited, he is not to think that she or others, primarily Norman Leys, are dissatisfied with his work: 'We are not only satisfied; we are *deeply* impressed. But that does not mean that we are willing to leave any stone unturned till we have made the best use of what you are doing, & that means also passing precise & clear information to the public. Is that clear?'[38] And so it goes on, Winifred expending her failing energies in cajoling and bolstering yet another of those around her.

Ballinger arrived in Cape Town in June 1928, his passage booked and paid for by Winifred in the hope, if not the expectation, that it would be refunded by the ICU. This refund never came,[39] nor at any time did any financial support for Ballinger from the ICU even though the understanding with Kadalie had been that the organiser's passage would be paid, his expenses whilst there and a salary of £350 per year. Any idea that a British trade union or the TUC might finance the enterprise had now been abandoned; the most that official support could muster seems to have been a £50 donation from the TUC to the ICU in January 1928.

Ballinger's telegram from Cape Town to Creech Jones of July 1928 summarised the difficulties he encountered: 'THREE MONTHS PERMIT INTERVIEWING AUTHORITIES MAY REQUIRE HOME ASSISTANCE COLOSSAL TASK ACCENTU- ATED FINANCIAL DIFFICULTIES ALLRIGHT PERSONALLY.'[40] The ICU was gravely in debt, the South African government sus- picious (hence the three-month permit, later to be shrewdly extended when Ballinger's ineffectiveness was realised) and his position amidst the Communists, the white unions, and the restive, ill-organised ICU membership an isolated and precarious one.

Some years later, in 1933, Winifred would describe what he found
when he arrived in Johannesburg:

> a Union drifting rapidly into chaos, branches disaffiliating
> as quickly as they could, rival organisations springing up
> like mushrooms, bailiffs in the headquarters, the treasury
> empty – that was what untrained and hot-headed leader-
> ship, cunning legal exploitation by unscrupulous white
> lawyers, provincial jealousy and personal feuds had made
> of the once flourishing ICU.[41]

Within a year of Ballinger's arrival, Kadalie had resigned in disgrace
and acrimony, the ICU was in schism and there was hardly any
coherent organisation left for him to advise. As Winifred admitted,
when she helped him to go to South Africa, she had sent him out
in ignorance: 'I had no notion when I talked to you about ICU conditions here in England that this was the sort of thing you would
have to face though from the history of early British trades unionism I suppose I should have guessed.'[42] Ballinger's position
henceforth deteriorated into that of a liaison offficer with ill-
defined duties towards black workers in South Africa and the
responsibility of acting as adviser and conscience to African sympathisers in England.[43] Where many men would have hastened
back to England, he persevered, rather as Bill in *Mandoa, Mandoa!*
persisted, with no clear purpose other than a dogged determination to keep the channels of communication open between Africa
and the West.

In the absence of financial support from the ICU, Ballinger's
salary became a matter of concern. 'A Trust Fund has been set up
to pay my salary,' he wrote to Winifred in August 1928. 'I suspect
the Fund is the sole creation of Mrs Lewis.' In fact it was Winifred's
idea but Mrs Lewis was responsible for the South African fund-
raising and administration. He continued: 'Is it at all feasible for a
few ILP'ers, and friends of the Natives . . . to be approached, to

subscribe my Salary and expense? Please do not on any account make yourself responsible for further outlays either for ICU or myself.'[44] But of course Winifred did make herself responsible; she described her role as that of 'Treasurer to the Ballinger Trust Fund' and this meant not only subscribing at least £100 a year from her own earnings but also assuming the major responsibility for fund-raising from others. A letter to Mrs Lewis in August 1928 typifies the kind of commitment she was prepared to make: 'I hope to collect some promises of money from a few friends, so that . . . I could be able to send on appeal from both you and Ballinger a sum (I hope up to £500, but I have no definite promises yet) . . . I am willing in cases of extreme emergency to sell some of my own shares . . . I do want you both to feel that we won't let you down.'[45] The papers she left after her death contain numerous drafts and copies of press appeals on behalf of the fund, notes for lectures she gave to promote its cause, and letters petitioning for money. 'I must have written literally millions of words about Ballinger since 1927,' she wrote to Vera in 1934. She continues in a manner which suggests that even as late as this, when there was evidence that little remained of the original aims of the Ballinger enterprise, she still believed it the most valuable exercise of her life: 'perhaps [these words] are the only words I have ever written which will deserve immortality. Well, well – better to be the willing scribe of one permanent movement for releasing the human spirit, than produce nothing but ephemeral fiction.'[46] It is a sad irony that her involvement in South African affairs is probably the least remembered of her many interests, and that her fiction, particularly *South Riding*, has proved to be the least ephemeral.

Attempts by Winifred and Creech Jones to secure income for the Ballinger fund involved enlisting the help of individuals: 'I think you and I,' he wrote to her, 'might take steps to get some of the members of the ILP Imperialism Committee with other known friends together and put the position to them, and for us to make an appeal to persons who can help.'[47] But this does not seem to have produced the desired result and Winifred was left to rely on random fund-raising, mostly from friends, and on what help she could obtain from the several societies sympathetic towards African affairs which sprang up during the 1920s and 1930s. The most significant of these was the London Group on African Affairs, 'a small sort of committee', as Winifred called it, which was started in 1930 by Frederick Livie-Noble[48] as a British extension of the work in Africa of the Joint Councils of Europeans and Africans. This body organised a widespread campaign for the Trust Fund in 1932 asking for suffficient money for 'a regular guaranteed salary [for Ballinger] of £400 a year for a term of years with another £400 for working expenses.' It also offered hospitality to visiting Africans to London and was responsible for many of 'Winifred's Africans' who found their way to Glebe Place. Its list of signatories included Lord Olivier, Leonard Barnes[49] H.G. Wells, Constance Malleson and Bernard Shaw, as well as Winifred herself. Also in 1932, she joined the Socialist League in the belief that it was about to start an Imperialism Committee. 'But about the future,' Creech Jones assured her in terms of depressing familiarity, 'do not be apprehensive – the new Soc. League Sub-Committee can look after policy and general political interests [and] for Ballinger . . . we should have a committee which can keep in friendly touch with the Soc. League Subc'tee . . . and to it you could pass your trust with perfect serenity.' He continues by saying how grieved he is that Winifred is so ill and that she does not seem to be making the progress she should. But for all their efforts, little secure income seems to have been generated from any of these sources, for late in 1932 Winifred wrote to Phyllis Bentley that 'my African Fund is £300.4.6 in debt', which she paid off with the royalties from the American sales of *Mandoa, Mandoa!* It is diffficult to estimate how much of her own money Winifred contributed to the Ballinger fund over the seven years of her involvement with it but it must have totalled thousands. She was also the cause of other funds flowing to it, both in her public speaking on its behalf and in persuading friends to make donations: 'Dear Norman Leys came into £800 insurance policy last week,' she wrote to Vera in 1934. 'As a result he decided to give me a present. He has sent me a little Crown Derby ash tray, & £5 a year for his life time for Ballinger. He really is a love.'[50] This reliance on personal contacts was probably the main source of income for the Ballinger fund during the early 1930s because there is little evidence that public appeals, such as that published in *Time and Tide* in June 1932, which stressed Ballinger's ability to stave off 'rising disaffection' amongst black workers, brought much financial assistance.

Winifred's increasingly precarious state of health from 1931 onwards made it even more essential for the fund to be placed on a secure financial basis yet this was not achieved until 1934 when, spurred on by the death of Howard Pim, the sympathetic if wayward accountant in Johannesburg who had managed the money sent out for Ballinger and had frequently subsidised the fund himself, Creech Jones and Winifred formed an organisation called the Society of Friends of Africa, with Winifred as its first chairwoman.[51] Its South African 'special correspondents' included Mabel Palmer and Ethelreda Lewis and its main advisers were Ballinger and the woman he had by this time married, Margaret Hodgson.[52] Friends of Africa seems finally to have provided the support group Creech Jones had so long been promising and which was essential to Ballinger's continued existence in South Africa. Writing with forlorn cheerfulness of him as late as January 1935, Winifred admitted that his appointment as technical adviser to the ICU had been a failure due to the 'limitations of trade-unionism among natives during their present economic, political, and cultural repression'. But with her customary optimism she then goes on to say that his new work in promoting co-operative ventures in farming, catering and retailing were proving to be real compensation for his lack of earlier success.[53]

The raising of money wasn't the only drain on Winifred's

strength and resources during these years. The list of her writings on South Africa were extensive; she wished to raise consciousness as well as funds. Thus, for example, in 1928 she wrote in the *Workers' Herald* (reported in the *Johannesburg Star*) on 'General Herzog's Native Bills' deploring the fact that, apparently without protest from the British government, British legal models, in particular the Defence of the Realm Act, were being harnessed to anti-trade union and racist legislation. In October 1930 an article by her in the *New Leader*, reprinted in the New York edition of the *Nation*, argued strongly and cogently, on economic as well as humanitarian grounds, against the segregationist policies being introduced by the governments of Kenya, South Africa and Rhodesia, and urged the British government at the next Imperial Conference to reaffirm its policy of promoting the interests of African natives in spite of formidable opposition from the 'United Africa' (white supremacist) enthusiasts. In 1929 she reviewed 'Writers of South Africa' for the *Bookman*, white writers of course, including Pauline Smith, Roy Campbell, William Plomer and Sarah Gertrude Millin, but she ended her review speculating on an interesting future when 'books begin to appear written by black men and women'. In 1930 she and Norman Leys led a protest against a BBC pamphlet accompanying a series of talks called 'Africa, the Dark Continent' which advocated a segregationist policy. This categorisation of people according to class, sex, race, and so on, was, of course, deeply antipathetic to Winifred's individualist ethos. Any belief that 'an African should be an African and a European a European', and that to claim, as the pamphlet did, that there was 'a fundamental difference of mentality' between them, was 'a false central thesis'.[54] More enlightened assumptions and policy (as in the case of Jamaica) were those of 'equal status before the law, together with a high franchise qualification'.

She was also concerned with the fate of black people in Britain and in 1931 became a member of the executive committee of the Quaker-inspired Joint Council to Promote Understanding Between

White and Coloured People in Great Britain whose objectives were to educate the British public in racial issues, to deal 'wisely with instances of Colour Bar as they arise', to liaise with similar organisations concerned with East–West contact, and to offer hospitality to African coloured visitors. She herself frequently offered hospitality to African students and in 1931 contributed to the payment for the education of one student, Alex Hlubi, at Fircroft College in Birmingham.[55] She also seems to have belonged, or at least to have had some connection with, a Communist-oriented group founded in 1933 called the Council for Promoting Equality of Civil Rights between White and Coloured Peoples,[56] whose moving spirit was Reginald Bridgeman. It is indicative of her commitment to racial equality that she was prepared to join forces with a group she was not generally in sympathy with. In this instance, her indignation over the Tshekedi case[57] on which Ballinger submitted lengthy reports, and which prompted Winifred into a flurry of press activity, over-rode any wider political misgivings she may have had about the Council which seemed especially suited to deal with such issues as the Tshekedi affair. Through the somewhat sensational publicity surrounding the dispute, she saw the means to the reforms she and Ballinger thought necessary: 'What we have done all the time is to keep interest off the purely personal aspect of the case on to the need for administrative reform in Bechuanaland. What may come of it, I don't know, but there has not been such a press on the protectorates for years.'[58]

In the last months before her death, Winifred was planning a visit to Liberia. This visit had been in her mind for some years and she had talked it over with Norman Leys. In 1931 when she was in Cottingham nursing her father he wrote to her with a 'bundle of reading' about East Africa in the hope she might be the person to write a book about it. 'Don't put off reading [it],' he wrote. 'It will do you good to travel into another world and live there for half an hour.'[59] Incompetent and corrupt in its government, Liberia, according to Winifred, was ripe for imperialist takeover and it was to help in resistance to this and in the preservation of Liberian independence that she imagined her role.[60] Yet it is diffficult to believe that she seriously thought she would go there. She told Ballinger on his visit to England in 1935 that she would not be able to do so but she also wrote to Phyllis Bentley on 26 August 1935, a month before her death, that 'on the strength of *Mandoa* the Liberian government has asked me to visit its republic as an official guest & write a report on what I think of it! So I am going to the Gold Coast & Nigeria first to study conditions for comparative purposes. I am supposed to start in November.'[61] Apparently her doctor, Edgar Obermer, had told her that she could go, 'to spare [her] the sense of frustration – wh. wd depress her & be bad for her.'[62] She may have had phases of optimism which allowed her to think her travels were not yet over but more probably she told people what they wanted to know or what she thought they could cope with. She appears to have died in the assurance that the Ballingers' work would continue, as indeed it did because through the Friends of Africa the financial support was sufficient to allow them considerable freedom to travel and write, particularly in relation to the Protectorates. But their effectiveness was minimal, their reports largely ignored by the Dominions Office and their presence easily accommodated into the South African political scene. The ICU, and Kadalie, had ceased to wield real power by 1930 and, in any case, Ballinger's connection with them had by then been severed. Even Mrs Lewis had to admit to Ballinger's very limited impact and the likely failure of the ICU: '[The ICU] will sink: they can only swim if a born leader turns up, & so far the heavens are bare. The only consolation therefore, for five years hard work on our part is (1) one good man in the country & likely to stay (2) a set back for the extreme left, as it undoubtedly has been since B's arrival (3) an insight into the mentality of the chamber of mines people & the farmers, who might otherwise have hidden the cloven hoof successfully.'[63] Writing in 1933, Winifred summarised what she considered to be Ballinger's impact:

he has achieved what no one else has been able to do.
There exists today in South Africa a small but significant
nucleus of educative and developing Trade Unionism; there
are young natives attending classes on economic and book-
keeping and history, who are learning and thinking and
waiting . . . there is a hope for the black helot, that one day
he may learn to exercise the only lasting vindication of his
neglected rights, the organisation and corporate self-
protection of the enfranchised citizen.[64]

In what Edward Roux,[65] writing in 1948, has called 'the tragic tale
of Kadalie', the most tragic element was the lost opportunity to
harness and direct the power of the ICU in its early stages: 'No
single mass movement of the black workers in South Africa has
ever even remotely approached the power that was in the ICU. . . .
For a time it had even seemed that it was going to change the
whole face of South African political and industrial relations.' Roux
and others have argued that persecution and internal disruption
were the chief causes of its collapse; whether sustained and official
support from the British labour movement could have seen it grow
into a mighty instrument of change is now a matter of no more
than regretful conjecture. As it was, its cause was left to enthusiastic individuals, amateurs for the most part, and to the kind of
informal groupings such individuals had the resources and stam-
ina to organise.

It is easy to accuse Winifred of political naiveté in her involvement in South African affairs. Like Ballinger, she seriously
underestimated the importance of racial issues to the development
of trade unionism in South Africa, believing, as she frequently
stated, that there were similarities between black workers and
working-class labour in Britain. 'In each case,' she wrote to
Ballinger, 'it is the standard of living & of civilisation rather than
the difference of race which separates people . . . the man living on
the margin of subsistence is much the same whatever his race.'[66] It

was all part of her belief in the importance of the individual who, if given equality of opportunity, can rise above conditions of race, colour, class or sex. It led her to believe too simply that racial equality could be achieved harmoniously through constitutional and educational means and through the work of well-meaning individuals. But some recognition of what she was trying to do must also be given, of the grandeur of her task, and of the pride she rightly took in her endeavours. That her mission was acknowledged by some discerning individuals at the time is suggested by a letter from Norman Leys of November 1933: 'Every morning when I awaken one of the first things that come into my mind, and often the very first, is the astounding fact that at the critical period of the struggle for the liberation of Africans in our time, a person with qualities exactly fitted to make that struggle an unexpected success has appeared. I shouldn't wonder if the fact that you are a woman may help to turn the scale.'[67] But also in her papers is a copy of a letter of 1933 from J. Frederick Green, National Treasurer of the SDP, to Creech Jones in which Green says that in his 'heretical' view the solution to South African problems is fundamentally economic rather than political and entails the destruction of the 'exploiting Trade Unions of South Africa and of their sham Labour Party'. His analysis also maintains that no British government, Labour or otherwise, will ever seriously offend the South African government ('When the Union closes the Basutoland frontier,' he rhetorically asks, 'will a Labour government order the fleet to Cape Town?') and it will certainly not interfere with the Union policy of restricting the native to unskilled labour. Such being the case, 'the blacks and "poor whites" of S.A. have got to work out their own salvation [because] I have no faith in any Government here, Labour or otherwise, doing it for them.'[68] It is interesting that Winifred kept this letter but there is no evidence in her non-fiction writing that the views it expressed ever shook her faith in what Ballinger represented, in the work he was doing, and in the propaganda activities she and Creech Jones carried out.

In her fiction the picture is more complex. Her own dogged and courageous support for Ballinger, and her belief that it might just be possible for one man to change a system based on entrenched prejudice and ignorance, are, of course, reflected in the staunch and pragmatic individualism of some of the heroines of her novels. Joanna in *The Land of Green Ginger*, Eleanor in *Poor Caroline*, and Sarah Burton in *South Riding* share an 'unlimited confidence in the power of the human intelligence and will to achieve order, happiness, health and wisdom'. But Jean Stanbury in *Mandoa, Mandoa!*, sensible and hard-working, very much a projection of Winifred herself, puts the case more resignedly: 'we have to work for the world as we know it as best we can . . . we have to go on'. The decision 'to go on' is taken in response to the intractable social and political problems the novel depicts, and the comic tension in the book derives from the muddle and waste of these problems and the various progressive reforms characters try to effect. Their motives range from Talal's vainglorious ambition to Bill's dutiful endurance: '[He] had no particular faith in his own action. He was upheld by no ideal of ultimate perfection. . . . Yet, while he stayed in the country, the runway would be kept clean and the office occupied. It was little enough; but it was something. It meant that he was not wholly useless; it meant he had kept faith, though he knew not with what power.'

Winifred began writing *Mandoa, Mandoa!* towards the end of 1931 during the aftermath of the October General Election in which the Labour government had been defeated and replaced by a National Government, marking the beginning of an era of economic depression and unemployment. The end of 1931 also saw the onset of her kidney failure, as yet undiagnosed, which caused very high blood pressure and its uncomfortable and frightening symptoms, 'When angry pulses leap, / And black blood lashes its frustrated power / Against tall cliffs of sleep.'[69] She worked at the novel in Clare Leighton's cottage in Monks Risborough, near Oxford, where she had gone to rest away from the pressures of her journalism and her home in Glebe Place, Chelsea, with its babies and their attendants. She later described how writing the novel had been a kind of escape at this time of breakdown: 'Sticking to *Mandoa* and to other work with me is not courage. It may be a kind of superficiality. Pain, sadness and regret bore me so that I would rather think of anything else. I welcome work as something positive and real that we can get a grip on.' What was to be her main interest in the story was the impact of modernity in all its aspects, but particularly industrialism, on a pre-industrial black society: 'During all my contact with Africa, I had felt that one day I should want to write a novel about the contrast between the two ways of life – African and European.'

Though the novel draws much of its material from Winifred's own African experiences, it makes indirect use of them. In particular, the novel's theme is that of commercial exploitation by foreign entrepreneurs rather than the industrial exploitation by white minority settlers which would have been central to her South African concerns. She explained her sideways approach to her African novel:

> I did not want to lay the scene in South or East Africa,
> because, knowing a little about them, I felt I did not know
> enough. I preferred to take an imaginary place, so that
> errors of factual accuracy could not divert me and my read-
> ers from the human story. I wanted to take as my Africans a
> race of Portugese-Abyssinians rather than Bantu, because,
> in the first place, I felt they would be more articulate, being
> more highly developed in social civilisation and less drawn
> in on themselves, and therefore better exponents of
> comedy. In the second place, the more I saw of Bantu, the
> more I realise that I could not hope to portray the working
> of their minds, the effects of tribal experience and the cor-
> porate symbolism which forms so important a part of their
> consciousness. In the third place, I wanted an independent,

proud and unconquered race, without the psychological complications which emerge after white rulers have enforced their superiority upon their black subjects.[70]

The immediate occasion which gave her the idea for the novel was the coronation in 1930 of the Emperor of Abyssinia, which, like all matters Abyssinian at this time, was extensively and rather luridly reported in England. In reading about Abyssinia Winifred was struck by the resistance of age-old traditions of court intrigue, slavery, fierce independence and idiosyncratic Christianity, to Western influences introduced by Haile Selassie. It seemed to her that the transitional nature of Abyssinian culture, and the exotic nature of the coronation, could be appropriately drawn on to expose the contrasts and likenesses between African and European ways of life, and they were such as led inevitably to a comic, even satiric, exposure.

Nowadays, particularly in view of Abyssinia's subsequently tragic history, white British novelists would be wary of writing comic novels about a struggling and, in Winifred's words, 'a bewildered black race' but in the 1930s Britain still had enough sense of imperial superiority to do so and, in any case, Abyssinia, under Haile Selassie, was courting Western condescension. *Mandoa, Mandoa!* was in a tradition of comic novels about cross-race conflict and misunderstanding, and its subject was very topical, a topicality also witnessed by an exactly contemporary novel, Evelyn Waugh's *Black Mischief*. Waugh knew Africa well and had been at the Abyssinian coronation and the aims of his novel were also to deal with 'the conflict of civilisation, with all its attendant and deplorable ills, and barbarism'. Being written at the same time as *Mandoa, Mandoa!*, it caused 'a literary steeplechase of the kind I thoroughly deplore,' Winifred wrote; '[it has] the same plot . . . so mine has to be rushed through.' In the event, *Black Mischief* was published in October 1932, three months before *Mandoa, Mandoa!*

The two novels have very differing comic emphases. In Waugh's case the satire derives from the hopelessness and absurdity of attempts to communicate across cultures, or even between individuals. Life is mischievous and the brilliance of Waugh's wit serves to intensify the pessimism of a novel based on this conception. *Mandoa, Mandoa!* is regretful rather than caustic in its sense of near hopelessness: the four Europeans of the International Humanitarian Association, in danger and discomfort, in turn silently express the isolation that undermines all human intercourse: 'there's no liking, no friendship, no love. . . . There is no real companionship. We each live in a private, distorted world . . . how alien we are. Not two people in the world share the same thought, the same mood.' At this lonely and frightening time of her life, these must also sometimes have been Winifred's thoughts, but so too was Jean Stansbury's optimistic version of the freedom and daring that isolation and danger can bring: 'I like the sense of things happening all over the world – and feeling the contact with curious enterprises.' There is a joyful and comic engagement with the 'curious enterprises' Jean encounters, particularly the political intricacies of the wedding of La'gola and the crowd of Western eccentrics it brings to Mandoa.

If the novel throws light on Winifred's experience of South Africa and of the Africans she met in London, it does so particularly in relation to the debate between 'progressives' and 'conservatives' amongst both black and white South Africans in the 1920s and 1930s which Winifred had rehearsed with Ethelreda Lewis. Talal, modelled on Kadalie, welcomes all the technology the West can supply; he is opposed by the old chief Ma'buta who wants to retain traditional customs and primitive rituals, including slavery and the hereditary power of the chiefs. The novel is sympathetically critical of both positions. Talal's infatuation with steamboats and motor cars is not only absurd, given there are no navigable rivers or roads other than mud-tracks, but also sharply questions the benefits civilisation bestows. Do such commodities represent the sum of Western achievement, and is

Talal's susceptibility to them an avenue to his and his country's exploitation? The slave trade Ma'buta manages is, of course, everything that denies human dignity and fellow feeling but European indignation is challenged by the novel's reminder that although physical slavery may have been eliminated in the West, it has been replaced by a wage slavery which causes the dole queues in London on Remembrance Day. The novel's conclusion is that 'progress' is inevitable; grudgingly it must be regarded as a desirable alternative to 'the amiable indifference and ferocious conservatism' of existing Mandoan society. What remains of Britain's imperial legacy is entrusted to the doubting Bill who ruefully sees himself as bringing to a 'primitive' people the 'three great gifts of civilisation – Profit, Power, Pity'. As an end-of-empire novel, *Mandoa, Mandoa!* is interesting in its ambivalence towards Western responsibility for colonial progress; it is also an exotic version of the question always central to Winifred's fiction: progress and innovation are inescapable and mostly desirable but their coming is inevitably at the cost of much that is treasured and valuable in traditional customs.

A footnote to Winifred's African adventure was the opening in December 1940, by the joint effort of the Friends of Africa and the Johannesburg City Council in the Western Native Township, of the Winifred Holtby Memorial Library, 'the first library to be built and equipped solely for the use of non-Europeans and . . . intended to serve native women as well as men.' Vera despatched all Winifred's books on South Africa, and an oil painting of her inscribed 'A Friend of Africans'.[71] The dedication speech was made by Mrs Margaret Ballinger, MP. The report in the *New Stateman*, on 11 January 1941, mentions the still segregated gathering and the 'slight hesitation of most of [the Europeans] before shaking hands with a native'. In 1963 it was transferred to Soweto, the Bantu population from the township having been moved there. The library was destroyed in the riots of 1976 and has not yet been rebuilt.

Perhaps the last note on Winifred's South African crusade

should be with her short story, 'The Voorloper Group', published in *Truth Is Not Sober*. It features a picnic in the wilderness outside Pretoria organised by someone called Maldon who is planning the publication of a new magazine which will be called Voorloper, the Forerunner. Maldon and his fellow white intellectuals, based on Roy Campbell and William Plomer, who had started a magazine called *Voorslag* (the Lash), consider themselves the forerunners of their new society, 'A great ox-wagon, slow, cumbrous South Africa trekking forward, and the figures running ahead.' But the story makes clear that the real forerunners of the new society are the two Zulu servants who use the flickering light from the camp fire 'to teach each other to read out of a child's primer'.

CHAPTER 7

'We are both here, Gordon and I'

After their wedding in June 1925, Vera and Gordon spent almost four weeks on honeymoon in Europe, on the whole a successful and happy time which Vera wrote of to Winifred with considerable frankness. She found the sexual side of marriage neither repulsive nor compelling and thought a little of it would go a long way. As far as Winifred was concerned, she wrote, one sexual experience 'would go as far as you ever needed'.[1] Winifred replied soothingly that perhaps she and Vera were beyond the kind of physical infatuation Gordon was experiencing: 'neither of us can be, or expects to be, carried away by our experience of love.'[2] Gordon, for his part, wrote to Winifred from Dover on his marriage night, acknowledging the void he was causing in her life – 'I know, my dear Winifred, what I am stealing from you' – but assuring her that he would take great care of Vera and that, so far, 'the child, contrary to all reasonable calculations, looks amazingly well . . . having a husband at present seems to agree with her.'[3]

But though marriage agreed with her, it wouldn't be enough for Vera and even at this early stage she was writing to say not only how much she missed Winifred, but that Gordon could never supplant her or the kind of literary companionship and encouragement she had provided. Winifred replied that a choice between them was not necessary: 'And then, of course, here I am. And even if I should marry, which is improbable but possible, here I always shall be. And the ideal of life will probably be, as you say, when you return to England & we are both here, Gordon and I.'[4] Already, then, the continuation, although under altered circumstances, of Vera and Winifred's close companionship was being affirmed and the idea of a three-sided relationship being contemplated.

In September 1925 Vera and Gordon set sail for the United States for Gordon to resume his post as Professor at Cornell University. Vera's dislike at being a Faculty wife, and her inability to secure journalistic contacts, made her even more nostalgic for her previous life with Winifred and she wrote from America on 11 October 1925 that she might not return there next year. Their continued togetherness was also in Winifred's mind when she wrote from South Africa, on 2 May 1926, that if Vera did return to America after Christmas she could return with her to America, and then cross America on her way to Manchuria, to visit Stella Benson. But, Winifred concludes, 'Whatever you arrange for, other things being equal, I should be able to fit in with quite nicely.'[5]

In the meantime, in the aftermath of Vera's wedding and departure for America, and before her own visit to South Africa, Winifred was busy teaching to earn money, and was going to Six Point Group meetings and giving lectures for the League of Nations Union. Life was full of social and literary contacts, even including a chance meeting with J.B.Priestley who had read, and advised rejection of, 'The Runners' and whose wife had died two days earlier. He and Winifred drank coffee for three hours and talked about Rose Macaulay, Yorkshire, sex, the post-war generation, the Sitwells and his life. Winifred was by now becoming a regular visitor to Stonepitts, Margaret Rhondda's home, and wrote Vera gossipy letters about the lavish hospitality and the other guests, who included Rebecca West. There were memorable social occasions, such as the visit to see Paul Robeson in the highly popular and acclaimed *Emperor Jones* at the Ambassadors, in an expensive seat costing 4s 3d. Robeson, she thought, was a 'magnificent creature & his acting uncannily good. The return of the negro to his primitive dark fears & superstitions, childishness & charm was done with amazing force.'[6] In September she went to Geneva to the League of Nations Assembly, repeating alone the journey she and Vera had made together in the autumns of 1923 and 1924. From Geneva she wrote long, informative letters to Vera, keeping her in touch with League concerns – disarmament, Armenia, the Protocol – and personalities: Austen Chamberlain, a 'puzzled, stiff-minded, honest person', his cold personality very different from Ramsay MacDonald's, Robert Cecil, 'looking more than ever like an amiable tortoise', and the over-cautious Duchess of Atholl.[7] She would also again go alone to Geneva in September 1930 when the Women's Equal Rights International was set up, with Helen Archdale as Chair, travelling from there to Paris to a meeting of the University Women's Club.

When she returned to London in the autumn of 1925, with the excitement of Geneva over, she settled into her life alone prior to her departure to South Africa. She stressed that she was not unhappy, in fact, 'very, very happy, but it's a sort of autumn empty happiness', as though she felt the height of her experience was over. 'I miss the feel of your fingers round my left arm when I walk through the evening streets. . . . But I enjoy the trees and the lamps and the theatre and my work no less.'[8] In the copy of Shaw's *St Joan*, a performance of which Vera had seen with Gordon on the day she had agreed to marry him, Winifred had written 'Ave atque Vale. July 5th 1924' and after their actual wedding she had written the poem 'The Foolish Clocks', which Vera quotes in *Testament of Friendship*. Equally poignant is the poem Winifred wrote in mid-December 1925, 'The Frozen Earth', the title she would give to a volume of poems published in 1935. The poem is subtitled 'Edward's Funeral March' and it and its later companion poem, 'Symphony Concert', subtitled 'For a dead musician', also published in *The Frozen Earth*, relate to Winifred's wishful belief, ever since the Italian holiday in which she and Vera visited Edward Brittain's grave, that she was linked to this dead brother, perhaps had in some sense taken his place. Grief over Vera's departure fuses with grief at the loss of Edward who recedes into a past almost beyond memory: 'You have grown too cold, too cold, too cold / To lift your limbs from the frozen mould / And visit me here in the garden.' 'Symphony Concert' was written in September 1931 amidst Vera's engrossed writing of *Testament of Youth* and was occasioned by a visit the month before to a Beethoven Promenade Concert: 'I suddenly found myself thinking of Edward, and the words came into my head "I am his deputy" and . . . the tears were rolling down my cheeks.'[9] As Edward's 'deputy', she is ashamed to have so dull a perception of music but it could not be otherwise since, for thirteen years, every song she has heard has been deafened by 'that last sound you knew, / The shrapnel splintering before it slew.'

Winifred arrived back in London from South Africa in mid-July 1926 and cabled Vera in New York that she was home. By this time Vera had planned to return to London herself after arguments with Gordon about the need to resume her writing career. 'I am beginning to look forward, more than I can say, to coming home,' she wrote on 16 July. 'It has been a queer year, of mixed pain and pleasure, delight and disappointment. Two conclusions only I have so far brought out of it quite clearly: 1. That I would not now for the world not have married Gordon or want not to have met him. 2. That marriage in general is an unhappy state, and to be avoided by anyone who is already quite happy single unless they are *very* sure that it is what they want, and have planned beforehand the conditions on which they intend to live together.'[10] It was a strange remark to make, partly a warning to Winifred about marriage and partly self-congratulation on having 'planned the conditions on which . . . to live together'. But Vera was to be at her most difficult and demanding around this time, with both Gordon and Winifred. The conditions she imposed on Gordon were that their home should be in England, with the result that he exchanged his full-time appointment at Cornell for a part-time one.[11] The part Winifred was to play in this relaunching of Vera's career was to be the same as she had been in the past, to become again one of two single women with independent but mutually supportive lives in journalism and fiction – *except* that for approximately half of each year Gordon would turn the two-some into a three-some. Naive and egotistical as Vera was, even she sensed that this reversal of what Winifred had expected, which was to be alone without Vera, would cause some bewilderment and reticence on Winifred's part. Vera voiced her misgivings in a letter of late June 1926, when Winifred was still in South Africa: 'Sometimes I feel anxious, because you said "I will meet you at Southampton if possible", but 18 months ago you would have said "I *will* meet you at Southampton." Is something very wrong at home, Sweetieheart, or is it that time and distance are making me apprehensive about you as I used to be about Gordon?' In *Testament of Friendship* Vera remembered this anxiety as 'some imaginary lack of response' in Winifred's letters which had caused her, Vera, to write 'suggesting a little sadly that perhaps she might not want to share the flat again during my six months in England'.[12]

Winifred's replies to these letters show contrasting ways of responding to Vera. To Vera's warning that most marriages are unhappy, Winifred replied briskly that she was inclined to agree that marriage is in general an unhappy state – 'but so also, in general, is celibacy. The resigned loneliness and masked inferiority of most virgins who have no creative passion to sublimate their Libido (I have been reading Freud, you may observe!) seems to me just as unfortunate as the disillusioned and often exasperated state of most married women.'[13] The comment applies common sense to Vera's dogmatism and at the same time is a mild reminder that although she, Winifred, may be a virgin she is one of those saved from loneliness and inferiority by her creative passion. The letter continues to say that good personal relationships are 'rare, sweet and dangerous – you with Gordon, I with my friends, especially you, and my liberty for creation.' This is a measured letter and also one which holds Vera slightly at arm's length, with Winifred reminding Vera that she has other friends and that she is free to do her work, which Vera had felt herself not to be.

But a slightly earlier letter from Winifred, in response to Vera's worry that she had changed and become cold and indifferent, is in quite another vein. Troubled, self-accusing and emotional, it assures Vera of her love and blames the alleged indifference on a kind of shyness: 'I do not find demonstrative intimacy an easy thing,' she explains; 'I had never thought to show such natural demonstrative affection as I find rises quite naturally now from my love for you. . . . Your presence breaks down a sort of inhibition that makes me otherwise unconsciously reluctant to show my feelings. . . . But this inarticulateness, this inhibition is always ready to rise up in me.' The letter continues vehemently – 'I need you every hour. Listen, my heart . . . you must believe these things – for they are true. I love you. I need you. I want to be with you,' and concludes by assuring Vera of the inclusiveness of her love for her: 'My little love, if you doubt – ask Gordon if it could be possible, having loved you, to cease. . . . We will make this winter a time of profitable work for you if we can. For me it will be pleasure. I wish that Gordon were to be here too.'[14] This not only signals willingness to help Vera's career, as in the past, but also accepts Vera's changed status, the marriage to Gordon. She had stressed that the happiness of Vera and Gordon was not painful to her, and recognised that Vera 'can give biological happiness to Gordon' which she cannot give to her. Now this happiness will be more than just tolerated; it will be rejoiced in and embraced. There never was any doubt that Winifred would gratefully share Vera's renewed London life on almost any terms that Vera would propose but at the same time she was anxiously aware – much more so than Vera – of the adjustments and compromises the new arrangement demanded of her, and also the possibly uncomfortable and unmanageable difference to their lives Gordon's presence would make. When Winifred writes, 'ask Gordon if it would be possible, having loved you, to cease. His answer will be adequate, perhaps, as my intention,' there is a capitulation on her part not only to Gordon's pre-eminent position as Vera's lover but also to the authority of his response. As husband, he can respond physically in ways that she cannot, and because of this he can speak of love in accepted ways that she may not. It is in this light that her protested inarticulacy may be read: 'I want so much to make you see, and I can only flounder stupidly in words,' but her 'stupidity' is that of a negotiator for whom there are no accepted means of communication, to whom the future is uncertain and in which she is only ever likely to be supernumerary, the surplus single woman, the 'maiden aunt' in the family. In her biography of Vera Brittain, Deborah Gorham has described Winifred's self-concept as patterned very much in these terms, as 'an updated version of the Victorian spinster. Like the model spinster, Holtby learned to cultivate selflessness as a duty and learned to take vicarious pleasure in the romances, marriages and the children of her sisters and friends.'[15] Though true to some extent, this description does make Winifred seem more of a victim than she was, and it underestimates the importance to her and to society of her life outside the Brittain–Catlin household. Some three years later, having fully sampled it, Winifred could vehemently state the case for the 'more amusing, agreeable, permanent and adventurous' lifestyles of modern maiden aunts who are, she says,

> working in schools and offices and factories; we fly aeroplanes and explore Africa; we remove appendices or lecture on the civilisation of Crete. . . . And where do we live? Some of us live alone. But those who prefer family life may

still enjoy it . . . living with their self-chosen families, as
independent equals, satisfying their natural instincts for
domesticity while helping to solve the economic problem of
the young couple. And are they not portents of the family
as it may be? A small community of equal, independent citizens, related either by blood or by affection and common
interest, living together by choice, not by necessity.[16]

During the fraught summer weeks of 1926 Vera tried to reassure
both herself and Winifred that the plan to live together would
work and, above all, that the relationship between herself and
Winifred would be the same as in her pre-marriage days. 'I don't
think in my heart of hearts I ever doubted you *weren't* different,'
she wrote to Winifred from America. The trouble was that people
thought that she, Vera, was different, that because she was married
she wouldn't want to lead the same sort of life as before: 'One
begins to suspect that even the people who know one best will take
for granted that marriage *has* made a difference.' She explained
how frustrating it was to be perceived as a married woman: 'when
people meet you and think you unmarried, their first question
always is "What is your job?" But when they know you are married
they ask: "What is your husband?"' The letter concludes: 'I am
longing to see you – more than I dare allow myself until I am actually within sight of Southampton. I am taking your letter with
me . . . for it makes me long to see you so much that it will miti-
gate the little pang which leaving Gordon always gives me.'

To have two loves, two kinds of intimacy, was what Vera wished
for, Gordon supplying the physical needs, including children, and,
however Vera may have protested against it, the status that went
with marriage and motherhood, whilst Winifred provided the
intellectual and literary support and the benign rivalry[17] that nur-
tured Vera's career. Vera loved and needed both Gordon and
Winifred very much and it was surely courageous and affirmative,
as well as integral to her feminism, to want to relinquish neither.

What is perhaps less admirable is the clumsiness and even the cruelty with which she pursued this aim. The letter quoted above includes a passage which was excised from *Selected Letters* and which illustrates a number of less attractive features about Vera's efforts to arrange a lifestyle which would accommodate her desires. Recognition of Winifred's generosity and perhaps of her own demanding behaviour prompted her to write: 'No wonder Lady Rhondda loves you, and Percy and Mr Hutchinson, and all the nice, nice people that I wished loved me, and who never do. The wonder is that you do love me, that you see more in me than what most people see – which is a combination of egotistical bitterness plus a kind of insincere prettiness plus an intermittent (and, as they think, designing) attraction for men.'[18] This wheedling passage is not quite honest (Vera never thought Margaret Rhondda 'nice'), it plays on the wartime events of Vera's life which made her bitter, and negates Winifred's heterosexual appeal (the implication being that, Percy and Mr Hutchinson notwithstanding, she isn't attractive to men, which is why people love her). At the same time it is highly seductive of Winifred, (correctly) attributing to her powers of love and perception beyond the common – 'you see more in me than what most people see'. It was an appeal that Winifred could not resist; if Vera needed to be demonstrably loved beyond the norm, Winifred needed to be needed, by the world in general but particularly by Vera. Her response to Vera's letter was to send flowers and a 'wee note' with the comment: 'You are sweeter and more foolish than ever.'

By the end of July Winifred seems to have grown used to the idea of the three-way household and her letters more outspokenly welcomed it: 'Of course I am keeping on the flat [it had been let whilst Winifred was in South Africa] – or rather, we are keeping it on. Any other notion never occurred to me.' There is also a more assured and full-blooded, although perhaps rather strained, assertion of her claim on Vera's affections: 'Oh, my dear, I have pictured so often going down to Southampton again, this time to meet my love, my love, my love. My ship is coming in, my sweet from the sea. Not yours, not Gordon's – mine.'[19] Perhaps there was a kind of license now in writing so passionately, Vera being safely married, the sexual question settled and Vera's heterosexual needs taken care of. Above all, there had to be rejoicing that their partnership would not be broken, the noble friendship of two emancipated women would continue; all that was required was that it should adjust itself to the inclusion of a husband for a little over a half of each year.

When Vera came to write of these crucial few weeks during the summer of 1926, the account in *Testament of Friendship* occupies no more than a page. The final move into a settled triangular household, into which would be born children – '[I] would have you miss nothing of the richness of life,' Winifred wrote encouragingly to Vera – is recorded with even greater brevity: 'When G. decided to change his American professorship to a half-time post so that our family could be born and reared in England [Winifred] suggested joining the household from which he would so often be absent. The Maida Vale flat, we agreed, would be too small [and in] September [1927] we moved into an upper maisonette . . . off the Earl's Court Road.'[20] This suggests that it was Winifred's desire that effected this arrangement, and though there is no doubt that Winifred did desire it, it was Vera's expectation that was the motive force behind it. There was nothing at all unusual in such an arrangement, she assured Winifred: 'Half the married couples in this town seem to have a sister living with them, and you are more to me than any sister.'[21]

So the Brittain–Holtby–Catlin household in the period to Winifred's death – 'this household that gives me so much pleasure', as Winifred described it – started in 117 Wymering Mansions in Maida Vale, which had been the home of Winifred and Vera as single women, and then in September 1927, three months before the birth of John Edward, they moved to the two top floors of 6 Nevern Place, which would accommodate the baby and a nurse and in which Winifred had a bedsit on the first floor. There were also servants – a housekeeper and a maid. It would have been unthinkable otherwise; at hardly any time during her life would Winifred be without domestic help of some kind. The same was true of Vera. Even in the Doughty Street days in the early 1920s, before the advent of 'Nursie', they had someone in to do the housework. Like many women of her class, Winifred could barely cook; in her papers from the early 1930s are painstaking recipes for simple dishes like macaroni cheese and cheese-and-potato pie, for use on the few occasions when she had to do so. One of Vera and Winifred's most tetchy exchanges occurred at one of the times when they did not have a servant, Vera accusing Winifred of letting the flat get dirty, to which Winifred had replied that, foolishly no doubt, she had not realised it was her responsibility. As ever she concluded the letter in peace-restoring mode: 'Good night, dear love, little gallant fighter – and thank you, my sweet, for being so patient with me so many times – I kiss your darling hands – (though I could smack your pretty face for calling me so subtly a fool), & I enclose a cheque for £3.11.3 which is, I believe, half Mr Dyplin's bill.'[22] In their final house together, 19 Glebe Place, Chelsea, to which they moved in April 1930, three months before the birth of the second baby, Shirley, such difficulties were never met with again. It was Vera's home, with Winifred as a kind of permanent lodger, and Vera employed Amy Francis, who, joined by her husband, Charles Burnett, in 1934, would be with the family for forty years. There was a nurse-governess for the children, and in 1934 a secretary came in daily to do work for Vera and Winifred. Altogether it was a full, busy, thriving household, to which, of course, Winifred contributed financially except for those times when she was staying in Monks Risborough or in a nursing home. Her letters to Vera and to Gordon are strewn with references to matters of household upkeep; a £100 from her father, for instance, 'has been given me with the express instruction that it is to be spent on other objects than Africans; so the Home will benefit' in its current need for redecoration.[23]

The house in Glebe Place was, then, both a family context for Winifred and a work-place, almost a cottage-industry environment in which she undoubtedly thrived, and in which she lived in practice the new role and status of the spinster she had so often advocated in theory. Though she often took what some people thought was undue responsibility for Vera's household, and was made use of frequently, she also was free to lead an independent life, to come and go as her work dictated. Where she all too often went when not at Glebe Place was to her other family in Cottingham, sometimes for weeks on end and usually in response to family disasters, Alice Holtby never hesitating to call her daughter back for every calamity that the Holtby and Winn families suffered: her father's prolonged illnesses and death, of course, but also aunts dying of cancer, uncles bankrupt and drinking themselves to death, nieces with congestion of the lungs. 'I move from catastrophe to catastrophe,' she wrote from Cottingham to Gordon in April 1933, and the following month, the crises having abated, she described to him the joy she felt in returning to Glebe Place, 'that makes me appreciate more than ever your hatred of exile.'

But Winifred was also cramped and intruded upon in Glebe Place, with no proper study or sitting room, her room not as big, Vera noted in her diary, as the cabin she and Gordon occupied on board the *Berengaria* on their way to America in 1934.[24] John Edward Catlin later remembered that Winifred's sofa was also her bed, and that the bookshelves which lined the room were used as a climbing frame by his sister Shirley.[25] As the children grew older she seems to have felt the need of a retreat from the clamour of family life and rented a 'single-room flat' in the King's Road as an office. 'I am just shifting my last things from Gordon's room,' she wrote to Phyllis Bentley in May 1935, 'then hurrying off to meet him. I've changed to the loft upstairs & am getting an office out. A bedroom at last!' Some of the pleasure in this kind of solitude had been dwelt on in *Mandoa, Mandoa!* where Jean Stanbury, who has had years of '"making do" on sofas, and awaiting invasion at all hours,' rejoices in a home of her own, 'into which she could shut herself night after night, and remain confident of privacy, blissfully undisturbed.' This is also what Winifred arranged for herself for those periods of time in Withernsea and Hornsea during the last two years of her life. Hilda Reid, whose testimony must be taken with some caution because of her dislike of Vera, believed that Winifred hoped *South Riding* would make sufficient profit, her Break Through, as Hilda saw it, to permit her to buy a house of her own.[26] And St John Ervine, the irascible drama critic and novelist she had met through Margaret Rhondda, was always urging Winifred to leave the Catlin household where he thought she was treated no better than a servant. But Winifred didn't leave, at least not permanently. For all its incovenience and hard work, the Brittain–Catlin household gave her a sense of community, of being needed and loved, which grew more important to her as work became more demanding and her health deteriorated.

There were, inevitably, problems. Gordon's loneliness during his months of exile in America made him in practice, if not in theory, regret the feminist basis of the marriage. His letters were full of complaints, and by 1929 he was openly contemplating having an affair, pointing out to Vera that this was not out of line with their modern thinking about marriage. Whilst acknowledging this, Vera was upset, not least because she was concerned to demonstrate that marriage and career could be combined successfully: affairs and the gossip that would accompany them might 'smirch or spoil or render less dignified . . . our relationship [and] the success of our marriage matters to the world, to society, to politics, to feminism . . . one happily married wife and mother is worth more to feminism . . . than a dozen gifted and eloquent spinsters.'[27]

Winifred's spinster life during these years certainly demonstrated how gifted and eloquent she was. By 1929 she had published three novels and was a highly successful journalist, writing for the *Manchester Guardian*, the *Nation*, the *Radio Times*, the *News Chronicle*, the *New Leader*, and many others, including above all *Time and Tide*, of which she was now a director. She was, in fact, at this time, much better known than Vera, and indeed than Gordon, and to two such ambitious people this must sometimes have made her an uncomfortable household member. She had also proved herself a successful teacher and lecturer, she was involved in political circles ranging from the ILP Imperialism Committee to NUSEC, she knew famous people and had many friends. An indication of her rising reputation was the inclusion in 1928 of a short work by her in the 'To-day and To-morrow' series, published by Kegan Paul. The series comprised commentaries, almost all bearing classical names, on a variety of contemporary issues and boasted a number of distinguished names among its contributors: Bertrand Russell, J.B.S. Haldane; C.E.M. Joad, Dora Russell, R.C. Trevelyan, Sylvia Pankhurst, Robert Graves, for instance. Winifred was one of the first of only a few younger writers (Rebecca West and Vera would later contribute[28]) who were asked to write one of these esteemed and popular little books. Hers was *Eutychus; or The Future of the Pulpit* and its title page describes it as 'A Short Treatise in the form of a Plain Dialogue, suggested as a possible epilogue to Fénelon's *Dialogues sur l'Eloquence*.' Eutychus is the plain man who 'likes a bit of religion in the right place . . . I like to be told what I ought to believe and how I ought to live and where I shall go to when I die.' He meets Archbishop Fénelon, who represents traditional Catholicism, and Anthony who is a modern rationalist, and they agree to debate the question of the future of religion. To Fénelon, the evidence overwhelmingly suggests that church authority and doctrine is very much alive; religious controversy rages over the new woman voter, alterations to the Anglican Prayer Book, Evangelical objections to phrases such as 'Sung Mass', the entry of women into religious observance, and so on, all evidence of the vitality of the church. Anthony replies that these controversies are merely passing fashions and that the real future of humanity lies with the scientists and psychologists (particularly the Viennese school), and the preachers of this 'religion' take as their text, 'Our kingdom is of this world', and its chief priest is H.G. Wells. This new secularism has many sects and preachers – Pacifists, Feminists, Communists, Imperialists – who offer salvation. The satiric form of the dialogue gives Winifred the opportunity to cast a slightly caustic eye over society's numerous and varied do-gooders. Eutychus falls asleep during Anthony's highbrow discourse and when prompted to speak gives a populist, democratic view in which the pulpit has passed to the people and to the media they understand and enjoy. It's a culture in disarray that *Eutychus* portrays, but vigorous, engaged and optimistic, and Winifred's enjoyment in it, and in the profusion of her ideas concerning it, are obvious.

Winifred had also used her increased solitude after Vera's marriage to develop friendships previously on the edge of her life. She had been corresponding for some months with Stella Benson, the novelist, who came to tea when she returned to England in the autumn of 1925 and was 'nicer even than her books – kinder, less ruthless, extraordinarily personal and real somehow. But she looks horribly ill. . . . She is ill much of the time. . . . I often forget what a strange distance lies between people who are ill and well.'[29] Stella Benson liked Winifred, though she thought her 'very intense and very much withheld'.[30] Vera was still at Wymering Mansions before leaving for America and remembered the tea party when she came to write *Testament of Friendship*. She too noticed how ill Stella looked and how otherworldly: 'Delicate, witch-like, remote, with her penetrating blue eyes and the chill whisper of a voice that her deafness gave her, she seemed a spirit from some distant planet temporarily inhabiting a crude, material universe.'[31] As traveller, adventurer and novelist, Stella inspired Winifred with awe, and also gratitude that she 'seems to want to know me'. Winifred would go on holiday with Stella and her husband, James Anderson, in June 1928, 'just for the inside of a week in a sort of revolt. I had so much work to do that I just decided to do none of it.'[32] She found Stella and her husband 'darling people . . . so charming together', and Stella for her part thought Winifred 'the Perfect Fellow Traveller'[33] and wanted her to travel in Manchuria with her. They would have had much in common, both hating exploitation, both unafraid of speaking out against it, both supporters of the League of Nations.[34] During Stella's final illness in 1933, in South China, Winifred wrote to her to praise 'the way you launch off into the wilds ignoring the dilapidations of the body', and she described her own bodily dilapidations: 'my head squeezed into an iron nut and my pulses pounding wildly with ferocious excitement.'[35] Far away and unable actively to be involved in Winifred's illness, a distant rather than a close friend, mortally ill herself with tuberculosis, Stella, like William Ballinger, who also was receiving treatment for tuberculosis in 1932, must have seemed a person she could confide in. Her relation with Stella was untrammelled and when she reviewed Stella's best known novel, *Tobit Transplanted*, in 1931 she could describe it wholeheartedly as funny, beautiful and unique: 'The landscape of China, the memorable individual animals, all the glow and strangeness of the whole pattern illuminate its rich and delicate liveliness.'[36]

Other friends and acquaintances also filled Winifred's spinster life. She began a friendship with Storm Jameson in 1927 – 'downright and pleasant & friendly, in a businesslike-don't-waste-any-time-sort of way' – and by 1929, after an angry beginning to the relationship over a review Winifred had written, was intimate enough with Rebecca West to stay in her villa on the Riviera.[37] Odette Keun, whom Winifred had met through *Time and Tide*, also became a friend and when the affair between her and H.G. Wells went bitterly wrong, she confided in Winifred, reading to her the 'essay' she was writing about him, 'the tears pouring down her cheek. . . . It has cost her nearly a nervous breakdown to write it. . . . She is a superbly courageous, indefatigible [sic], tormented

seeker after truth.'[38] Throughout, of course, there was the friendship with Margaret Rhondda whose wealth was such that she could
afford to rent villas or pay for hotel suites in exotic locations and
invite friends and friends of friends to join her. There was such an
occasion in August 1929 when Jan and Edith Smeterlin (as Edith
Mannaberg she had been Winifred's friend at Queen Margaret's
School) were there with Winifred – 'We had long talks about sex
and snobbery' – and another in July 1931 in St Lumaire and the
Haut Savoie with the journalist Marie Scott-James.

Winifred's relationship with Gordon was an altogether more
complex one and a major testing ground for both the ideal of
semi-detached marriage Vera desired and the friendship between
Vera and Winifred. Vera was very anxious that Winifred and
Gordon should get on together and occasionally accused Winifred
of coldness towards him. 'I was astonished by your suggestion
that he likes me more than I like him,' Winifred replied to one of
these accusations; 'apart from the fact that physically he has no
appeal for me – who has? Harry did once, I think, but not now) I
like him quite dangerously much.'[39] Gordon also had good inten-
tions towards the triangle he found himself in, including a
willingness to continue corresponding regularly with Winifred.
But aspects of his personality as it emerged in the correspondence,
even during its early stages, jarred on Winifred. Apart from his
pompous and opinionated manner of writing (with 'principal sentence[s] lost in the surrounding interminable forests of subordinate
clauses,' as he described it himself), he was full of self-pity, hating
Cornell and believing himself 'quite dead', with nothing but relent-
less work until 'I have hammered this next book out of myself.' He
admits he ought not to be writing to Winifred like this but perhaps
it is better that he does, 'otherwise Vera will get the benefit of it
and – well: that's that.'[40] His letters to Winifred became reposito-
ries of his misery in Cornell and requests for both advice and help:
whether he should return to England and should he do so, if, by
personal contact, she could 'ferret out anything which, however

unimportant, pays livelihood +£100 and is not entirely unsuit-able.'[41] This was to be the pattern of his correspondence and his relationship with Winifred: she was to serve as a mediator between him and Vera (even buying presents from him for Vera), and she was also to assist his career and help to get his books published. His letters were extraordinarily frank and outrageously self-centred, and in this they established an uninhibited intimacy with Winifred which seemed to ignore or be quite unconsciousness of the possibility of any sexual attraction between them.[42] His letters suggest he was fond of her, often beginning with 'My darling Winifred' and disclosing his frustrations and despairs in extrava-gant terms. In some respects he wrote to her as if she were a man, with lengthy discussion about politics, economics, academic affairs, and even occasional smutty jokes – 'You can tell Vera! I never tell Vera these things . . . You won't. And why not? For same reason why I not.' Yet her position as the unmarried 'sister' in the household allowed him to seek for sympathy in a way he probably wouldn't have done if she had been a man. This use of her as a cor-respondent sometimes made him unfeeling, as when he wrote to say of her illness that though it was a 'damn shame', he envied her the financial freedom, and the necessity of living where she chose and doing what she wanted that illness brought with it, whereas he was 'damned to live in this tower of barbarism'.[43]

On Winifred's side, the courtesy and helpfulness of her letters to him before his marriage to Vera continued for some time, along with bulletins on Vera's and then John Edward's health: 'She is as happy with him as she can be. She must give a little disquiet as a hostage to ill-luck.'[44] An example of how supportive she was of his career is the letter she wrote on the *Realist*, the short-lived maga-zine of which Gordon was a founder member, in which she listed the good points as they struck her and her friends, notably Margaret Rhondda, and, very tactfully, the weaker aspects like the editorial notes and the lack of advertisements ('Isn't that awfully expensive?').[45] Winifred was by now an experienced journalist with editorial expertise, and this was valuable advice but the *Realist* foundered anyway, too high-minded and also, as the absence of advertisements suggests, too commercially naive to succeed.

By the middle of 1929, however, after two years of Gordon's complaints, the tone of patient explanation became more emphatic and began to be tinged with exasperation which would eventually tip over into a satiric vein which Gordon did not seem to notice. The collapse of her tolerance came finally in 1933: 'Vera has gastritis; both children have whooping cough; the night-nursery ceiling leaks. Now, now clearly, is the time to write and commiserate you upon your misfortune in escaping domestic bliss.'[46] Vera was in the final agonising throes of *Testament of Youth* and Winifred felt that Gordon's sad letters required brisk response, including an account of her sexual adventures that week, as a rejoinder to his hints and disquisitions on the affairs he contemplated having: 'Last week I broke a record by having two improper proposals & being kissed by three different men within twenty four hours. . . . But really it is very tiresome that I feel less emotion than if I had been caught in a thunderstorm – some concern as to my clothes, some admiration of the elements in action, and complete mental detachment. . . . I have neither disgusts nor pleasures in it . . . but a nausea for the hypocracy [sic] of sentimental & pseudo reverent phrases whispered as the prelude to activity so completely unsentimental and vigorous.' Adding to demands for emotional sympathy was Gordon's constant pressure on her to help place his articles in English journals; her contacts were too popular, she soothingly told him, to be of use to someone with a first-class mind like his: 'Now, if you were a vulgar little whippersnapper like Godfrey Winn & wrote "Why I am afraid of Bachelor Girls", I could be of the greatest possible service.' What further tested her politeness was Gordon's reaction to the portrait of him in the last three chapters of *Testament of Youth* in which he is portrayed as 'another stranger' who will redeem the losses of the war. Relations between Vera and Gordon became very strained during this period and Winifred was concerned to set them right again: 'Really, Gordon, there is *nothing* in [*Testament of Youth*] that could in any way offend your taste or damage your reputation.'[47] 'Are you not possibly mistaken?' she wrote in another letter; 'Is it not possible that, far from doing you harm, this might do you actual good? . . . Only the irremediably vulgar could find cause for ridicule in a record so dignified.' In the same letter, written from Cottingham soon after her father's death, when she has had to answer 350 letters of condolence, she reprimands him for his complaints that his career has taken second place to Vera's: 'If you have altered your way of life, so has Vera. The sparse literary product of the past seven years has not entirely been unrelated to housekeeping, children, & your interests: she has corrected your proofs & typed your articles; she has done a million chores of varying kinds; she has taken responsibility for your father (albeit unwillingly); she has taken complete responsibility for the children. . . . And always it seemed to me that the division of labour was pretty fair – & perhaps – if I may suggest it – rather heavier on Vera's side than yours.'[48]

And so it went on through the spring of 1933, with Winifred in Cottingham moving from one family crisis to another, and Vera also requiring emotional support during revisions of the typescript of *Testament of Youth* (including alterations and deletions required by Gordon) and the anxious time preceding its publication and the reception by critics and public. Winifred's intervention over the trouble with the last chapters of *Testament of Youth* was probably crucial in the survival of Vera's marriage. Whilst she thought Gordon 'hypersensitive' she recognised that his perception of the academic world as 'dessicated [sic], inhuman [and] suspicious' was what mattered: 'he has to live in it,' she wrote to Vera. 'Therefore I think you had better accept his suggestions as far as you can.'[49]

There is no doubt that Gordon's self-esteem suffered not only from the success of Vera, but of Winifred too. Their working relationship, in which he must have seemed an intruder, was also not easy for him to accept although it gave him more freedom to travel and engage in politics than a conventional marriage. After Winifred's death he was to write to Vera: 'You preferred her to me. . . . It humiliated me and ate me up. That's why of course I could not read *South Riding* and probably never shall be able to do so. . . . The point is, not sex but preference is what matters.'[50] Perhaps to assert his influence more strongly, and enabled to do so by Vera's great success with *Testament of Youth*, in the spring of 1935 he decided to resign his professorship at Cornell to return to England to concentrate on a political career. As his letters to Winifred show, he had been thinking about doing so for some years and to some extent Winifred had encouraged him, or at least had encouraged him to leave academia which he believed was prejuduced against him: 'I should like to see you snap your fingers at the lot from the security of a non-academic job,' Winifred wrote in 1926. As Paul Berry and Mark Bostridge have shown,[51] the decision to leave an academic career turned out to be an unwise one which involved relinquishing what was probably Gordon's true vocation, to be a political scientist rather than a practical politician.[52]

Winifred's support of Vera during the writing of *Testament of Youth* was unfailing and unstinting, not only in writing and talking encouragingly to Vera herself but also in keeping alive the book's interest with publishers, particularly Gollancz. After it was accepted for publication, she wrote lovingly and generously from Cottingham, where the protracted final illness of her father was taking its course: 'All the time, whatever I am doing, I am conscious of a note of happiness & relief because of your book.' So accustomed was Winifred to feeling Vera part of her, that the book's success was also her success. 'I am glad because *my* judgement is justified too. I know now that all my hopes for what you may do with the book are going to be justified. It will be the instrument to give you that power you need to work for the things you care about & fulfil your destiny & myself.'[53] When the book was finally published, Winifred wrote the notice for it, a kind of extended blurb, and she had to do this in a rush because the original introduction by Phyllis Bentley was not satisfactory. Gollancz told Winifred 'anything up to 1,000 words' but when she had written her piece she thought the size of the notice and how she had done it were inadequate.[54] Yet it was published, describing *Testament of Youth* as 'like no other book yet published' and praising in particular its setting of personal experience against 'a heroically-sustained panorama. . . . [T]he individual stories illuminate with their fortuitous symbolism the great march of European tragedy.'[55] To later generations *Testament of Youth* is indeed like no other book. As Storm Jameson said in her review for the *Sunday Times* in September 1933, 'its mere pressure on mind and senses makes it unforgettable' as an account of the experience of war by a woman participant and from a woman's point of view.

Vera's portrait of Winifred in *Testament of Youth* was inevitably going to cause disquiet amongst their friends. Vera's unforgotten hurt at the debate in which she felt she had been humiliated jostles with her memory of the tall, popular, golden-haired Northerner, too humorous and hearty for Vera's war-torn nerves. Yet the whole portrait is overlaid by the knowledge of more than ten years of successful friendship so that the immediacy of its hurtful beginning is softened by the memory of what it will become, as, for instance, when Vera describes Winifred's boisterous arrival in Mr Cruttwell's study whilst admitting to the obstinacy with which she, Vera, disregarded the sensitivity and strength of Winifred's face. Hilda Reid thought Vera's attitude at Oxford and in *Testament of Youth* made insufferable assumptions that no one had endured as many losses in the war as she had. But this does less than justice to the element of self-criticism – Vera confesses that she was 'tense and hard and disagreeable' – in *Testament of Youth*, or the tribute the book pays to Winifred's life-restoring effect: 'I felt like an icicle beginning to melt in the gathering warmth of the pale spring sunshine.' Hilda's comments were made many years afterwards but someone who was less reticent at the time of publication was Phyllis Bentley, giving the death blow to a friendship with Vera which had begun swiftly and which had almost as swiftly deteriorated.

Phyllis Bentley was Winifred's friend. They had met in 1928 when Winifred went to give a course of university extension lectures in Halifax, Phyllis's home town. 'I envied [her] with all my heart,' Phyllis wrote in her autobiography: 'Tall and fair and handsome . . . that lovely speaking voice, that precision of English, that flat in London, that post on *Time and Tide*, those interesting well-cut clothes, that Oxford degree.'[56] Winifred stayed with Phyllis and her widowed mother 'once or twice' and she and Phyllis met occasionally in London, and also corresponded. In the slump years of the late 1920s Phyllis's mill-owning family had begun to fall on hard times and partly to chronicle the fluctuating fortunes of the West Riding wool industry and partly from a need to earn money Phyllis began to write the novel which would bring her considerable fame during the next decade. Apparently she was encouraged in this by Winifred: 'Stick to your own genre. . . . No one else is playing your game.' *Inheritance*, the family saga of the Oldroyds, was published in March 1932 to immediate acclaim. At the time Winifred was away from London in Monks Risborough, and this was followed by a spell in a nursing home in Courtfield Gardens in April. When Vera visited her in March they talked about the forthcoming *Inheritance* and how Gollancz had liked it so much that he telegraphed its acceptance. 'Wish something of this kind could one day happen to "Testament of Youth",' Vera wrote in her diary. With Gordon away as well as Winifred, Vera was feeling trapped in domesticity and her anxieties about the writing of *Testament of Youth* could not, as usually happened with her work, be talked over with Winifred. Phyllis, whom Vera had met the year before in Winifred's company, represented the successful author, published by Gollancz, that Vera herself hoped to be. There was also the question of Phyllis's 'grey life, tragic through negation',

in Winifred's words, which Vera believed should be compensated
for not only by success but also by a little smart London society. So
it was with a mixture of envious curiosity and condescension that
Vera asked Phyllis to stay with her at Glebe Place, an invitation
Phyllis accepted, journeying to London in May 'radiant with happiness' to occupy Winifred's room for a week. Vera had mentioned
the invitation to Winifred who 'seemed a little surprised – as P.B. is
her friend not mine – but thought she might like to come.'[57] Phyllis
was, apparently, equally surprised and also apprehensive but on
this first visit everything went well. Phyllis listened attentively to
Vera's worries about *Testament of Youth*, managed to buy smart
clothes which enabled her to look less 'provincial & all hung about
with beads and things' and was highly appreciative of the party
Vera gave in her honour. On her second visit, only a week later,
Winifred was at home too, the doctors having 'found enough what
is the matter with her to continue the treatment at home.' But
within a few days, an argument between Phyllis and Vera over the
'respective merit of critical & creative qualities in literature' developed into a row with Phyllis in tears in her room and Vera trying
to make amends. After an overwrought interview they came down
to supper to find Winifred, 'calm, tactful, never surprised by anything . . . sitting in the window-seat reading the *New Statesman*'.[58]

The relationship between Vera and Phyllis recovered for a while
to the extent that Winifred and Vera discussed together how they
might help Phyllis: 'her dark, intense misery & the tragedy of grief
& frustration, & whether there was anything we could do to . . .
soften her, make her happier & more attractive.' When Gordon
returned in June he too seems to have made Phyllis welcome and
she liked and was at ease with him. But Vera's account of this
summer describes Phyllis as full of resentment and complaint
about her Halifax life, always bursting into tears and being hurt by
other people's happiness, and it's clear that Vera thought her both
sexually and socially frustrated and envious of Vera's own lifestyle
and personal fulfilment. Phyllis was particularly touchy and

suspicious at this time; she was infatuated with Vera, being, as she explained to Winifred, 'naively romantic about feminine beauty' and to some extent Vera was infatuated by Phyllis too, warmed by her flattery and by the apparently beneficial effect she had on Phyllis: 'the fact that I really seemed to want her had been a new revelation to her of her own possibilities & power to attract & life wouldn't be so intolerable so long as she kept in close touch with me & my world.' But Vera's world was also Winifred's and it's difficult to judge just how much she felt threatened and dispirited by finding herself in this newly-forming triangle. She was on the edge of the relationship between Vera and Phyllis, or at least taken for granted; she certainly features little in Vera's journal entries at this time. Winifred was around, in the household, going to meetings and parties, carrying on as best she could with her own work for *Time and Tide* and for Ballinger but the interest in Vera's life and in her journal was in Phyllis, so much so that Winifred's illness, whatever the doctors had discovered was the matter and that could be treated at home, is hardly mentioned, nor is there much about Winifred's current books, *Virginia Woolf* and *Mandoa, Mandoa!* Was Winifred jealous at the way Vera and Phyllis had 'fallen in love with each other'? As far as Vera records, Winifred was amused, perhaps exasperated. Hearing how a bad-tempered letter from Vera had made Phyllis 'tremble all over & quite incapable of food or work [Winifred] merely remarked' according to Vera: ' "You've been the most important person in too many people's lives, you little bitch!" ' It is a remark which could have meant almost anything from affectionate admiration to intense resentment.

In November Vera went to Halifax to give a lecture and was ill with gastritis whilst there. The disappointment of the visit for Phyllis was compounded by two delirious and injudicious letters Vera wrote to Phyllis on her return home. Phyllis was offended and wouldn't accept an apology although she eventually wrote to Winifred saying she hadn't realised how ill Vera had been. Lavish present-giving followed but there was no mending the quarrel;

'she's too ill & neurotic & put off me to care anymore about what happens to me,' Vera wrote in her diary. The relationship soon deteriorated even further over Phyllis's grudging dustjacket description of *Testament of Youth* and over the portrait of Winifred in the book. Vera did respond to the extent of reducing the amount of text on the Somerville quarrel, omitting Winifred's actual speech at the Somerville debate: 'It would be worse than death to me if people thought . . . that I was making use of this book to be slyly spiteful towards you, my dearest of dear companions,' Vera wrote to Winifred.[59] As for Vera and Phyllis, in Vera's terse words, 'We decided in 1933 that it would be wisest for us to stand at a little distance.'

Phyllis disappears from Vera's journal after 1934, except for references to her American tour but a conclusion to the affair was given in Phyllis's autobiography, *O Dreams, O Destinations*, published in 1962, where she wrote warmly of the good days of her friendship with both Vera and Winifred, the intellectual and political interests the household offered her and, most valued of all, 'the delicious feeling, which Winifred and Vera both took pains to foster in me, of being welcome, wanted.' As far as the rift was concerned, she recorded that, 'for Winifred's sake at first, later when she was lost to us for our own, we became reconciled . . . and when we meet or correspond, do so in entirely friendly fashion.'[60]

Winifred's efforts to smooth over the quarrel between Phyllis and Vera at first took the form of a bluff cheerfulness: 'Now ain't it queer how differently people see things?' she wrote to Phyllis in April 1933 about *Testament of Youth*. 'I feel so flattered by the portrait of a noble, self-effacing, thoughtful & unselfish Winifred . . . that I can't find any connection between the creature & myself at all. . . . So do calm your boiling blood, my lamb. After all one personal portrait has little to do with the grand sweep of the book.'[61] Later letters adopt a different tone, explaining Vera and Phyllis to each other: Vera 'will never again be in such a state of tension as she has been during the short time you knew her. . . . If you multiplied by three times what you felt at the end of writing *Inheritance*, you'd get something of the same result.'[62] And to Vera she explained that 'Phyllis is a tragic person, whose limitations call for more love & patience & understanding than – say – the warm rich natures like Storm Jameson's,'[63] and, more harshly, that Phyllis was 'one of those people congenitally incapable of feeling deeply anything which does not immediately & directly concern themselves.'[64] Winifred maintained a steady concern for Phyllis throughout the quarrel, always saying how much she and Vera would like Phyllis to come on holiday with them, commending her on her books and encouraging her writing. But, as Phyllis recognised, to quarrel with Vera was, at the very least, to create a distance between herself and Winifred. Though Winifred kept her friendship with Phyllis alive to the end, it did not flourish, and her comments to Vera, particularly over the American tour Phyllis undertook in 1934, so much less successful than Vera's, were pitying and exasperated. Rather pathetically, Phyllis wrote to Winifred, thanking her for her mediation: 'I shall be so glad to hear from you sometimes, Winifred, & see you if I come to London, but Vera and I must keep apart.'[65] All through the ebb and flow of the Vera–Phyllis relationship, Winifred kept calm, apparently undisturbed by the intensity of the association in its early days, and willing to help when it began to go wrong. She was very ill by this time and such flushes of feeling and pangs of disaffection must have seemed remote and insignificant; she also knew that Vera would return to her when the first enthusiasm of this relationship had waned, just as she had when the excitement of her early days with Gordon had faded. Once again, though, in a triangular relationship in which she found herself, she had played, or had attempted to play, the role of mediator. Did she ever wish to be otherwise – demanding, passionate, intractable, one of those on whose behalf mediation is undertaken? Mediators are powerful people, seeking future results rather than immediate gratification, and are sometimes scheming and manipulative. In an exaggerated form they are the Alderman

Snaiths of the world, channelling and savouring the passions of others, with 'an odd masochistic pleasure to be found in this contact with energy . . . – a sort of vicarious satisfaction, a novel response to unfamiliar stimuli.' Winifred's sympathetic portrayal in *South Riding* of the repressed, secretive little Alderman is not a crude self-portrait but it is a shrewd recognition of the energies which propel mediation, its sources in unfulfilled desires, its goals, for good or evil, of resolution and movement forward, its temptations towards manipulation. Comparing his own passionless life with the emotional turmoil of those around him, Snaith uses an image[66] which echoes the description Winifred gave of hers, that of a stream: 'he felt that he was nothing – a stream of water, cold, metallic, barren, without colour or form.' Yet he also rejoices in this invisible strength: 'After all, water had power, he thought. It does not only reflect pictures, it turns wheels, it irrigates valleys, it drives dynamos . . . When he died the entire face of the South Riding would have changed, because he once had lived there. I shall do better than any of them, he told himself.'

Throughout the second phase of Winifred and Vera's relationship, after Vera's marriage, their support for peace movements continued, although their alignments began to alter in response to the changing international situation. In her pacifism, as in her feminism, Vera all along had been influenced by the work of Olive Schreiner and followed Schreiner in *Woman and Labour* in believing that women are biologically less bellicose than men: 'Because women produce children, life and the means of living matter to them in a way that these things can never matter to men.' Her emphasis on the difference between men and women is at the root of the conflicting emotions in *Testament of Youth* where, as she admitted, war is most bitterly regretted yet the virility and romance of men going into war – 'this glamour, this magic' – is still acknowledged as a proper masculinity. It was a nostalgia for the 'crest and spur of the fighting cock', to use Virginia Woolf's words,[67] which will surface in Vera's novel of 1936, *Honourable*

Estate, where the greatest erotic appeal belongs not to the enlightened husband of a progressive post-war period but to the soldier-lover who is killed in battle. With Winifred the approach was different. Although she had suggested in 1926 that women's child-bearing capacities made them less ready than men to endanger life, she believed this was circumstantial rather than innate. Her stress on the importance of the human individual regardless of gender, class, race or colour, made her less extreme and less essentialist on questions relating to women and pacifism.

The relationship between feminism and pacifism in the interwar period grew increasingly complex and various. By the early 1930s women counted for up to a third of active peace campaigners, if the number involved in Dick Sheppard's influential Peace Pledge Union, at the height of its success in 1936, is anything to go by. Many of these women were also feminists but not all feminists were pacifists. The question of whether feminists should support war had been vigorously debated in the suffrage circles before and during the First World War. As Martin Ceadel has shown, the peace movement between the wars became increasingly divided into pacifists and what A.J.P. Taylor has called pacificists who represented 'a non-pacifist strand within the peace movement,' accepting, however reluctantly, that military force may be necessary as a last resort. Pacifism, by contrast, was 'an ethic of ultimate ends' opposed to force under any circumstances.[68] As the 1920s drew to a close and the prospect of another war became more threatening, pacifism, as opposed to pacificism, became less tenable than it had been in the idealistic period after 1918. The relinquishing of a pacifist position was very painful to many women, and in the extreme case of Helena Swanwick may have led to her suicide in 1939. Storm Jameson declared herself a pacifist in *No Time Like the Present* in 1933 but by the next year her equivocation is apparent in the collection of essays she edited, *The Challenge to Death*, where she and most of her contributors tacitly assume that war may be necessary in certain circumstances. By

1940 she had left the Peace Pledge Union, acknowledging the delusions of her earlier position: 'I brushed out of the way the uncomfortable reflection that a pacifist could support the idea of an armed League only if she assumed that the bombs of the International Air Force would never be dropped. . . . Looking back, I see that in 1933 I was blinder than a bat to the real tragedy of our time.'[69] In 1940, Maud Royden, a Christian pacifist whom Winifred had heard preach 'magnificently' on several occasions, would sum up the agonising realisation: 'The unbelievable thing had happened – there had come into the world something that was worse than war.'[70]

Vera's progression through the 1930s was towards pacifism away from the pacificism implicit in her membership of the LNU. Her disillusionment with the 'right-wing' League of Nations, whose leaders, she believed, had become 'sorry apologists for the new militarism', led her to sponsor Dick Sheppard's Peace Pledge Union, and her 1937 essay, 'No Compromise With War', marks her final break with the League, 'this gilded angel of internationalism . . . the reincarnation of the Triple Entente which made the previous war inevitable by dividing Europe into two hostile camps.' Over the Spanish Civil War she called herself 'an uncompromising pacifist': 'I hold war to be a crime against humanity, whoever fights it and against whomever it is fought. I detest Fascism and all that it stands for, but I do not believe that we shall destroy it by fighting.' Her pacifism would be the final blow to her friendship with Hilda Reid, who remembered watching searchlight practice with her in wartime London, exasperated by what Hilda regarded as Vera's naive statement that 'she wished they wouldn't do it'.

Winifred's death in 1935 meant that she did not have to make the decision that Vera and others of their circle faced when the Peace Pledge Union took its radical pacifist stand in 1936 and forced its members to choose between this and the partisan and powerless collectivism that was all the compromised League seemed to offer. But the evidence from her work suggests that almost certainly she would not have followed Vera into pacifism but would have remained constant to the pacificist attitude that membership of the LNU implied and that her experiences in the decade from 1925 to her death confirmed. She had never been as passionate and single-minded a peace-worker as Vera and although as a journalist she wrote frequently about the need for peace, her fiction certainly was not as preoccupied with war and its causes and prevention as Vera's. Only *The Crowded Street* features a war-time experience, in the description of the bombardment of Hardrascliffe (Scarborough). Even *South Riding*, written in 1934 and 1935 within sight of planes engaged in bombing practice over the North Sea, makes only passing references to war, its heroine fleetingly 'haunted by the spectre of another war' and enraged that 'the greed and folly and intellectual lethargy, the departmental pride and wanton folly of an adult world' should endanger the children in her care. Of course, in a less specific sense, this, her last novel, is anti-war in its emphasis on human fellowship: 'we are not only single individuals, each face to face with eternity and our separate spirits; we are members one of another.'

This sense of collective as well as individual responsibility had led Winifred to join not just the LNU but the Union of Democratic Control (UDC) in the mid-1920s and to become a member of its Executive Committee in 1927. The UDC had been formed in 1914 with the objective, as its name suggests, of planning for the democratic management of the peace in post-war Europe. It was particularly concerned that foreign policy should be under parliamentary control, openly debated in the House of Commons rather than secretly designed by the War Office as had seemed to be the practice hitherto. Such accountable procedures might lead to settlements which would be less punitive than in the past, neither humiliating the defeated nor rearranging national boundaries. As it turned out, these objectives were far from what the Treaty of Versailles effected, but the UDC continued its campaign under the dedicated and inspired leadership of Dorothy Woodman. By the time Winifred joined the UDC, it was beginning to change from a generally pacifist organisation to one which could envisage war as a last resort. By the early 1930s two issues in particular – the rise of Fascism and the build-up of armaments – seemed to make change in this direction a moral imperative, and these were to be the two issues that Winifred's peace writings would focus on.

Winifred also joined the National Council of Civil Liberties when it was founded in 1934. Though this was not specifically a peace organisation, it was concerned with the protection of individual freedoms, including pacifist freedoms, as in its campaign against the Incitement to Disaffection Bill or its monitoring of pro-Mosley behaviour by the police. As Kingsley Martin, editor of the *New Statesman*, said, the National Union of Fascists' demonstration at Olympia in 1934 was a test case concerning police neutrality in the face of right-wing violence: 'The police watched from outside [and] should have interfered when the [Fascist] violence became obvious.'[71] Vera was present at the demonstration and testified against the Blackshirt violence, as did Naomi Mitchison and Storm Jameson, but Winifred was in Withernsea at this time, and, as it turned out, staged her own single-handed counter-demonstration at a Blackshirt rally there. During the summer of 1934 she was an observer at Blackshirt rallies for the NCCL.

The question that oppressed her most was what could she do about the 'wanton folly' that on all sides would lead to war? Nothing except to write: 'I don't know what to do about it,' she told Vera, 'except to go on . . . trundling the little wheelbarrow of propaganda across the world.'[72] The furore over re-armament during the early 1930s provided a spur and a focus for her peace propaganda, resulting in some of the most impassioned and incisive journalism of her career. Her position in the debate, like that of many pacificists (like Dorothy Woodman, for example, whose pamphlet, 'The Secret International: Armament Firms at Work', went into eight impressions between 1932 and 1934) was that

arms should no longer be manufactured privately; this would bring
about a desired limitation in armaments because the profit motive
would be removed. Winifred's essay, 'An Apology for Armourers',
for Storm Jameson's collection of peace essays, The Challenge to
Death, is an ironic defence of arms manufacturers whose support
for war is justified by their responsibility to sell arms for profit.[73]
In Winifred's view, in addition to the nationalisation of arms
manufacture, disarmament should proceed on the basis of 'all-
round abolition, within a limited period, of every type of weapon
forbidden to Germany by the Treaty of Versailles.' This was the
subject of a deputation presented to Prime Minister Ramsay
MacDonald and the Foreign Secretary on 10 November, led by the
Archbishop of Canterbury, with signatories from the professions,
arts, industry and peace movements, Winifred being one of the
four literature deputees.[74] In January 1935, she wrote one of her
most forceful articles[75] – for the socialist magazine Labour, having
joined the Independent Labour Party the year before – attacking
government duplicity in blocking the LNU's attempt to discover by
means of a questionnaire what the citizens of the country desired
in regard to foreign policy and the abolition of the private manufacture of arms. At first supported by all parties, the proposal had
finally been blocked by the government, which, Winifred tren-
chantly pointed out, was to play a double game of paying
lip-service to the idea of international security whilst surrendering
none of its national sovereignty, including the freedom of big business to manufacture arms and profit by their sale. The likely
outcome of the questionnaire, whereby it would become apparent
that the populace supported the League system, would be a serious
embarrassment to the government.

A plan for a lecture on 'The Psychology of Peace and War', given
in the early 1930s, remains in Winifred's papers, and is an indication of how far she had come from the simple optimism of her
early days as a speaker for the LNU. Then there had been an
assumption that appeals to reason were what was required; 'now'

it was not so simple. There were psychological causes for war, amongst them the dark erotic impulse to death as well as life, and the code of aggression and honour bound up with a militaristic notion of masculinity. The lecture plan doesn't develop these ideas but they point to the position she began to articulate in her play, *Take Back Your Freedom*. Flawed as it is, the play is one of the earliest attempts in the 1930s to see the causes of war as related to the *construction* of masculinity and femininity: Arnold Clayton is trapped in masculinity of a fascist nature because his mother has been trapped in a feminine role which has left her unfulfilled and disabled from participation in public life. If Winifred was less extreme in her commitment to peace than Vera in that she seems to have supported the taking up of arms as a last resort where Vera held implacably and courageously to an uncompromising pacifism, in another respect, in her tentative linking of feminism and pacifism, Winifred was more imaginative and bold in her thinking. Vera's feminism, which was founded more in a belief in the essential difference between men and women, led her into a closed position in which war could only be understood in terms of sexual opposition. Winifred's reluctant feminism, which always stressed the insignificance of the differences between men and women and affirmed their common humanity, led her to view that difference as largely constructed, and therefore amenable to change and reform.

If Winifred had lived, the divergence in the attitudes of Vera and herself to war and peace would have become more obvious. It is unlikely it would have caused a rift in their friendship; Winifred would have developed and acted on her own ideas whilst supporting Vera in her controversial stance and comforting her during the ensuing opprobrium.[76]

CHAPTER 8

A reformer-sort-of-writer:
Virginia Woolf and the woman's novel

I feel the whole world is on the brink of another cata-
strophic war, & to go & shut oneself up in a cottage writing
an arcadian novel, when one might be trying to shove it
one infinitesimal fraction of an inch in the other direction –
seems to me a kind of betrayal. That's the worst of being
50% a politician. I can't get out of my head my responsibility for contemporary affairs. If I were a pure artist, I should
know where my duty lay. As it is, I compromise all the way
& do nothing well. You are safe: you are an artist. I am a
publicist, & a darn good one when I exert myself; but I
want to write this particular novel & the one after – (I have
three in my head!) – & yet I feel that it's my business to
stand by the people shouting against war.[1]

Winifred wrote this, to Phyllis Bentley, in the winter of 1933
shortly before she took a cottage in Withernsea and began to write
what became *South Riding*. She had expressed similar sentiments to
Lady Rhondda: 'I shall never quite make up my mind whether to

be a reformer-sort-of-person or a writer-sort-of-person. . . . Only I trust my judgement as writer . . . much more than as a worker for causes, and I actually enjoy writing more.' To Vera she had said, 'I have no illusions about my work. I am primarily a useful, versatile, sensible and fairly careful artisan. . . . I am, primarily, a publicist. At odd moments I write works of the imagination – stories, satires, poems and plays. They are very uneven in quality. They have moments of virtue.'[2]

When Winifred and Vera decided to become independent women living in London rather than returning to live in their parents' homes, they had a choice about how they would support themselves. They could, and did, teach, and in Winifred's case there was the opportunity, which she turned down, to become a university lecturer. The Sex Disqualification (Removal) Act of 1919 meant that, in theory at least, they could have entered the Civil Service and most of the professions. Yet in both their minds was the goal of writing 'works of the imagination'; other activities were a means to this end. In this approach to their life's mission, they inherited a Victorian tradition, partly a romantic notion of becoming women novelists and partly a business sense that this is how middle-class women earned a respectable income and perhaps also gained fame. They were by no means alone in this; many of their friends – Hilda Reid is another such example – also took to fiction, not out of absolute necessity but from a wish to earn an income of their own and a belief that this was the most creative and honourable way to do so. The ghosts of the Brontës haunt the women novelists of the post-war period in this as in many other respects.

When Winifred published her first novel in 1923, and Vera hers also in 1923, the literary scene was dominated by the great Edwardians: Arnold Bennett, H.G. Wells and John Galsworthy. *The Forsyte Saga*, published as a whole in 1922, epitomised the middle-brow success of this time, and set the mould for a type of novel, large and sprawling, which follows a family's fortunes through two or three generations. What we now think of as Modernist fiction, when it was not banned, as in the case of Joyce and Lawrence, remained with some exceptions the culture of minorities.[3] For middle-class, university-educated young women beginning to write in the post-war years, recent precursor female novelists were scarce. There was the feminist Olive Schreiner[4] – particularly influential on Vera – or, at the other extreme, a very popular writer like Baroness Orczy with her phenomenal success, *The Scarlet Pimpernel* (1905) (which would be produced as a film by Alexander Korda in 1933, five years before he produced the film version of *South Riding*) or Ethel M. Dell whose best seller, *The Way of an Eagle*, was published in 1912. But the middle ground of fiction seems to have been largely unoccupied by women in the Edwardian period. With the end of the war, however, young middle-class women began to write fiction as never before: historical novels, such as those by Hilda Reid or Naomi Mitchison, autobiographical fiction about their experiences as modern women, such as Rebecca West's and Vera Brittain's, and novels about their cultural backgrounds as in the case of the Jewish writer G.B. Stern or the rural writers Mary Webb and Doreen Wallace. E.M. Delafield is a good example of the emerging professional or semi-professional woman writer of the time. Eight years older than Winifred, her life was enlivened by her war service as a VAD, which she turned into a novel, *The War-Workers* (1918). This was followed by her Women's Institute and magistrate experiences as a married woman which she likewise drew on in her fiction. She wrote over forty novels in all, some of them addressing social issues like divorce and the single woman at home, but her most successful works were her satires of middle-class domesticity, culminating in *The Provincial Lady*, a series of stories published in *Time and Tide* in 1930. The time for such a writing career for a woman was propitious. As Nicola Beauman has argued,[5] the years between the wars 'were the heyday of fiction written by women': better educational opportunites, greater confidence from the changing political climate and, as Rebecca West was not slow to point out, some reduction in the competition due to the death in the war of so many men who, had they lived, would have kept 'certain appointments between their imaginations and pen and ink'.

Winifred's first novel, *Anderby Wold*, published in 1923 and quietly but encouragingly reviewed, gave her the obligatory mixture of pleasure and pain in the writing: '[it] is great fun; but ye gods, the sorrow of wrestling with a style like mine!'[6] The novel's focus, on the necessity for change and the fortitude demanded from those for whom change is painful, also traces the general changes which she saw overtaking farming during and after the war: 'no one can say I don't get my knowledge of farming conditions first hand.' The novel introduces themes which will recur in her subsequent fiction: the conflict between tradition and innovation, between those who want to act precipitately or autocratically and those who are pragmatists or democrats. The setting of the Wold countryside of her youth is one she will return to in *South Riding* and which is present in several of her short stories, 'Harking back to Long Ago' and 'The Second Alibi', for instance. There is also a rapprochement between an old and a young woman. Tentatively sketched in the relation between Sarah Bannister and Mary Robson in *Anderby Wold*, it will be developed more fully in that between Eleanor and Caroline in Poor Caroline, and between Emma Beddows and Sarah Burton in *South Riding*. In all three instances the women's bond is formed through the affection they hold for a man; it makes the older woman jealous and bossy towards the younger but eventually is the means of strengthening their affection and respect for each other. In contrast to this is the failure of heterosexual love in *Anderby Wold*, which will be played over in all later novels except *Poor Caroline*. Mary Robson's snatched embrace with David Rossitur is interrupted by her husband, followed by his stroke, and then finally by Rossitur's death. In *The Land of Green Ginger* Joanna's husband dies, in *Mandoa, Mandoa!* the moment when Bill and Jean might become lovers is thwarted by the 'long-trained habit' of inhibition. Robert Carne and Sarah Burton's night of passion is thwarted by his heart attack and he spends the night in her arms as a gasping invalid and not as a lover. In most of Winifred's fiction there is the ghost of a love story structuring the development, an echo of the great romance plots of nineteenth-century novels, plots she cannot quite escape from but which she cannot endorse wholeheartedly. Marriage is no longer seen as a woman's happiest fate but it is only in *South Riding*, her final novel, that the female protagonist finds a positive alternative to it. Winifred's novels track the enlargement during the inter-war period of women's life choices and roles: Mary's resigned marriage undertaken for economic reasons, Muriel's accepted but directionless singleness, Joanna's vaguely liberated passage into widowhood, Eleanor's 'semi-detached' and Jean's pragmatic marriage, lead on Sarah's part to a passionate devotion to a life of work which can withstand the depredations of romantic love. In this spectrum of female sexual and economic destinies, Winifred drew on the lives of women she knew and on her own life but her characters are types also, they characterise problems and issues which faced women during the inter-war years. Winifred's sense of history and the topical scene which made her a competent journalist made her also into a successful condition-of-England, particularly a condition-of-England's-women, novelist too.

Appropriately, all Winifred's novels, even *Mandoa, Mandoa!*, her most exotic and invented novel, not only use recognisable locations but are set in or near current time. *South Riding* is the outstanding example of this, in that she used not only the location of the triangle of Yorkshire which runs from Hull to Spurn Point up to Bridlington, but the novel is placed squarely in contemporary time, even to the extent of incorporating the Silver Jubilee celebrations of 6 May 1935. Its substance is the depressed and poverty-ridden early 1930s precisely located in the conditions and circumstances of this area of Yorkshire: the decline in farming, the

Local Government Act of 1929, the workings of the East Riding County Council with information drawn, so she said, from her mother's wastepaper basket, the public enquiry into the land-purchase scandal in Hull in 1932. Her mother was terrified that Winifred's use of such recognisable material would lead to libel prosecutions, claiming that if Winifred had lived she would have tempered what she had written. She may have done so to some extent under pressure from her mother, but the typescript of *South Riding* suggests nothing significantly unfinished in what Winifred left unpublished. It is a fair copy and Vera's 'correcting' of it did not involve having to decipher numerous alterations or complete half-formed sentences. Alice Holtby would have been equally alarmed at Winifred's journalistic tendency of using family material that was interesting or relevant as part of her fiction. She coolly appropriated material from the lives of family and friends, as, for instance, in her brisk use of a relative's bankruptcy as components in the character of Carne in *South Riding*:

> Just had to give a bankrupt relative £40 to prevent the
> bailiff distraining his race horses. He has glorious old furni-
> ture & Mother is going over to get some for me. He says
> she can take what she likes. . . . He lives miles away the
> other side of York – married into the 'County,' lived right
> above his means, kept a racing stable, which he hopes to
> sell after York races at a profit. If the bailiffs came, they'd
> take the horses for his debts. His aristocratic wife went mad
> & is now in an asylum. *What* a family we are, to be sure.[7]

This kind of magpie quality, where all that came to hand could be turned into fiction, produced in *South Riding* the large, sprawling, incident-packed novel of community life which looks back to *Middlemarch* rather than to the dynastic novels of Galsworthy. This concern for the details of a particular locality mark *South Riding* as a regional novel, one of those noticed in Phyllis Bentley's PEN pamphlet on *The English Regional Novel*, published in 1966, where she argued that the golden age of the regional novelist was 1840 to 1940, because improvements in communications made regions self-conscious of their identity, yet before mass communications were to rob areas of their individuality. The economic and social distresses of the inter-war period gave the form a 'fresh impetus [and it] flourished numerically more than ever before'.[8] Phyllis Bentley included Winifred in her list of regional authors of the 1930s, alongside J.B. Priestley, Leo Walmsley, Storm Jameson, Lettice Cooper, herself, and, somewhat equivocally, Hugh Walpole. The flaws of the genre were affectionately satirised in Stella Gibbons's *Cold Comfort Farm*, published in 1932, but it was its merits that attracted Phyllis Bentley: its verisimilitude, 'a conscientious presentation of phenomena as they really happen in ordinary everyday life on a clearly defined spot of earth,' and its essentially democratic nature, 'a belief that the ordinary man and the ordinary woman are interesting and worth depicting.' Winifred classed herself with this group of writers with pride and affection although she also saw the limitations; in 1932, reading Arnold Bennett's *Lord Raingo* (1926) she described it as 'too knowing. We second-rate provincials are. I am.'[9] But to St John Ervine, who had long scolded her for wasting her time on *Time and Tide* and in writing flimsy satires like *The Astonishing Island*, *South Riding* was the summation of her career, the novel about the land of her childhood he had urged her to do: 'for God's sake stop being a pamphleteer,' he wrote to her in 1933. 'The Almighty meant you to be an artist. That is why he gave you that good brain and your genial and kindly and receptive nature. . . . Produce the book I've begged you to deliver these years and years past.'[10]

Winifred's responsiveness to the contemporary scene, the receptive nature of her fiction, was, perhaps inevitably, at the expense of sustained psychological exploration of character. The brisk insight, the telling sketch and the illustrative incident tended to be her strengths rather than deep enquiry into the processes of consciousness. Even when the character she is developing has an obvious autobiographical bearing, the manner is not confessional but has the distance of reportage, as though it is somebody else's life which is being written about. Those characters who resemble her – Joanna in *The Land of Green Ginger*, or Jean in *Mandoa, Mandoa!* – have personalities one can recognise as similar to Winifred's but they don't add much to a knowledge of her states of mind or feeling. The emotional crises of their lives are underplayed, rather as Winifred in life underplayed her own crises. *Mandoa, Mandoa!* comes nearest of Winifred's novels to expressing her disappointment over Harry Pearson but the scenes where Jean meets Bill, the character based on Harry, are hasty, summarised and observed rather than felt. For example, Jean sees Bill coming along the path with his two negro servants, wearing white, with a white helmet in his hand, 'lordly and preoccupied'. 'And suddenly she was swept by blind, unreasoning, melting, feminine panic. Without a thought, she slipped behind the moon-flower bush, and stood hidden while he went past her up to the hotel.' The scene dissolves, within a few hundred words, in common-sense analysis on her part of his faults and her critical attitude towards them. A little later they hold a conversation in which, in emphasising her point, Jean places her hand on his arm:

> That startled him. He clutched her hand, crying, 'My
>   dear –!'
> She felt the strong shock of emotion flow through her.
> For a moment, anything might have happened.
> 'Good heavens, he loves me. He feels . . .'
> They waited.
> Every instinct, every memory, hung between them. Their
> past and their future stood balancing on a breath. Then
> long-trained habit intervened. Jean drew away.

The emotional tension ebbs away as quickly as it is summoned and a cheerful or resigned matter-of-factness takes over. This happens in the second of the two scenes of their meeting; after Jean and Bill have gone their separate ways for the night, she gets undressed for bed: 'she felt she was laying aside more than her dress and petticoat. She was laying aside physical and emotional adventures; she was laying aside her husband and her children.' The words from a Herrick poem come to her mind – 'And I am glad, yea, glad with all my heart' – and she concluded: 'Well, if not with all her heart, with a good deal of it. She had her work, and Africa, and a thousand human contacts. "Settled by a majority vote," she thought wryly.'

Winifred was writing in these two episodes about a relationship in her life which preoccupied her deeply and naggingly by virtue of its irresolution. Yet the expression of this is neither therapeutically indulged nor more than hintingly confessed to. Jean's response to Bill is a minor aspect of the novel, overtaken by its interest in African affairs, exotic personalities, clashes between cultures and generations. It may be that Winifred's abilities as a novelist were not great enough to command scenes of great feeling, including sexual feeling, but this doesn't quite suffice as an explanation because, interestingly, she did write movingly, albeit briefly, of the emotions of minor characters: Midge Carne's terrified re-enactment of her mother's madness, Lily Sawdon's destruction of the dog, Rex, Agnes Sigglesthwaite and the lambs. In this last instance, the experience was again based on Winifred's own; staying at Monks Risborough in 1932, knowing by this time that her illness was fatal, she too had an epiphany out walking in cold weather in which the gaiety of new-born lambs had given her 'a curious form of spiritual intoxication', not uncommon in those who have received a sentence of death, in which 'she heard a voice within herself saying: "Having nothing, yet possessing all things".' Yet this intensely autobiographical origin to the scene is quickly dissolved in a matter-of-fact decision by Agnes, in 'a new energy of defiance', to carry on, and she is, in any case, only a very minor character in the novel, one of the spinster figures who provide a foil for Sarah as well as a protest against wasted lives and talents.

As far as the major figures of her novels are concerned, their interest does not lie in the psychological complexities of their characters. Of course, her heroines (her major protagonists are all women) have stories to tell, achievements to record and disappointments to overcome but their function increasingly is to be a register of the lives of others and of the social problems they present. Her second novel, *The Crowded Street*, is the most centred on the subjectivity of its heroine, Muriel, of any of her novels but after this story of a girl who represents a direction Winifred herself might have taken, the novels follow a depersonalising progression. Joanna in *The Land of Green Ginger* still retains some of the developmental quality of Muriel but the comic detachment of *Poor Caroline* and *Mandoa, Mandoa!* renders Eleanor and Jean little more than observers of the scenes around them. In *South Riding*, Sarah Burton holds great interest thematically in her opposition to conservative forces, and the narrative of her love story is an important structuring device running through the novel's episodes, but it is only one thread amongst several, contributing to the network of ideas in the novel rather than of prime interest in itself. Her presence is justified less on account of her emotional life than as a vantage point from which the social landscape can be viewed. The division in Winifred's life and work between politician and artist, or reformer-sort-of-person and writer-sort-of-person, was always only ever one of emphasis and expediency. In *South Riding* the division is bridged in the form of the social problem novel in which the fictive elements support, enliven and humanise the documentary, reformist purpose of the novel. The novel is also a mature embodiment of all Winifred's most fundamental beliefs: her pacifism, her equalitarian feminism, her belief in social democracy and in the value of education, in the importance of the individual human being and of the individual's obligations towards society.

The bitter economic depression of the early 1930s brought forth other works of a similar kind – Walter Greenwood's *Love on the Dole*, for instance, or, in different vein, J.B. Priestley's *English Journey* – but there were not many novels, particularly novels by women, in the 1930s which undertook the same panoramic, *contemporary* view of society as *South Riding*. What distinguishes it from novels like Storm Jameson's *The Triumph of Time* or even Lettice Cooper's *We have Come to the Country*, which is set in an unemployment centre in the 1930s, is the range of issues *South Riding* addresses. Education, birth control, unemployment, poor relief, landed versus commercial interests, the care of the insane, local authority building programmes, local authority reform, the single woman – all issues Winifred had written about as a journalist now come together remarkably as a fiction about a community, a regional tale perhaps but also a social problem novel of wider significance. Winifred herself claimed that it was the only novel about local government – a claim which still holds good? – and this unpromising framework permits her the scope to write about the state of England and at the same time to suggest reforms which might bring about improvement. The impersonality of approach this large-scale scenario necessitates (there is a cast list at the front of the novel of over a hundred and fifty, though some of these are exceedingly unimportant, a few of them are animals and some are dead) enables Winifred to combine both sides of her working nature, the reformer and the writer, to become in *South Riding* a 'reformer-sort-of-writer'. It also preserves something integral to her character: an absence of self-centredness, a lack of interest in, a reticence about, perhaps even a boredom with, herself, which is compensated for and redeemed in an intense interest in and concern for others.

Winifred's journalistic sense of what makes a good story took her in *South Riding* over dangerously libellous ground as far as the East Riding County Council was concerned. The East Riding was one of the most conservative areas in the country and its County

Council particularly resistant to welfare reform, proudly reducing its rates in the early 1930s to the lowest in the country.[11] The cost of this was achieved by reductions in all the statutory responsibilities that had been laid on local government; roads, education, public assistance, health, maternity and child welfare had all been pared to the bone. For the poor of the population in the care of this far-flung County Council, life in these pre-Welfare State times was as harsh and insecure as anywhere in the country; there was no medical or maternity provision, no tertiary educational opportunities apart from what could come from the scarce and competitive 'scholarship' system, no building programme for council houses, no programmes for improving transport, sanitation and public health. Because this was a rural, traditionalist and thinly populated area, it received none of the publicity of other depressed areas of Britain, such as Tyneside or the mining communities, until, of course, *South Riding* illustrated in fictional form the range of deprivations the community endured: from the lack of proper housing and of maternity care for the Holly and Mitchell families, to, at the other end of the social spectrum, the ruination of Robert Carne through having to pay privately for the treatment of his wife's mental breakdown. Though never so notorious, *South Riding* was concerned to do for its author's backgound what *Love on the Dole* aimed to do for Walter Greenwood's urban Lancashire.

Greenwood always maintained that his writing was not 'literature' but documentary. In Winifred's case, though the documentary element is pronounced – there is an almost schematic accumulation of abuses and deprivations – here was a novel-writer's ambition to complicate the issues by embodying them in credible human beings. The local land-purchase scandal, which shocked Hull at the Public Enquiry set up in 1932 to investigate rumours of malpractice, is an illustration of this ambition. The enquiry, headed by the Recorder of Blackburn, found that the Chairman of the Housing and Town Planning Committee, in conjunction with a local builder and possibly another councillor, had 'improperly used his position and influence on the Council to promote his own financial ends'.[12] The local newspapers reported the enquiry extensively and so too did Winifred, sitting in Hull's Guildhall making pencil jottings and sketches of the proceedings. It was fascinating material relating in complex ways to the belief she expresses in the Preface to *South Riding* about the ability of a community to act corporately 'against our common enemies – poverty, sickness, ignorance, isolation, mental derangement and social maladjustment'. The Snaith–Huggins–Dolland scheming in *South Riding* closely resembles the Hull scandal, much to Alice Holtby's discomfort and anxiety, but where Walter Greenwood might have made these men into outright villains, like the money-lender Sam Grundy in *Love on the Dole*, in *South Riding* Huggins is shown as weak rather than bad and Snaith's actions are viewed in the context of his abused childhood, his repressed homosexuality and his genuine wish to see the South Riding a better place. Conversely, Carne, the 'good' person who opposes the malpractice, is shown as a reactionary figure whose neglect and traditionalism have been one of the causes of the South Riding's descent into poverty. What the novel tries to do, as it states in the Preface, is to unpick the 'complex tangle of motives prompting public decisions' in the knowledge all too easily gathered at the Public Enquiry that 'the motives of those who take part in it [are] not all righteous or disinterested'. As Mrs Beddows says towards the end of the novel, 'all this local government, it's just people working together – us ordinary people, against the troubles that afflict us all'.

Shortly before the Public Enquiry in Hull took place, the Chairman of the Housing and Town Planning Committee travelled to a hotel in Scotland and committed suicide. Winifred would certainly have heard about this baleful journey yet it did not deter her from writing about the scandal. Perhaps her own impending death gave her a kind of right to use the material from the enquiry, even in the knowledge that all in the area would connect fiction with fact. Perhaps also in the portrait of Snaith, whose motives have been complex, subtle and not all bad, some exoneration for the disgraced councillor could be found. There was, nevertheless, a kind of ruthlessness about her use of the scandal. She had always turned life into fiction and this was too good a story, too instrumental to her purposes in the novel, to turn away from it in squeamishness.

As a prolific journalist, particularly as a reviewer, Winifred was fully aware of the various kinds of novels written in the post-war years and how *South Riding* would take its place amongst them. She reviewed books by both men and women but was understandably especially interested in women's fiction and in the rise of the woman novelist during these years. In 1931 she reviewed five 'Novels of the Year' for the *Bookman* and the first two on her list represent opposite extremes of what women were writing at this time. The two novels were *The Corn King and the Sprinq Queen* by Naomi Mitchison and *The Waves* by Virginia Woolf, and Winifred was quite aware in her review that the distinction between the two novels was primarily one of form. Although Naomi Mitchison's book is about distant civilisations and Virginia Woolf's about the present, it is not so much in their choice of action and setting that the difference lies but in the way the characters' lives are presented. In Mitchison's case this is by 'a direct, full, varied . . . handling of the external show of things . . . one simply knows that this is the real world; that real people lived in it; that this is how they lived. These concrete and intimate details of manner, thought and life . . . are handled . . . as though she were telling us something that had actually happened and that she had seen.' Woolf's fiction, by contrast, is dominated by 'the subconscious monologue, the extreme development of symbolism, and the sustained unity of conception. [*The Waves* delves] deeper and deeper into a very small, very constricted area . . . the regions of human experience lying outside our bright, busy world of deliberate speech and action.' The year after this review she published *Virginia Woolf*, her only full-length critical study and the first one in English on Woolf.

Winifred was fascinated by the rich contradictions of Virginia Woolf's life: as a child her decorous life in town contrasting with her free, adventurous times in Cornwall, her father's impressive literary learning with her mother's playful ironic way of expressing herself. Winifred interestingly excavated the relationship between Virginia Woolf and Julia Stephen, having discovered a little, forgotten book in the British Museum called *Notes from Sick Rooms* by Mrs Stephen which gives clear proof that 'Virginia inherited the instinct to write from her mother as well as her father'. In spite of, or perhaps because of, its homely advice about beds, diet and hygiene, there is in this little book 'that peculiar humour, consisting of irony and extravagance . . . and something of the wondering, contemplative mind' which characterises Woolf's writing. In evidence, Winifred quotes a passage from Julia Stephen's book about 'Crumbs in Bed': ' "The origin of most things has been decided on, but the origin of crumbs in bed has never excited sufficient attention among the scientific world." '[13] That could have been written by Woolf herself, in Winifred's view.

Virginia Woolf is the work in which Winifred took stock of herself as a novelist. Vera rightly described it as 'the profoundest of Winifred's books' because it meditates upon the differing ways in which art expresses its moral responsibility; it also shows Winifred coming to terms with her own powers through a respectful and sympathetic analysis of her opposite, and it is significant that she wrote it not long before she started on *South Riding*, surely knowing how different her own book would be from Woolf's work:

I took my courage and curiosity in both hands . . . and chose the writer whose art seemed most of all removed from anything I could ever attempt, and whose experience was most alien to my own . . . I found it the most enthralling adventure – to enter, even at second-hand, that world of purely aesthetic and intellectual interests, was to me as strange an exploration as it would have been for

> Virginia Woolf to sit beside my mother's pie and hear my
> uncles talk fat-stock prices and cub-hunting. I felt I was
> learning and learning with every fibre of such brain as I
> have. To submit oneself to another person's mental atti-
> tudes, to sink oneself into their experience – it's almost like
> bathing in a strange sea.[14]

Although Woolf was sixteen years older, Winifred obviously
thought of her as a contemporary, one who had slightly earlier than
herself confronted the conditions of being a woman writer in the
twentieth century. As all her work testifies, in Winifred's view such
conditions included a greater debt of responsibility towards society
because of the new opportunities, knowledges and rights open to
them. Women writers were, more fiercely than ever, 'torn between
their obligations to art and their obligations to society'. They were
also, she thought, distracted by the claims of psychoanalysis and its
obsession with sex and sexual difference. In a passage very revealing of her own position as an equalitarian feminist, Winifred
mourns the fact that at the time when the woman writer 'might
have climbed out of the traditional limitations of domestic obligation by claiming to be a human being, she was thrust back into
them by the authority of the psychologist. . . . Her impulses, her
convictions, every notion that entered into her head came to her,
somehow or other, from her womanhood. Her sex was really all
that mattered about her.'[15] Such ideas have even infected Virginia
Woolf; in A Room of One's Own, Winifred argues, Woolf has allowed
this notion of sex difference to influence her ideas about male and
female creativity. She acknowledges that Woolf's ideal is 'a human
communism of intellectual experience', the androgynous mind
represented by the taxi ride in A Room of One's Own, but the very
ideal of male and female coming together in the taxi ride implies an
irreducible maleness or femaleness in the protagonists. Winifred's
hope is that so fundamental a division does not exist; certainly one
cannot know that it exists. In this lies a central point of opposition

between herself and Woolf: 'looking round upon the world of human beings as we know it, we are hard put to it to say what is the natural shape of men or women, so old, so all-enveloping are the moulds fitted by history and custom over their personalities. . . . The time has not yet come when we can say for certain which is the man and which is the woman, after both have boarded the taxi of human personality.'[16]

Winifred is also critical of Woolf in regard to her condemnation of the Edwardians, particularly Arnold Bennett. A careful reader and admirer of Woolf's criticism, she takes issue with her labelling of Bennett and other Edwardians as 'materialist'. In the first place, she suspects Woolf of inconsistency; at times, as in *A Room of One's Own*, Woolf herself is a materialist: 'Marx himself has hardly put the materialistic interpretation of psychology more clearly' yet Woolf blames the Edwardians for their interest 'not with the spirit but with the body'. In adopting a writing practice in opposition to the materialism of the Edwardians, Woolf has limited her scope: 'the immense detailed knowledge of the material circumstances of life . . . is beyond her. She will remain . . . shut off from intimate contact with Hilda Thomas of Putney and Edgar J. Watkiss, who lays lead piping among the bowels of Bond Street.' What Winifred fears is that the refinement, interiority and introspection of Woolf's approach has resulted in fiction which, however brilliant, reneges on its social responsibility. Literature, in Winifred's view, should address itself to the social conditions of its time, it should help to write history, not in any crude programmatic way but by careful observation of 'the material circumstances of life' which are the conditions in which people live and the pre-conditions of their consciousness of themselves.

The final chapter of *Virginia Woolf* is on *The Waves*, 'the most delicate, complex and aesthetically pure piece of writing that [Woolf] has yet produced', and the one that Winifred responds to most equivocally. Although she admires the novel 'as extraordinarily rich in texture', it nevertheless represents a limitation and probably an ending. More than the previous novels, *The Waves* has withdrawn from the world of practical reality into 'an extraordinary [Winifred uses this word repeatedly of *The Waves*; it is of course a word Woolf herself uses repeatedly] transparency and fluidity . . . as though human life were already melted into a watery universe.' In such writing there is no place for humour, satire and 'the trappings of flesh and bone, surnames, positions and continuous narrative', or any of the insights and analyses of the social commentator or historian-narrator. *The Waves* represents a split in Woolf's creativity; her political and social interests have migrated to her non-fiction writing, leaving the novels unworldly and elitist. For there are in Woolf, Winifred suggests, returning to the notion of Woolf's divided literary inheritance from her mother and her father, 'two streams of thought': 'one practical, controversial, analytical; the other creative, poetical, audacious.' From the evidence of *The Waves*, Winifred's prediction is that these contradictory impulses will continue to develop separately: 'her novels will grow more subtle and intricate as her criticism grows more orderly, stiffened perhaps into some kind of system.' The danger for Woolf as a novelist is that 'she is unlikely ever to command the allegiance of a wide contemporary public . . . there is still only a minority which prefers *To the Lighthouse*, with its demands upon the reader's intelligence and imagination, to a novel such as [J.B. Priestley's] *The Good Companions*, which tells a pleasant, full and easy tale.' Though Woolf wrote essays about the common reader,[17] in fact, her own fiction was not for the common reader.

Woolf was always acutely aware of criticism of her work and it is impossible to believe that she did not take this first book about her with a high degree of seriousness. At the time of the publication of Winifred's book, *The Waves* was attracting more adverse criticism than Woolf's previous novels, particularly of a kind which commented on the novel's remoteness from 'the material circumstances of life'. Leonard Woolf came to believe that the change in her next novel, *The Years*, was in response to these criticisms,[18] of which Winifred's book was an important element. Winifred could not be ignored, either as a critic or as a woman. As a critic and journalist she wrote for a middle-of-the-road, intelligent, but not necessarily intellectual readership whom Woolf, at least at this time of her life, wished to appeal to. As a woman Winifred belonged to the world of political activism and of social causes, including feminism, in which Woolf herself was passionately interested but not actually involved. By the early 1930s Winifred had, of course, come into quite frequent contact with Leonard Woolf through his membership of the Independent Labour Party Advisory Committee on Imperialism and in her attempts to persuade the left to support Ballinger and through him the ICU. She and Vera had also come to know him in connection with the League of Nations. In their support for pacifism and feminism Winifred and Vera were very obviously examples of the new 'woman citizen' of the inter-war period. Their long friendship, with its survival of Brittain's marriage, was also a challenging example of an alternative lifestyle. Altogether, in so many respects, she and Vera were very different from Woolf, not least, Winifred noted in relation to herself, in their different social backgrounds. This class distinction is recorded mockingly by Woolf: 'She is the daughter of a Yorkshire farmer and learnt to read, I'm told, while minding the pigs.'[19] In spite of these intimidating differences, Winifred had thrust herself upon Woolf, asking for interviews for the purposes of writing a book about her, and soliciting information from her friends, particularly Ethel Smyth, whom Winifred already knew slightly through *Time and Tide*. It was a bold undertaking on Winifred's part to write the first book on Woolf, and a significant one too, for in the coming together of Winifred Holtby and Virginia Woolf, the range of inter-war novel-writing by women was encompassed.

According to Woolf's letters to Winifred,[20] which ran from the end of January 1931 to the end of January 1933, they met at least four times, once during the writing of *Virginia Woolf* and three

times after it was published. In her letters to Winifred, Woolf was
coyly polite, to the point of condescension and insincerity; when
she wrote of Winifred to others, or in her diary, she was usually
rude, exaggerating her provincialism. She was also dishonest,
saying she had not read *Virginia Woolf* when she had, and she was
sometimes cruel ('poor gaping Holtby'). But on one of the occasions when they met, in late January 1933, they apparently talked
fruitfully about professions for women. Afterwards Woolf wrote to
Winifred:

> I was afraid that Mr Doggett and other interruptions made
> your visit rather a scramble but it was my fault if we wan-
> dered into Yorkshire and professions and so on. I have it at
> the back of my mind that I will re-write a paper on profes-
> sions that I read a year or two ago; and thus tend to pick
> peoples brains which is a proof that you had the brains –
> not that you were a moron as you say. It was very good of
> you to send me the information – I think it will be very
> useful. I want to keep rather more closely to facts than
> usual. And I am not at all well up in the subject of profes-
> sions.[21]

She was referring to a paper read to Philippa Strachey's London
branch of the National Society for Women's Service in January
1931, and to the conception of what would eventually become *The
Years* and *Three Guineas*: 'I have this moment' she had written on
20 January 1931, 'while having my bath, conceived an entire new
book – a sequel to A Room of Ones Own – about the sexual life of
women: to be called Professions for Women perhaps – Lord how
exciting!'[22]

The meetings between Woolf and Winifred after the publication
of *Virginia Woolf*, when there was no longer the need for them to
meet to discuss it, were an intriguing development. They seem to
have been at Woolf's instigation,[23] and it is tempting to see in

Winifred some representative figure of importance for her writing at this time, particularly in their talk about 'Yorkshire and professions and so on' and how Woolf's writing will develop during the next few years. Physically, Kitty Malone, in *The Years*, could be modelled on Winifred: five foot nine in height, 'like a cart-horse beside most girls of her own age . . . her mouth too big and with strong white teeth.' The Rigby family, Kitty's mother's family, had been 'the wives of Yorkshire squires for generations', and she, Kitty, 'would have liked to know all about Yorkshire; & so something about the lives of English people all through those centuries.' Kitty had wished to study history, but unlike Winifred's, her father would not permit it: 'he pronounced against Cheltenham, "for one reason" & "against" Somerville Hall for another.'[24] Winifred's modern education, in being a Yorkshire farmer's daughter who did go to Somerville College, marked a profound change in the lives of middle-class women which Woolf was at pains to register in *The Years*. Woolf was also concerned to show a change in the status of unmarried women at the time for which Winifred provided a very satisfying model. In *The Years* Eleanor's busy 'social conscience' work, her full and contented life as a single woman, and particularly her sense of community, represent aspects of the 'woman citizen' ideal for which Winifred was an exemplar. Furthermore, Winifred's sustaining philosophy was a loss of the individual in the collective self and *The Years* probes this as an alternative to self-assertion and territorial individualism: ' "My life's been other people's lives," Eleanor thought – "my father's; Morris's; my friends' lives; Nicholas's".' *The Years* predates *Testament of Friendship* by two years, and in 1938 Woolf could not have known how Winifred described her own life: 'I never feel I've really had a life of my own. My existence seems to me like a clear stream which has simply reflected other people's stories and problems.' But she did read *South Riding* in 1940, whilst writing *Between the Acts*, and Winifred's Prefatory remarks to her novel – 'we are not only single individuals, each face to face with eternity and our separate spirits;

we are members one of another' – are echoed in *Between the Acts* in the vicar's closing speech after the pageant: 'To me it was indicated that we are members one of another. Each is a part of the whole. . . . We act different parts; but are the same. . . . Surely, we should unite.' Of course, the common source for both writers is the Epistle to the Ephesians[25] and there is no direct evidence of influence yet it is tempting to believe that, even unconsciously, Woolf absorbed and re-used what Winifred wrote. What is certainly of interest is that these two remarkable women, so different in so many respects, each recognised in the other complementary qualities needful to their function as women and as writers. As Woolf said about Winifred's book on her, 'I felt [it] to be a painstaking effort rather to clear up her own muddles than to get the hang of mine.' She could equally have said that Winifred and Yorkshire and professions for women (and their sexual lives) were necessary to clear up *her* own muddles about the women's movement and about women and fiction during the 1930s.[26]

When *Testament of Friendship* was published Woolf read and didn't like it: '[Winifred] had a good deal more to her than V.B. saw [and] deserved a better, she said.'[27] In the enigmatic and less than honest letter to Vera thanking her for sending a copy of *Testament of Friendship*, Woolf wrote: 'I was puzzled by something about [Winifred] when we met. . . . I felt she was oddly uncertain about something important . . . I think I see now what it was.' Unfortunately Woolf did not explain what 'it' was but continued that she felt about Winifred 'that she was only at the beginning of a life that held all sorts of possibilities not only for her but for all of us'. Reading the biography prompted her to read *South Riding*, which she also did not like:

I think (so far) she has a photographic mind, a Royal Academicians mind. Its as bright as paint, but how obvious, how little she's got beneath the skin. That's why it rattles on so, I think. One's never pulled up by a single

original idea. She's seen nothing for the first time, for
herself. I feel, as I do when God Save the King strikes up,
that I could sing the whole book straight through. . . . She's
a ventriloquist, not a creator. Sometimes, of course, she has
the very words on her lips. But they don't come from the
heart.[28]

What did Woolf mean by 'a photographic mind, a Royal
Academicians mind'? Presumably she meant an observational
rather than an interpretative and innovative talent, conservative,
conventional and guided by the expectations of a certain kind of
readership. In some respects this criticism rings true, as does
Woolf's telling comment that 'She's a ventriloquist, not a creator.' It
is also possible that Winifred would not have objected to such a
description, and that likewise she would have recognised, had she
lived long enough to review it, that *The Years*, though a novel of the
'material circumstance of life' more than anything else Woolf wrote,
was qualitatively different from *South Riding* and served a quite
different purpose.

The kind of readership *South Riding* was written for was one
which would not easily have taken to reading Woolf's novels, but
which represented a huge section of the reading public, particularly
the female reading public, and which may be described as a middle-
brow readership. A self-ironising glimpse of this readership is given
in *South Riding* itself when Miss Sigglesthwaite writes to Sarah
Burton describing her new life since she was persuaded to retire
from Sarah's school: 'I am installed as daily companion to an old
lady living here who is almost blind. [I] read to her. . . . You would
be amused at her literary tastes, and so am I. I shall soon become
quite an expert in the works of Ruby M. Ayres, Pamela Wynne and
Ursula Bloom. Do you know any of these novelists? I assure you
that they have opened up a new world to me.' Winifred could, of
course, have added her own novels to Miss Sigglesthwaite's list.

The novels Miss Sigglesthwaite reads to her old lady would

almost certainly have been borrowed from a subscription library –
Boots, W. H. Smith's or the more expensive Times Book Club – and
the books she brought home would characteristically be written by
women. Though often innovative in content, the novels would
not be experimental in style but would employ familiar literary dis-
courses, showing no obvious cleverness of manner in relation to
the reader and succeeding in addressing a heterogeneous audi-
ence with an 'apparent artlessness and . . . insistence on
ordinariness'.[29] There was a rich crop of such novels during the
inter-war period; to take only a sample from the years around the
publication of *South Riding* supplies a context to Winifred's novel:
Phyllis Bottome's *Private Worlds* (1934), Doreen Wallace's *Latter
Howe* (1935), Storm Jameson's *Love in Winter* (1935), Dorothy L.
Sayers's *Gaudy Night* (1935), Elizabeth Bowen's *The House in Paris*
(1935), Lettice Cooper's *The New House* (1936), Rosamond
Lehmann's *The Weather in the Streets* (1936). Winifred knew some
of these writers – Lettice Cooper, Margaret Storm Jameson – and
reviewed others, particularly in journals for women or likely to be
read by women, like *Time and Tide*, the *Schoolmistress*, *Radio Times*,
and *Good Housekeeping*. There was a network of women writers
and readers, serious if not highbrow, which flourished at this
period as perhaps has not happened since. It related especially to
middle-class women and in its scope and engagement it captured
the change in the lives of such women in this crucial period. This
is the background to *South Riding* and from which it takes its
enduring strengths and popularity.

Up to *South Riding*, Winifred's fiction had earned little income.
Poor Caroline, for example, which had received the top fiction recommendation of the American Book Society, did not sell 1,000
copies in the USA.[30] Surprisingly, *Virginia Woolf* sold 500 copies
within the first three months of publication, more than any of the
novels to date, perhaps because it supplied a need to have a highbrow writer explained, particularly by someone with Winifred's
clarity, unpretentiousness and accessibility. This was, however, as

nothing compared with the success of *South Riding*: 16,000 copies were sold within five days of publication, 40,000 in the first year in the UK at 8 shillings a copy, and nearly 20,000 in America. It was the English Book Society choice in March 1936, and the next year it was awarded the James Tait Black Memorial Prize. The film rights were bought within a month of publication by Victor Saville for £3,000 and the novel was made into a film in 1938. By the provisions of Winifred's will, Somerville College received, via the Dorothy McCalman Fund,

> the profits on any manuscripts unpublished at the time of her death, which should subsequently be published. In accordance with her wish the income from royalties thus received was used in the first instance to endow a scholarship commemorating the name of Dorothy McCalman (1922–25),[31] limited to candidates who have been earning their living for a period of three years or more before applying for admission to the College, and who could not enter without financial assistance.[32]

To date the college has received nearly £300,000 from the bequest, far more than Winifred could have dreamed of. *South Riding* has, in fact, never been out of print and has had several bursts of popularity, usually coinciding with transmission in other media. For example, there was a BBC radio dramatisation of it in 1949, it was Book at Bedtime in 1971, and it was again dramatised in five episodes on radio on Sunday evenings in 1973. In 1974 Yorkshire Television serialised the novel and in September of that year, to coincide with the serialisation, Fontana brought out a paperback reprint of 250,000 copies at 60 pence each. The novel's popularity may be gauged by a comparison with the sales in the same year of one of the best-selling novels of all time, Agatha Christie's *Murder on the Orient Express*, 500,000 copies of which were issued at 35 pence each, timed to coincide with the film adaptation starring

Albert Finney as Poirot. Finally, Virago Press acquired *South Riding* in 1988, to complete their publishing run of Holtby's fiction, and since that date has sold nearly 40,000 copies of the novel. All through its history it has made its way as an enduringly popular and marketable product on its own appeal with very little institutional patronage; it has never been an A-level text, nor has it featured very often on university syllabuses.

At first reading the novel appears conformist and traditionalist, the ventriloquism that Virginia Woolf spoke of. It is subtitled 'An English Landscape' and this seems to confirm a nostalgic stereotype of Englishness (even of *Yorkshireness*), particularly in its stress on practical compromise and a muddle-through philosophy which purportedly were to become the saving qualities against German mechanistic efficiency in the 1939–45 war and which may have contributed to the novel's popularity. The pastoral suggestion in 'Landscape' is fulfilled in the novel's agricultural concerns, and its focus on the small town of Kiplington. The ending celebrates the coming together of the citizens of Kiplington for the Silver Jubilee, their differences temporarily reconciled, huge Union Jacks fluttering from the town's buildings. It is a heartening scene, and the thoughts of Sarah Burton, the heroine, summarise the message the book has advanced: 'This is what it means – to belong to a community; this is what it means, to be a people.'

This homogeneity is, however, something of a delusion, and the achievement of whatever compromise is reached at the end of the novel is recognised as perhaps excessively costly. The undermining of its own outer conformism begins early in the novel, when the nostalgia evoked by 'An English Landscape' is rapidly dispelled in the first two scenes in the novel, that of a council meeting, followed by that of Midge Carne looking at the 'dull landscape' from the decaying mansion she shares with her father. Both scenes end with the resounding defeat of the Carnes, the Conservative gentleman-farmer Robert Carne losing the election for the position of Alderman to the revolutionary Socialist Joe Astell, and Midge

Carne collapsing into hysteria. The battle lines between capital and labour, between tradition and reform, paternalism and free enterprise, privilege and equality of opportunity are drawn up and it seems that the forces of English conservatism are to be routed. But even here there is no certainty and the novel mocks revolutionary pretensions right from the very start in the melodramatic and totally inaccurate responses of the young reporter Lovell Brown, as he watches the council meeting:

> Here was World Tragedy in embryo. Here gallant Labour, with nothing to lose but its chains, would fight entrenched and armoured Capital. Here the progressive, greedy and immoral towns would exploit the pure, honest, elemental and unprogressive country. Here Corruption could be studied and exposed, oppression denounced, and lethargy indicted.

Sarah Burton brings to this English landscape a progressive, practical feminism which will complicate the various and conflicting political and social forces which the council meeting has announced. Sarah too has an extremist's imagination, a fighting belief in 'the power of the human intelligence and will to achieve order, happiness, health and wisdom' but this must be moderated by what is practicably possible to achieve as a teacher striving to 'equip the young women entrusted to her . . . for their part in that achievement'. At the end, Carne is dead and Astell dying, two of the many deaths the novel features, and the centre ground of Kiplington is left to Sarah Burton and her ageing mother-figure, Mrs Beddows. Joe Astell writes from Clydeside, 'I'm a militant again, thank God, quit of compromise . . . we can't build anything permanent on these foundations.' But he is a finished man and has to recognise that change may come more from 'the bricks and mortar' of Sarah's type of gradualist good citizenship, which he despises, than the 'bloody, brutal prospect' of revolution. If *South*

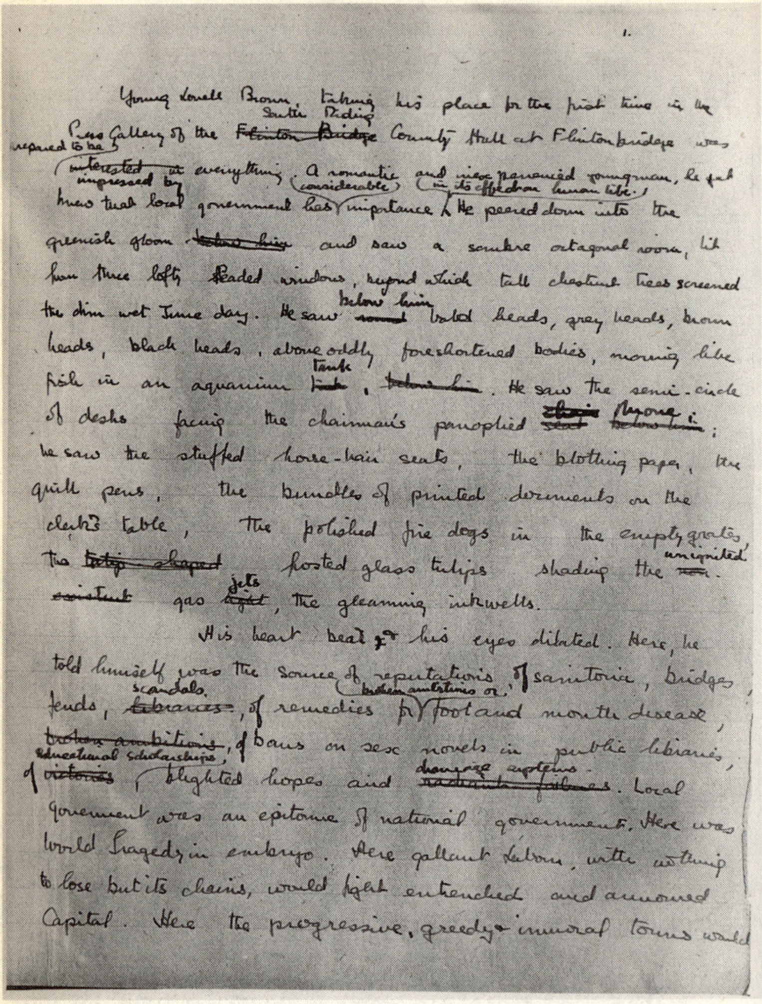
1.

Young Lovell Brown, taking his place for the first time in the Press Gallery of the South Riding County Hall at Flintonbridge was impressed by everything. A romantic and inexperienced young man, he felt considerable awe in its effect on human life. knew that local government has importance. He peered down into the greenish gloom and saw a sombre octagonal room, lit from three lofty leaded windows, beyond which tall chestnut trees screened the dim wet June day. He saw below him bald heads, grey heads, brown heads, black heads, above oddly foreshortened bodies, moving like fish in an aquarium tank. He saw the semi-circle of desks facing the chairman's panoplied throne; he saw the stuffed horse-hair seats, the blotting paper, the quill pens, the bundles of printed documents on the clerk's table, the polished fire dogs in the empty grates, the frosted glass tulips shading the unignited gas jets, the gleaming inkwells.

His heart beat & his eyes dilated. Here, he told himself was the source of reputations, of broken ambitions or, of sanatoria, bridges, feuds, scandals, of remedies for foot and mouth disease, of bans on sex novels in public libraries, educational scholarships, of blighted hopes and dangerous careers. Local Government was an epitome of national government. Here was World Tragedy in embryo. Here gallant Labour, with nothing to lose but its chains, would fight entrenched and armoured Capital. Here the progressive, greedy & immoral towns would

The first page of the holograph of *South Riding* (Hull).

Riding is an English landscape, it is an England in which revolution is denied, and the opposing forces of left and right – Astell and Carne – are becoming, and perhaps even *ought* to become, extinct. Carne's *angina pectoris* and Astell's tubercular lungs function as symptoms, in their respective ways, of fatigued or wasted and violent energies. It is not without significance that these figures from the extreme right and left are men. *South Riding* is a thoroughly feminist novel, not least in its appeal to a largely female readership not accustomed to think of itself as revolutionary or even as reformist, but in Winifred's view still capable of bringing about change.

A sense of this is captured in a conversation between Sarah and Joe Astell about the relationship between politics and education and she describes the three kinds of girls she teaches: those to whom ideas of love, marriage and children are all-sufficient; those who haven't thought seriously about what they want; and those to whom 'the words exploitation, injustice, slavery, and so on start the wheels going round'. 'I don't think you can change the first and third groups much,' she says. 'The middle group you might alter a bit – but many women, like many men, never grow up.' Winifred herself belonged to the third group but *South Riding* is addressed to the first two groups, in particular, the middle group of women whom Winifred wanted to help to grow up, and to whom so much of her journalism had been addressed. The novel's educative drive is towards this middle group whose opinions and lives as *women* are still capable of being altered 'a bit'.

South Riding is a radical text in relation to this middle group of women in several respects but the most important has to do with Sarah as a model of singleness and independence, and the novel's consequent refutation of the claims of romantic love as the only satisfactory destiny for a woman (at the manuscript stage the novel was subtitled 'A Romance' but this was not crossed out). Sarah's unmarried, lonely state is not taken lightly; she is not unattractive to men nor unattracted by them, she has been engaged to be married three times, she falls unexpectedly and violently in love with her political opponent, Carne. But although there are echoes of *Jane Eyre* in the novel, there will be no Ferndean at the end of the story. Carne loves only his mad wife, who outlives him, and even a modern revision of the romance element, in which an adulterous affair might have intensified the relationship, is thwarted by the heart attack Carne suffers when he visits Sarah's room. If the novel eschews a happy ending, it also skirts a tragic one; Carne dies because his horse rears on the cliff path, not because he commits suicide; Sarah thinks after his death that she wishes to die but as her plane threatens to crash she realises this is a false wish. Although Sarah, the character, makes an extreme statement about romantic love – 'I tell you here and now that I would have given all I have for one night – one hour . . . I should not have cared what happened to me afterwards' – the text carries her on beyond this towards a 'serene old age' of usefulness and public service, and, in the figure of the elderly Mrs Beddows, to 'gaiety . . . kindliness [and] valour of spirit'. At a time when women still outnumbered men by a million and a half, and when many of these 'superfluous' women must have had memories of unfinished love affairs and frustrated sexual passion, *South Riding* offered an alternative model for life. Sarah Burton's is not the spinsterhood of rejection and defeat – 'she knew herself to be desirable and desired, withheld only from marriage by the bars of death or of principle' – but a transcendent second best. In the total scheme of the novel, what Sarah will do outweighs the loss of Carne and even of personal happiness and its narrow satisfactions. 'I shall build up a great school here,' she says; 'I shall make the South Riding famous.'

Just how potentially changeful and even subversive *South Riding* was in the context of its time is illustrated in the changes the film version introduced. The film also was successful, bringing popular as well as critical approval: 'a scrupulous, authentic picture of English life for the first time on any screen', said the *Daily Mail*, and even the *New Statesman* thought it 'something positively real'.[33] But the film's construction of English life departs significantly from the novel. The initial image, accompanying the opening credits, is one of rolling farmland with a team of horses ploughing. Superimposed on scenes like these is a tribute to Holtby's purpose in the novel: 'she strove to preserve for us a part of the changing England that is typical of the whole.' This is not at all what the novel does, nor, to be fair, does the film which shows, albeit to a lesser degree, the end of the gentleman-farmer, feudalistic way of life of the Carne family. The film does, however, save Robert Carne from death, although it teaches him a lesson or two in the process, particularly about the need to abandon his aristocratic pretensions and instead to form an unlikely alliance with the Socialist Joe Astell, both of them motivated by commitment to the community and in opposition to unscrupulous business men, Snaith, Huggins and Tadman. It is a curious political conclusion in its linking of aristocrat and socialist against commerce and trade as the means to save England. This alliance in the film between Carne and Astell is echoed in the equally unlikely friendship that grows up between Midge Carne and the working-class, scholarship girl, Lydia Holly.

But if the film ties together class elements in a simplistic manner, it neutralises yet more thoroughly the sexual politics of the novel. The film is glamorised by the presence, in flashback, of Carne's mad wife, played by Ann Todd, whose wild beauty and imperious manner create some of the dominant images of the film. In the novel, an incident related briefly by a servant, in which Muriel Carne forces her horse to go upstairs, is given full scope in the film (in a scene which recalls a similar episode in the box-office success, *Gone with the Wind* of 1936), and the servant's humorous conclusion to the tale in the novel, in which the terrified horse had urinated on the bedroom floor, causing a permanent stain on the ceiling of the room below, is entirely omitted. In the film, Carne has no shadow of heart disease, and though he is tempted to commit suicide in order to pay his debts, he is roused from this by

Sarah, to whom he has already declared his love. She tells him of the plot to buy land fraudulently and on the strength of this he routs the dishonest upstarts at the next council meeting. Muriel Carne, in the meantime, has conveniently died.

The film does acknowledge some of Sarah's 'new woman' qualities: she cares about her school, she is outspoken and unprudish (though by no means as sexually liberated as her counterpart in the novel), and Carne is enough of a new man to admire her progressiveness, even allowing Maythorpe Hall to become the new buildings for the girls' grammar school (not the mental institution it becomes in the novel) on the payment of the mortgage. But the pre-eminence of love in a woman's life is upheld, death, age and indifference have no part in the lovers' story, and Sarah herself is silenced at the end, except as sustainer of the man and his adoring companion in the singing of 'Land of Hope and Glory'. There is no such singing at the end of the novel, but instead a speech of exhortation by Sarah to her schoolgirls to 'Question everything. . . . Question every one in authority.'

Vera saw the film on its opening night and later commented that 'A more realistic film could be made today, showing Sarah Burton and Robert Carne as the star-crossed middle-aged semi-lovers whom Winifred created, and depicting Mrs Beddows as a patriarchal seventy-four instead of the glamorous sixty-six presented by young-looking Marie Lorh.'[34] Odd, to describe Mrs Beddows as 'patriarchal', but otherwise an interesting recognition that the film spoke to and of its own time with far more conventional reassurance than the novel. Indeed, the film seriously misreads the novel in the interests of compromise, traditional values, and unity across class divides; these interests are best served by the presentation of heterosexual love as victorious and as a regenerative and purifying force in society. To recall some of the events occurring at the time the novel was published and the film produced is to understand how great was the need for consolidation of national identity along traditional, even nostalgic, class and gender lines. In 1935 Italy invaded Abyssinia; in 1936 German troops entered the Rhineland, the Spanish Civil War was fought and Franco was recognised by Germany and Italy; 1937 was the year of Guernica and of Italy leaving the League of Nations, and it saw the intensification of the Mosley anti-Jewish marches; in 1938 there was the Munich crisis. In this year, the year of the film of *South Riding*, stunned by the 'sudden crescendo of international tension', Vera made plans to evacuate her children to America in the almost certain knowledge, which all shared, that war was coming again to Europe. Ever since its inception, British (and American) cinema had tended to be a conservative medium and never more so than in the years before the outbreak of the 1939–45 war. At such a time, no popular film, or even serious middle-brow film, could refuse to endorse the message of national consensus and therefore of love between the sexes as legitimately triumphant. In this filmic revision of the novel, the radical elements are diluted, and what was innovative and progressive in Winifred's 'English landscape' is safely sentimentalised.

CHAPTER 9

A woman in her time

The onset of Winifred's fatal illness was heralded by sickness on a flight to Paris in August 1931 and a violent headache which left her almost speechless with pain. She was on her way to join Margaret Rhondda in St Lumaire for a working holiday in which she hoped to press on with her study of Virginia Woolf. At the time the flight was thought to be responsible for the indisposition but the headache recurred during the holiday, particularly when she went for a few days into the mountains to visit Marie Scott-James. Months of travelling to Cottingham every weekend to help with nursing her father, plus the enormous amount of journalism, fund-raising and public speaking she constantly undertook, were blamed for what appeared to be symptoms of overwork. On her return from holiday she took charge of Vera's children whilst Vera and Gordon took a holiday in France and then, with the coming of the General Election of October 1931, she threw herself into ener-getic canvassing for two of her friends, Charles Roden Buxton and Monica Whately, both of whom were Labour candidates, and both of whom were defeated. Within days of the election Winifred collapsed, again with sickness and headache and, as Vera described it, with 'the ominous yellowish pallor which was to become so familiar during the next four years'.[1]

As Vera said, 'At first nobody took Winifred's illness very seriously.' A spell in bed, a restful break in Clare Leighton's cottage at Monks Risborough in Buckinghamshire and a Christmas holiday in Tunis with Margaret Rhondda were prescribed but in November, before the Tunisian holiday could take place, Winifred collapsed again, with the same symptoms as before. This time she went to a nursing home in Courtfield Gardens where no satisfactory explanation for her collapse was found, except that her blood pressure was exceptionally high. She stayed in the nursing home until after Christmas, was advised to rest completely for several weeks, and early in January 1932 Vera took her to a convalescent home in Sidmouth. She returned to London in late January but within a few days had another attack and the planned departure for Monks Risborough, where she was to complete her convalescence, was postponed until mid-February when she seemed well enough to travel. She had many visitors at Monks Risborough – St John Ervine and his wife, Clare Leighton and Noel Brailsford, Harry Pearson newly back from the RAF, Monica Whately and, on one occasion, her mother and Lady Rhondda at the same time; such a good idea, she told Vera, because she could 'leave them together happily & come to bed, & lie in the dark, with my wireless playing to me! Bartok – with Bartok conducting.'[2] Vera could not visit her for some weeks because she had caught chicken pox from the children; as ever when apart, they wrote to each other almost daily, Winifred's letters the only alleviation, Vera wrote, in a 'dismal wretched world'. For Winifred, the enforced rest – she was writing very little, and in bed for much of the time – did not bring the desired results; her blood pressure was higher in Monks Risborough than it had been in London and the specialist who had been consulted, Halls Daly, seemed unable to offer a convincing diagnosis, let alone a cure. It was with some relief that, through

Clare's recommendation, she was referred to Dr Edgar Obermer, the German-Austrian arterial specialist, in April 1932. 'I am so egotistical,' she wrote to Vera, 'that I am enchanted at all the ego-centric concentration on my symptoms – I've never felt so important in my life.'[3] Obermer diagnosed renal sclerosis, Bright's disease, and apparently told her that she might have only two years to live. She did not tell anyone this at the time and Vera was readily reassured, even when she learned that Winifred had irre-versible kidney damage, writing quite cheerfully in her diary that 'though having to live partially as an invalid, [she] need never be much worse if she follows his treatment & the routine he has sug-gested. She can write as much as she likes but not activise a great deal.'[4]

Obermer's regimen, which he set out for her in a series of letters in 1932 and 1933, comprised a carefully regulated, protein-free diet, a restful lifestyle, and drugs, particularly sedatives called Padutin, Tiodine and Impletol, taken either by mouth or by injec-tion.[5] He took an exceptional interest in her case, charging her a mere £10 a year for his consultations, and he wrote to her with blunt forthrightness about her condition. 'Your kidneys have def-initely lost over half of their functioning cells, which have been replaced by fibrous tissue. This is called renal sclerosis. . . . Unfortunately there is no means, and never will be any means, of restoring the destroyed kidney cells. . . . What has to be done in your case, is to adapt you to the altered circulatory conditions which are demanded by your sclerosed kidneys, and at the same time to institute measures in an attempt to prevent the sclerotic or fibrous process from proceeding any further.' Winifred annotated Obermer's letters. He had, for instance, recommended a fast-day once a week but this had given her far worse headaches: 'appar-ently when there is no blood much in my stomach helping me digest food, it goes to my head. So he now makes me eat bulky but meatless meals, & I've had far fewer headaches.' The distressing nature of Winifred's disease, and also of the many medicines and injections she was prescribed, are apparent in Obermer's commiseration over what he refers to as 'night curves' and her general inability to sleep well, the throbbing and pounding of her pulses and the panic and anxiety of the illness and the fear of death it brought. Most of this she withheld from Vera, who was in any case obsessed with the writing of *Testament of Youth* and with her troubled relationship with Phyllis Bentley.

The last three and a half years of Winifred's life were a heroic balancing of the needs of her illness with the demands of her work and her commitment to friends and family. The first full year of her illness, 1932, was in some respects her quietest year, probably because for some of it the belief was still that her complaint was caused by overwork and could be cured by rest. After that, in the light of how seriously ill she was, the wonder is she did so much and lived so long. At Christmas 1931 she had had a postcard printed which said that she was in a nursing home and would not return home until the spring, 'and no correspondence is being forwarded'. During the first half of 1932 she did very little journalism although she was working on *Mandoa, Mandoa!* But by May 1932 she felt her condition had stabilised sufficiently for her to spend five days of each week in Monks Risborough and two in London, mainly seeing to *Time and Tide* business. She returned to London permanently in August and after a spell in Cottingham gradually began to resume some of her earlier activities, including taking part in a deputation to the Prime Minister about re-armament. By early 1933 a fairly regular pattern had developed of writing, some social and political activities, and a very few lectures, punctuated by days in bed when severe headaches signalled that her blood pressure was exceptionally high; sometimes the systolic reading was as high as 240. Inevitably there were times when she could not follow even this gentle regime. She records, for instance, that she had felt particularly helpless on a 'torrid day' in December 1932 when Vera was ill (this was on her return from Halifax), 'I had been ordered to take a day in bed; the housemaid was sent home with bronchitis . . . and Shirley was sick on the nursery floor.'

Because she remained fairly active and rarely complained, people tended to overlook her illness with almost wilful insensitivity. Her desire not to be treated as an invalid was partly responsible but also she had always been of service, always there to help, and those closest to her could not break the habit of relying on her to the point of exploitation. The long weeks in Cottingham in the spring of 1933 during her father's last illness and Alice's early widowhood, Margaret Rhondda's demands on behalf of *Time and Tide*, Vera's domestic emergencies, all these fatigued her and wasted her energies. There were, in addition, her own political and writing commitments. She could have refused to continue in the old ways of service but to do so was antithetical to her, and perhaps also at this time of greatest need she needed more than ever to be indispensable. October 1934 was a typical month with several book reviews completed, *Time and Tide* commitments fulfilled, particularly Notes on the Way, five South Africans in London 'wish[ing] me to be their chief entertainer & friend', an NCCL meeting of women's clubs to protest against the Incitement to Disaffection Bill which was to receive its third reading at the end of the month, an aunt staying, and Gordon and Vera in America, so Winifred with ultimate responsibility for the children. And all the time she was 'deep in *South Riding*' although whilst Gordon and Vera were away she managed to work on it for only four hours. Years later, in one of his angry outbursts to Vera, St John Ervine recalled how all these demands had competed for her failing energies. He had tried to persuade her not to complete 'one of her bloody little notes' for *Time and Tide*, 'And she said, "Oh, but I must. It's so important!" It wasn't important, Vera. . . . Nothing she did in that office was worth the trouble of doing. Her job was to write *South Riding*, more and more novels about her own people, and she footled away her energies on bloody causes that were dead before she began to write about them.'[6]

It was to escape such dissipation of her energies that she rented a cottage in Withernsea, on the Yorkshire coast about fifteen miles from Hull, during the spring of 1934: 'real rural discomfort – no hot water, outside sanitation', but it helped her complete her essay for *Challenge to Death*, and to gather her thoughts and her material for her novel. She repeated the escape in the spring of 1935 in Hornsea, also on the Yorkshire coast, this time to bring *South Riding* near to completion. The rooms in Hornsea were kept by three sisters, the Misses Brooks, '& I am to have the back sitting room which has French windows facing down the garden, because that looks South & is bright and cosy, & the bedroom above it.' Hornsea was near enough to her mother, who wasn't well, and an aunt and uncle dying of cancer: 'I wrote my novel and sick-visited.'[7] There was a suggestion she might visit America later in the year even though her blood pressure was still over 240, 'though kidneys improving. But lectures & travelling make me feel like Hell.'[8]

At the end of July 1935 Winifred went to Malvern, with Margaret Rhondda, where she met George Bernard Shaw and reviewed his play, *The Simpleton of the Isles*, for *Time and Tide*. She was really very ill by this time, suffering acute attacks of headache and sickness, and the photograph of her with Shaw and Margaret Rhondda shows her thin and strained although eager and apparently cheerful. Vera and the children, with their governess and Edith and Margaret de Coundouroff had gone on holiday to Wimereux in France. Winifred had probably gone with them too, and had then returned for the Malvern visit, with the intention of rejoining them after Malvern and after a few days of working on the last stages of *South Riding*. Gordon was in Cambridge seeing Lloyd George, and also intending to join the party in Wimereux at a later stage. But on the morning of 2 August Mrs Brittain phoned Winifred to say 'that Vera's father had walked out of the house in the night & she did not know what had happened to him'. After summoning Gordon to deal with the police and relatives, and anxious to spare Vera the shock of a telegram, Winifred travelled to

Wimereux to fetch Vera home, arriving exhausted and ill at lunch time on 3 August and returning with her to London the same day. Mr Brittain's body was found on 5 August in the Thames at Twickenham, and the inquest returned a verdict of suicide. The strain of the search and discovery exacerbated an infection Gordon had picked up on a recent visit to Russia and soon after the inquest he 'went down with a sort of sceptic fever', as Winifred described it, '& was really dangerously ill'. Vera cared for him at Glebe Place while Winifred, armed with plenteous supplies of Padutin, and the still uncorrected manuscript of *South Riding*, travelled again to Wimereux to join Edith and Margaret in caring for the children. 'Hilda Reid came with me and has been an angel,' she told Phyllis Bentley, and she wrote frequently to Vera assuring her that the children were well and no trouble and that she was having a restful time. She was, for her, 'extremely idle', Hilda recalled: 'sunbathing, playing with the children, sitting in the little cafe opposite, with that *cassis-siphon* that seemed to have all the effect of champagne. . . . Her face, very white and lined with fatigue, lit up with the old animation.' This period of enforced inactivity proved welcome. As Hilda said, 'The accident of illness had given time to . . . *South Riding*. . . . She corrected its last pages at Wimereux. She was pleased with it.'[9]

Winifred wrote to Vera on 26 August, the last letter she would write to her, except for scribbled notes, confirming plans for her return with the children. The letter is full of concern for Vera and for Gordon, and concludes: 'I shan't write again, but I shall wire if there is any change of plan. It's a lovely day again today, & two more days on the sands won't hurt the children as well as giving you a few more hours' peace. So expect us on Wednesday. 5.21 isn't it? Dear, dear love. v s v d l. W.'

But on her return to Glebe Place at the end of August, her Cottingham family demanded her attention. Her brother-in-law had unexpectedly remarried and 'dumped my nieces on my mother . . . without yet one word to mother or anyone.'[10]

Winifred hastened to Cottingham for the weekend and this frantic journey undid the benefits of Wimereux so that she returned exhausted, scarcely able to walk, and could hardly concentrate on an interview she and Vera had with the Society of Authors. Obermer ordered her to spend two or three days in bed, believing that arsenic injections he had tried on her might have made her worse.

Vera seems to have become frightened, perhaps fully for the first time, by Winifred's symptoms – continuing sickness and headache – on the night of Monday 9 September when she brought her down from the attic to sleep in her bed, and she slept in an un-made-up bed in Shirley's room, 'so as to be near her'. She began to record in great detail Winifred's distressing last days, as though the precise writing down of symptoms, appearances, visits and feelings was a necessary act of control over a world collapsing around her. Obermer was brought in the next day and told Gordon how seriously ill Winifred was, yet she had defeated his calculations so often in the past that her current attack might not be the end. But she should, he thought, be more expertly nursed and suggested the Elizabeth Fulcher nursing home in Devonshire Street where she could be cared for by his assistant, Dr Bowde, 'a young German with Nazi views who is practising in England & is a specialist on kidney diseases.'[11] Vera left her there in a large, quiet room with roses and books, and returned home 'feeling very depressed & sad'. She cancelled her planned holiday in Monte Carlo with Gordon and over the next week visited a rapidly weakening Winifred who was restless and distressed, whose eyesight was deteriorating and who could get no sleep even though the doctors tried all manner of injections 'until there seemed to be bruises & sore places over the whole of her poor arms & body'. On 17 September Winifred scrawled Vera a note: 'Darling, Did the gale keep you all awake? We were nearly blown out of bed. . . . I'm prostrate on my back after injections and mayn't move about at all. Hence bad writing. Doctors seem to think they can give me a new

head & kidney & set me up for life. Writing *too* awful. Won't
inflict you. Dear Love – W.'

After some hesitation, Vera decided Alice Holtby should be told
of Winifred's condition, and Alice travelled to London with Edith
de Coundouroff on Tuesday 17 September, spending the afternoon of the next day with Winifred, and returning to Cottingham
on the evening train, to be sent for again on 23 September. Vera
was both impressed and appalled by Mrs Holtby's optimism and
stoicism which seemed to her 'incredible – a combination of temperament & old age, I suppose'. Relations between Vera and Alice
Holtby would be very strained over the next few days, with Vera
resenting what she thought of as Alice Holtby's 'colossal egoism'
which caused her to 'hold court' in the next room, and Alice trying
to seize control of events in opposition to Vera. Margaret Rhondda
once more proved a valuable diversion, subduing her own feelings
to act as go-between amongst all those now gathering round the
dying Winifred – Violet Scott James, Amiya Chakravarty, Edith,
Hilda Reid, and, towards the very end, Harry. Primarily to avoid
alarming Winifred, Vera and Gordon had gone to Brighton on 20
September for the holiday that should have been in Monte Carlo,
but they took only two days of it because an urgent summons that
Winifred was unconscious brought them back to London again.
Whilst she was in Brighton, Vera received Winifred's last note, a
barely legible reply to a letter Vera had sent about the hotel she and
Gordon were staying in: 'Darling, why not move to the Metropole
if plush bores you? Had lovely supper last night, two chicken
sandwiches & slept all night and O. says I can have tomato-juice
cocktails & biscuits every morning. Sorry to be so gastronomic but
this is news for *me*. Do have a holiday. I am so much better.
Overwhelmed by offers of visits. Edith will do everything. Give G.
my love. I wish you both shared my passion for the Pavilion.
Funniest institution in the world, I think, Love. W.' Her humour
and cheerfulness persisted throughout, partly on Vera's account but
also from the long-trained habit of grasping at life to the full,

determinedly relishing its riches and absurdities, rather like a character in one of her short stories who responds with fear but also with exhilaration to the news of his imminent death: '"I am going to die. I am going to die," cried the merchant in his heart. And he knew that life was sweet.'[12]

Winifred died in the early hours of 29 September, Vera and Gordon with her, having disobeyed Alice Holtby's instruction that since Winifred was in a morphine coma there was no need for anyone to be there. Vera, therefore, with Gordon a shadowy figure in an armchair behind her, witnessed Winifred's death, holding her hand or her wrist, thinking of the words 'When thou passest through the waters I will be with thee: I will not fail thee nor forsake thee,'[13] and listening to the changing breath rhythms which became the 'one final, lingering sigh, and then everything was at an end'. Thus Vera claimed Winifred's death, despite Alice Holtby, and made it her own, just as she would make the publication of *South Riding* her own tribute to Winifred, despite Alice Holtby's objections, and in *Testament of Friendship* would write her own version of Winifred's life. Some of this desire to exclude Alice Holtby coloured Vera's account of Winifred's memorial service, conducted by Canon Dick Sheppard, on 1 October at St Martin-in-the Fields, when it seemed fitting to Vera that the coffin on its passage up the aisle paused between her and Harry, Alice's view of it blocked by Harry. At the end of the service the Holtby family went out first and the congregation hung back to let Vera go next, 'a tribute to my friendship with Winifred which moved & touched me when I recalled it afterwards', though at the time she was too upset to register much that was going on, except that Alice Holtby was again 'holding court' outside the church, and Winifred's other friends – Phyllis, Margaret Storm Jameson, Hilda, Edith Smeterlin, Margaret Rhondda – were kind and helpful in their different ways. The same day she and Gordon, with Margaret Rhondda and Hilda, travelled to Cottingham, where most effficient preparations had been made – 'everything ready, everyone comfortable' – in readiness for the funeral. Setting off from Cottingham at 10 o'clock the next day, two cars made their way the 35 miles to Rudston, Mrs Holtby, Hilda and Lady Rhondda in the first car, Vera, Gordon and Edith in the second one, on a funeral journey which was a tour through the landscape of many of Winifred's novels and short stories:

> We drove thought the flat land of Holderness first, and then through Beverley with its beautiful Minster – to which Winifred & I walked one day from Cottingham, over the fields – till finally the flat land began to rise, & we passed through Driffield & were among the Wolds of which Winifred had so often spoken to me[14] – those undulating curves of land that she told me, almost when I first met her, had become part of her being. And suddenly we were in Rudston, where the sheds covered the recently unearthed tessellated pavements of the Romans,[15] and we were passing Rudston House – ivied, solid & spacious, with its lawns & dells – where Winifred was born, and opposite, folded into a curve of the hill, stood the small church with its triangular roofed tower flanked by the ancient pagan monolith about which her story[16] was broadcast only last August, and the village churchyard where she was to lie . . . how fitting it was that she should be brought back here, 'bringing her laurels with her', as one of the onlookers said.[17]

After lunch at Cottingham, Vera, Gordon and Lady Rhondda travelled back to London, 'leaving Edith & Mrs Holtby alone in the house looking forlorn and sad.' 'What an annihilation of a family & a lifetime,' Vera wrote. 'Grace, Mr Holtby & Winifred all gone within little more than seven years, & the oldest of them all surviving her entire household.' These were the only sympathetic words Vera had to say about Alice Holtby in her diary account of Winifred's death and burial. In *Testament of Youth* a version of the comment is given at the point where Alice Holtby responds to Winifred telling her about the 'understanding' between her and Harry: 'And Winifred's mother, on the point of losing, at seventy-seven, the last of those who had made up her life, responded gallantly: "Mind? Why, I'm delighted! . . ." '[18]

What now lay immediately before Vera was the correcting of the typescript of *South Riding* and the ensuring of its publication. She was the more anxious to see this under way because she feared, rightly, that Alice Holtby might raise objections. She had, according to Vera, disliked the 'Prefatory Letter to Alderman Mrs Holtby' which Winifred had asked that she be shown, never seeing 'its intense pathos and beauty [but only] the possible effect of it on her own position on the East Riding C.C!' Under the terms of Winifred's will, made in July 1932, Alice was the executor and Vera the literary executor 'with full authority to publish any of my hitherto unpublished manuscripts'. Alice Holtby's fears that *South Riding* might damage her, or hurt other people – as indeed it did – by being too candid in its portrayal of local characters, made her write 'grousing' letters to Vera, and, after the novel was published, angry letters to Hilda Reid denouncing it as a 'travesty'. On account of it, she resigned from the East Riding County Council – 'I could not have sat among them again'[19] – but Vera was unrelenting, correctly believing that this was Winifred's most fitting memorial. Amidst the darkening landscape of Europe, with Germany violating the Treaty of Locarno, it was published on 2 March 1936, by Collins, and was chosen as Book of the Month for March. 'Why, why couldn't this have happened before?' Vera wrote. 'Why couldn't she have lived to know it? Oh, my poor sweet! And in her life she always felt that no book of hers really came off.'[20]

In the sure knowledge that nothing could at this stage prevent its publication Vera went to Cottingham on 11 February where she found Granny, as she often called Alice Holtby, 'not critical or aggressive and seems to have resigned herself to *South Riding*'. It would be Vera's last visit to Cottingham because soon Alice Holtby would move to Harrogate. She gave Vera a photograph of Winifred's grave, but this fragile truce between Vera and Alice Holtby would be placed under severe strain when Vera came to pay her larger debt to Winifred, to write a biography of her.

At the time of Winifred's death, Vera had been once again keeping a diary that was intended, in Alan Bishop's words, as a 'full, continuous, personal record of her daily life, against the background of national and international events'.[21] It was a sequel to her wartime diary which had petered out in 1917. This second diary was begun because, as Vera wrote in her brief Foreword, 'Life [is] too interesting now for its events to remain unchronicled; always doing exciting work and meeting worth-while people.' She had had the idea for it in mind for some time but was 'induced to come to the point' by Phyllis Bentley. She noted that she was thirty-eight, that John Edward and Shirley were no longer babies, and that though the formative years of her life were behind her, 'yet I feel that all my achievements that matter belong to the future and will one day come to pass'. The implicit purpose behind this diary was a second *Testament*; just as her diary from the war years had served her well in writing *Testament of Youth*, so this new diary would furnish a further autobiography, one that would take forward a record of a pioneering personal life which would be representative of historical change, particularly in the lives of women. She could not know that the central event in compiling this diary, and in forming the *Testament* that would arise from it, would be the death of her friend. As Alan Bishop has noted, the new diary traces a pattern increasingly and bitterly reminiscent of the old; 'it begins in optimism and moves towards despair', not only over the loss of Winifred herself but also what she and Winifred had worked for. As she left the nursing home on 28 September 1935, in the sure knowledge that Winifred was dying, a newspaper placard confronted her: '"Abyssinia Mobilises". Everything that Winifred and I had lived & worked for – peace, justice, decency – seemed to be gone.'[22]

The record of Winifred's death in the diary is both heartfelt and moving and also written with a certain literary self-consciousness, even in the midst of the harrowing details and the irritation with Mrs Holtby. It would be too strong to say that it was written deliberately with publication in mind but it possesses a polished articulacy which makes it more than a private outpouring of grief or a record of facts, though it is those things too. So the description of the visit to the undertaker's to see Winifred in her coffin is a complex mixture of precise detail, personal anguish and a romantic and even ceremonial stateliness. It is written by Vera the grieving friend and also by Vera the successful author of *Testament of Youth*, a comparison Vera herself invites by the mention of how in death Winifred seems 'more completely gone & extinguished than those who died in the War':

> though she was still lovely and tranquil, it was with a different loveliness & tranquillity from my last glimpse of her face at dawn on Sunday, when the warmth and colour of life still remained in it. Her features, now, had the stillness and colour of a beautiful wax-work – the wax-work of a nun or a bride; her lips were just parted in a tiny fixed smile; she looked altogether happy & serene as a statue is serene, but the life & the light of her had gone clean away. . . .
>
> Clearly, definitely, with an annihilating thoroughness, the Winifred I had known for sixteen years had vanished; that generosity, that eagerness, that lovely kindness, had utterly departed and its place knew it no more. Whether it had become nothing I did not know. I felt it had, despairingly. If it existed, it had gone, very far away, and was nowhere near me; the only trace of it . . . lay in the sweetness that her character had given to her face. Her closed eyes, & her eyebrows, alone seemed the same; but they were those of the Winifred I knew at college, rather than the Winifred of

recent years, who used lip-stick, & eye-brow pencil. Until I
saw her in death, looking so young, with her fair eyebrows
which had grown a little in the nursing-home, & the pur-
plish tinge beneath her eyes (as I had so often seen it in
sleep when she was tired) just where her fair eyelashes
rested, I hadn't realised that make-up, by adding sophistication, causes people to look older, not younger.[23]

Within three weeks of Winifred's death, when Vera and Gordon
were in Fowey, in Cornwall, for a brief holiday before Gordon
would begin canvassing in earnest as a Labour candidate for
Sunderland in the General Election of November 1935, publishers
began to ask Vera to write a biography of Winifred. She felt no
more able to write one immediately than she had felt able to write
about the war until some years afterwards. There was in any case
her own novel *Honourable Estate* to finish and the typescript of
Winifred's novel to correct. Vera had decided that this should be
called by the title Winifred had finally settled on, *South Riding*,
and not, as had also been suggested by Winifred at an earlier stage,
Take What You Want, which, Vera thought, 'suggests a snappy, trivial book; and Winifred's is great & ought to be a classic'.

Unexpectedly, Vera found comfort and support from her publisher Victor Gollancz who was sympathetic both to Vera's grief and
to her reluctance to write a biography too quickly. He suggested
that the book should not be a formal biography but a biographical
novel of the same kind as *Testament of Youth*, and when Vera said
that she wanted to write not just a portrait of Winifred but of a
woman in her time, he was enthusiastic: ' "That's the title! We'll call
it 'A Woman In Her Time' & add in sub-title that it's the story of
Winifred Holtby." '[24] As it turned out, the eventual title was suggested by Gordon who made the crucial suggestion that the
friendship between Vera and Winifred should be the biography's
focus. It thus became a tribute to women's friendship, a demonstration that 'the type of friendship which reaches its apotheosis in

the story of David and Jonathan is not a monopoly of the masculine sex.'[25] It took its middle place in what would become a trilogy
of Testaments tracing Vera's life as a forward-thinking, twentieth-
century woman: war survivor, modern friend, wife and mother,
political activist, good citizen.

Vera began reading Winifred's files, in preparation for the biography, in February 1937. One of her first discoveries was letters
from St John Ervine to Winifred containing unflattering references to herself, which left her depressed for several days. She
wrote an unposted reply which she clipped to his letter. In 1939,
further accusing comments from him decided her that the 'time
had come for the worm to turn' and she wrote him a long, frank
letter enclosing her earlier one. As well as reproaching him for not
making his accusations directly to her instead of to Winifred, she
went on to defend Winifred's choice of her, Vera, as a friend. It is
an important letter because it explains, with great credibility, the
basis of their relationship, and something also of the nature of
friendship itself, its shared memories, its tolerance of difference,
its endurance:

> just possibly she did get something out of me which to her
> represented an adequate return for all the immense and
> immeasurable services she did me . . . although we didn't
> exactly grow up together, we grew mature together, and
> that is the next best thing. . . . We were completely at ease
> with each other as two loving sisters are at ease. When she
> was with me [she] could, so to speak, completely unbutton
> her personality. . . . Now when you are in pain, the only
> person whose society is tolerable for long periods of time is
> the person with whom you can be completely
> unbuttoned. . . . When she was sick I held the basin and
> emptied it. She didn't mind me because she was used to
> me, but she would have hated anyone else doing it. . . . She
> turned to me when her best friends exhausted her. She

loved them dearly; it is probable that she respected
them . . . more than she ever respected me; but I gave her
rest and relief when she was at the end of her tether. . . . I
was her intellectual inferior, of course. You were right in
saying that she had more creative power in her little finger
than I had in the whole of my body. . . . But I don't think
those qualitative calculations ever entered into our relationship with me. . . . She realised that beneath all my egotism
lay a perfectly just and balanced appraisment of comparative human values, and that though I frankly enjoyed and
deliberately sought the adulation that is always given to the
apotheosis of the commonplace, I wasn't deceived by it in
the very least. . . . I do not want you to go on thinking that
Winifred – so generous, so gallant, but so clear-headed in
her judgements – was a self-deceived and exploited fool.[26]

This movingly generous letter, perhaps the most honest comment
Vera made on her relationship with Winifred, brought an apology
from St John, and, more important as far as Vera was concerned,
an assurance that Winifred 'had nearly raised the roof off my head'
when she had received his censorious letters.

By the time this happened, during early 1939, Vera was going
through Winifred's papers more intensively, sometimes with great
anguish, particularly over Winifred's letters to her: 'Wept all morning over W.'s 1926 letters with their reminder of just what we
lost – *I* lost.'[27] The writing began in earnest in March, amidst
alarms at Hitler's invasion of Czechoslovakia, plans to evacuate
John Edward and Shirley if war should be declared, and her own
continued involvement with the Peace Pledge Union. It was completed quickly, in just four months, with an urgency born of the
fear of war. The completed typescript was taken to Harold
Macmillan on 9 August, and it was published on 2 January 1940,
in a cover of Winifred's favourite blue colour and bearing a repro-
duction of Howard Lewis's portrait of Winifred.[28]

When she was beginning work on the biography in 1937, Vera promised that it would not be

> the pious and formal biography sometimes written of dead authors by their friends . . . Winifred was far too vital and radiant for a conventional memoir. . . . Her biography might be written as a poignant tragedy of exceptional artistic promise cut off before maturity by untimely death. I want rather to treat it as a story of superb fulfilment, spiritual and intellectual, achieved during a brief span of crowded years, by one of the most remarkable young women of her time.[29]

To record Winifred's vitality and radiance and her remarkableness was undoubtedly Vera's intention but the very closeness of Winifred's achievements to Vera's own political and personal concerns made this a difficult task, and the later recasting of the biography, apparently at Gordon's prompting, as a record of a friendship, imposed a limiting perspective on what Vera would write, particularly of the years she and Winifred spent together. Like all biographies, *Testament of Friendship* made over the material it drew on: Winifred's papers and books, Vera's memory of her, what others remembered or had written about her, and Vera's own letters and the diary record of the last three years of Winifred's life. The subtly shifting use of information is easy to trace when letters or diary are compared with the finished biography. For instance, the description of Winifred's youthful appearance without make-up after she was dead is transposed to a week before she died, to the time when Vera and Gordon returned from Brighton. That cosmetics are ageing is described as an 'irrelevant discovery' whereas in the diary it isn't irrelevant at all but part of the shock and wonder that the nakedness of a beloved, newly dead face imparts. It is an insignificant detail but it points towards a tendency in *Testament of Friendship* to distance what is being told, to give a commentary on it, perhaps to make it more sophisticated and intellectual. *Testament of Friendship* is about an exemplary life and an exemplary friendship and this seems to prompt Vera to play down its untidy, unresolved elements. This is most significantly manifest in the narrative with which Vera binds together the multifarious aspects of Winifred's life, a narrative which she announces in the Prologue, part of which I have already quoted:

> From the days of Homer the friendships of men have enjoyed glory and acclamation, but the friendships of women, in spite of Ruth and Naomi, have usually been not merely unsung, but mocked, belittled and falsely interpreted. I hope that Winifred's story may do something to destroy these tarnished interpretations, and show its readers that loyalty and affection between women is a noble relationship which, far from impoverishing, actually enhances the love of a girl for her lover, of a wife for her husband, of a mother for her children.

So this is not only a biography of a friendship but it is of a friendship that leads to something beyond itself, to an ideal woman, one who has a successful career, who is loyal and affectionate towards women, but whose destiny and fulfilment is crowned in marriage and children. This ideal woman also carries no taint of lesbianism, for it can only be in this sense that 'tarnished interpretations' can be construed. But Winifred fitted this pattern of an ideal woman only partially; she was a loyal and affectionate friend but she did not marry, and she did not and could not have children. Vera deals with this dilemma first of all by means of a kind of surrogacy in which Winifred lives a complete life through her, Vera's, heterosexual fulfilment. This is conveyed in *Testament of Friendship* in the numerous mentions of Winifred's commitment to Vera's children, particularly the elder, John Edward, and is reinforced in Vera's third testament, *Testament of Experience*, in a passage meant to evoke admiration:

None of her books published in her lifetime had sold
remarkably, so she helped mine to sell magnificently. The
only man whom she really loved failed her, so she identified herself with my married happiness. Her burdens were
great and intolerable, so she shouldered mine which were
often trivial. When she learned that she must never have
children, she shared in the care of ours.[30]

Winifred as a woman whose own life is incomplete, and who lives
vicariously through Vera, determines the other roles Winifred plays
in Vera's narratives. She is the older foil to Vera's feminine youth-
fulness in *Testament of Friendship*, as in the account of her being
mistaken for the bride's mother at Vera's wedding, or when she is
reported as having been described as 'Too long i' the tooth'[31] by the
handsome burglar on board the SS *Barrabool*. She is aunt to the
children and an aunt or mother to Vera too, just as at some points
she is her brother Edward, and her chivalrous escort and companion, all roles in which she shoulders Vera's burdens and
supports her ambitions to be a modern woman successfully com-
bining a career and marriage.

Perhaps aware that Winifred had been subsumed into her,
Vera's, life-story, Vera engineered the 'journey's end' conclusion to
Winifred's life and to Winifred's biography by pressuring Harry to
propose marriage to her. But in this attempt to give Winifred a life
of her own, Vera did so on her terms: a successful career woman
and also one who eventually gained romance. Throughout her
post-war years this was an ideal of feminism – career *with* marriage – that Vera embraced, and somehow Winifred had to be
fitted into this model. Winifred did love Harry and in the last
years of her life she in some measure intensified her relationship
with him, but theirs was only ever a subdued love story and it is
doubtful that Harry would have come to Winifred's bedside if Vera
had not sent for him; he would not even have known she was so
seriously ill. Margaret Rhondda's verdict on the relationship

between Winifred and Harry, that it mattered neither as much nor as continuously as Vera made out, should be borne in mind as counterbalance to Vera's version.

It remains, however, profoundly distressing that Vera wrote a script for Winifred which in its ending was a travesty of her friend's life. Winifred's complicity in this script is puzzling. Perhaps she really believed that Harry had loved her 'all through' and that finally they would be united, a belief which contradicted the judgement of her mature years. Perhaps 'all through' meant something entirely different from Vera's interpretation. Or perhaps Winifred colluded with Vera's scheming, to please her and Alice Holtby, knowing, as Harry did, that it was a contract which would not have to be kept. In trying to imagine Winifred's state of mind at this late stage of her life I have come to think that a complex mixture of these motives was at work: a longing to be loved and comforted in her extreme weakness, a nostalgia for the past, and a wish to please those who were so busy around her, particularly Vera whose distress at all times must be alleviated. Her mind on the borders of consciousness, it must have seemed easiest to go along with what others thought best, to be, at the end, a reflection of the wishes of other people.

In 'A Garland for Winifred', the loving and touching poem Hilda Reid wrote probably in 1931, Hilda explains why Winifred is like a poplar tree:

> Moved by every far distress,
> Rooted deep in steadfastness,
> She's like a beacon, and she stands
> In the low and marish lands
> Like a sacrificial pyre,
> Herself the victim and the fire.

Writing in very different mode, but at almost the same time, Freud in *Civilisation and Its Discontents*, published in 1930, in discussing

various groups of people in relation to how differently the love
instinct is expressed, describes one group who value loving more
than being loved; they turn away from sexual love and transform
the instinct into an impulse with an inhibited aim, 'directing their
love not to single objects but to all men alike. . . . What they bring
about in themselves in this way is a state of evenly suspended,
steadfast, affectionate feeling, which has little external resemblance
any more to the stormy agitations of genital love, from which it is
nevertheless derived.'

Freud's comments are relevant because of their contemporane-
ity, as though, as a keen observer of human nature, he was simply
noting a kind of person not uncommon during the post-war years.
St Francis of Assisi may have been a supreme example in previous
times but his character and lifestyle, Freud maintains, are not
exceptional at the time of writing, and are generally highly
regarded.[32] Winifred herself invites inclusion in Freud's group by
her frequent comment that it is loving which is important, not
being loved. In her maturity this compensating thought was able to
temper her response to Harry's neglectful behaviour and Vera's
egoism. It was a learned response; what began in her youth as the
sort of brave lie that people say on being rejected became in her
maturity a creed to be lived by, so that when she answered her
mother's question in 1933 about her ambitions in life she could do
so in terms of a general and not a personal good: 'I want there to
be no more wars; I want people to recognise the human claims
of . . . all oppressed and humiliated creatures. . . . And I would like
to be used as one of the instruments by which these things are
done.' Although always anxious to assure her mother of the moral
usefulness of her life, nothing in her life or her writing at this time
suggests that this statement was made only to placate her mother,
that it was hypocritical or said for effect. Hilda Reid, writing as a
friend of long standing, gives a particular emphasis to this sacrifi-
cial sense of obligation which came to dominate Winifred's life. It
was a willing dedication, not imposed upon her, and though she

was a victim, she would not have thought of it in those terms because the energy and passion came from herself: 'Herself the victim and the fire.'

If one imagines the growth of her personality what comes to mind first is the bright, eager, extrovert little girl, anxious to please, to be liked, slightly bossy and peremptory, born into a well-off household with a strong, almost feudal sense of rural responsibility and an active work ethic. Though the church at Rudston was no fire-breathing place of sin and punishment, it too endorsed the lessons of social responsibility and duty to God. When Winifred later lost her faith in God, the habits of moral obligation were not lost also, but directed ever more fervently towards social ends. In a normal course of events, such a woman would have married and had children, perhaps serving her family and local community more zealously than most, perhaps also possessing an uneasy sense that there should be more for her to do, 'alternat[ing] between a vague ideal and the common yearning of womanhood'.[33]

But the 'normality' of this destiny for a daughter was compromised from an early stage by Alice Holtby's decision to publish Winifred's poems and then that she should go to Oxford. Winifred was clever and lively, teachers were encouraging, Winifred seemed almost like a boy in her adventurousness and courage, almost the son that Alice Holtby may have wished she had had, and that Winifred perhaps wished she had been. Also, Winifred was plain, or at least not conventionally pretty. In these respects a man's education was appropriate, for financial reasons – Winifred might never marry – and also because it vicariously satisfied the desire for larger things that Alice Holtby undoubtedly had. Harry's failure to become the romantic, boy-next-door lover and husband confirmed this less than feminine destiny. Even more far-reaching was the effect of the war on women entering citizenship at this crucial political period. Winifred and her kind, who were now receiving many of the privileges of men, had survived where so many men had not and this left a legacy of debt, guilt and responsibility greater than women had felt in earlier times. In Winifred's case it powerfully contributed to the sense of immunity from suffering which fuelled all her reformist endeavours. She was indeed a woman in her time, highly representative of a generation of women who now thought of themselves as deputies for men as well as pioneers for future generations of enfranchised women. Her kind of feminism, which stressed the likeness between men and women, not their difference, affirmed this commitment.

The progression towards the 'evenly suspended, steadfast, affectionate feeling' which characterises Winifred's later years was intensified by the development of her relationship with Vera. The complementarity of their personalities was important but beyond that Vera too was a woman in her time, representing, so Winifred believed, all that was courageous and forward-looking. Not only had she suffered more from the war than Winifred, but after it she pledged more – career, marriage, children – for what seemed like an ideal of feminism. The need to inhibit personal wishes was imperative in the face of this greater good that Vera embodied. The period around 1925 – Vera's marriage, Harry's continuing unreliability – was climactic for Winifred because it seemed to seal the pattern of service she and Vera were separately to follow. Afterwards, particularly in the mission she found in South Africa, she matured into the ability to value loving more than being loved. When she discovered that she was seriously ill, and unlikely to live for much longer, this further intensified the detachment from self. Her epiphanic experience at Monks Risborough when she broke the ice for the lambs and heard 'a voice within her saying: "Having nothing, yet possessing all things"'[34] was a confirmation of her life's direction.

If this detachment of generalised benevolence was achieved at the expense of sexual satisfaction, this would not have been a shocking or untenable sacrifice to Winifred. About Radclyffe Hall, author of the notorious novel of lesbian love, *The Well of Loneliness*, she wrote: 'Radclyffe Hall taught me a lot. She's all fearfully wrong,

I feel. To love other women deeply is not pathological. To be able to control one's passions is. Her mind is all sloppy with self-pity & self-admiration. She's not straight in her mind. . . . We should shake off this *tyranny of sex* & use it only in the stabilising power towards the creature with whom we decide to continue the human race if we do decide.'[35] Yet to categorise Winifred as a repressed lesbian, or a sexual 'invert' in the Radclyffe Hall sense, is too simple. In the first place, her fulsome way of writing should not be over-interpreted. Vera's exceptional sensitivity to imputations of a lesbian relation between her and Winifred led her to excise all endearments in *Selected Letters* but to take the opposite line and read into them a highly charged lesbian desire would be to over-look a mode of address common between women of their class at the time. Winifred was certainly very attuned to the physical features of the women she knew – Vera's delicacy of frame, Jean's red hair – and she had a great sense of women's beauty, and the beauty of women's clothes. But at the same time she had a physical appreciation of men too, and her long tolerance of Harry had partly to do with his good looks, his film-star blond, clear-cut leanness. Almost certainly she had some kind of sexual experience with him during 1934 and at various times during her life contemplated marriage and the having of children. I think one has to return to her own comments about the construction of sexuality, made variously in her later years, that 'feminine' and 'masculine' are very artificial categories and that the human personality is, in varying degrees, an admixture of both. 'We do not . . . know,' as she had written at the end of *Women*, 'though we theorise and penalise with ferocious confidence – whether the "normal" sexual relationship is homo- or bi- or hetero-sexual.' Perhaps like many women, given an appropriate context and a willing partner whom she loved of either sex, she could have been lesbian, heterosexual or both. Vera's enclosing of Winifred within a heterosexual narrative, for purposes largely to do with her own heterosexual agenda, diminished the individuality of Winifred's notions of sexuality, and also diminished her distinctive achievements in making a celibate life fully worth living.

This cannot be stressed too much. Winifred was a spinster when the term supposedly held horrors for women and when there inevitably were many spinsters around. Winifred embraced the name and the condition of spinsterhood and campaigned on its behalf not pityingly or complainingly but with a genuine sense of its potential for love and usefulness. Like her heroine of *South Riding* she could say, 'I was born to be a spinster, and by God, I'm going to spin.' In this she refuted the sexologists of the period with their easy equation of spinsterhood and frustration. Such reductive categorisation was the opposite of her philosophy of human nature, which was that the individual is unique and that distinctions such as male or female, black or white, celibate or married, although important, are secondary, and must be minimised in the progressive endeavour to liberate the human spirit into useful well-being. Perhaps this staunch humanism sometimes concealed depths of loneliness and despair, and Margaret Rhondda was right in seeing in the character of Caroline, in *Poor Caroline*, aspects of a self-portrait which revealed 'a dead-sea-apple feeling and fear underneath your balanced surface'. But Winifred would have replied that the balanced surface is what matters because it is this exterior, public self which is instrumental in creating a good society. The inner self, whatever its fears and regrets, is of value only to the extent that its energies can be channelled into the general good.

Vera thought that in her maturity Winifred seemed to change from the extrovert young woman she had first met to someone 'who displayed critical, satirical and ruthless characteristics quite other than those of an extrovert'.[36] Vera attributed this change to the 'secret endurance of pain and the certainty of frustration by death'. But to Margaret Rhondda, who knew Winifred both before and after the onset of her illness, this was a misinterpretation of Winifred's character. Reviewing *Testament of Friendship* for *Time and Tide* in January 1940, she admitted that no two people ever see a third from the same angle and so it was to be expected that her memory of Winifred would be different from Vera's. Nevertheless she must record that although she didn't see Winifred as a less 'good' person than *Testament of Friendship* showed, 'I do see a gayer, more humorous, happier person'. Vera had quoted Winifred's comment that 'everybody's tragedy is somebody's nuisance' as an example of the 'ruthless realism which so seldom escaped outside her thoughts'. But to Margaret – and, indeed, to most people, one might add – this was a mistaken interpretation: 'I should have said . . . that that capacity for seeing the little along with the big was an example of the kind of salty humour which not seldom but always seasoned her talk and made her such a first-rate companion.' Hilda Reid likewise recorded what good company Winifred was, how, even in the last weeks of her life in Wimereux, though deeply fatigued, she amused guests in the hotel 'with her almost incredible stories'.[37] This was not only a side of Winifred that she may have subdued in relation to serious-minded and rather humourless Vera, but also one that Vera did not wish to promote in her biography of Winifred. This was to be the dignified record of a remarkable friendship which would provide lasting inspiration for later generations of women. The salty humour and outrageous stories might not fit in with such a testamentary undertaking.

Paradoxically, in exalting the significance of this noble friendship, Vera, however unwittingly, deprived Winifred of her independent status as a successful woman of action. She was livelier, more famous, more heroic and less pathetic than Vera paints her, and also fun to be with and to know, with a public presence which commanded respect and affection in literary and political London. It was because of this reputation that the Woolfs asked her to write an autobiography, not because she was Vera's friend. Not just the bravery – which Vera was only too ready to celebrate – but also the glamour of Winifred's life – an aspect less to Vera's purpose – is captured in brief in her rather unlikely acquaintance with H.G. Wells which Vera partially describes in *Testament of Friendship*. After Winifred heard from Dr Obermer that she might not live for more than two years she invited herself to tea with Wells; 'astonished but benevolent', in Vera's words, he agreed to see her and they talked for two hours. '[S]he had never enjoyed herself more in her life.'[38] What Vera doesn't say is that the previous month, March 1932, Wells had called to see Winifred in Monks Risborough, when she happened to be out. Her reputation, particularly her connection with *Time and Tide*, were such that he first attempted to make contact; her call to him was therefore reciprocal, not the audacious step of a distant admirer that Vera makes out. From that time on Winifred and Wells remained on good terms, and the easy, slightly jocular flavour of their exchange, as well as Winifred's zeal for, presumably, the Ballinger fund, are captured in a letter from Wells of June 1932: 'Dear Winifred Holtby/Importunate woman. I am not as well off as Shaw & have ten thousand dependants to his one. But here is five *pounds*. That gives Shaw pride of place as richest contributor. Yours, H.G. Wells.'[39] 'Importunate' is a good description of Winifred: not in that she demanded much for herself but that she demanded much from life, from herself, and from what she believed to be the human capacity for good sense and benevolence.

Notes

Abbreviations

WH	Winifred Holtby
VB	Vera Brittain
GEGC	George Edward Gordon Catlin
PB	Phyllis Bentley
HR	Hilda Reid
AH	Alice Holtby
MR	Margaret Rhondda

Manuscript sources

Hull	The Winifred Holtby Collection, Local Studies Library, Hull Central Library, Albion Street, Hull.
McMaster	The William Ready Division of Archives and Research Collections, McMaster University Library, Hamilton, Canada.

Published sources

PB & MB	Paul Berry and Mark Bostridge, *Vera Brittain: A Life*, London: Chatto & Windus, 1995.
CF	*Chronicle of Friendship, Vera Brittain's Diary of the Thirties, 1932–1939*, edited by Alan Bishop, London: Gollancz, 1986.
LF	*Winifred Holtby: Letters to a Friend*, edited by Alice Holtby and Jean McWilliam, London: Collins, 1937.
SL	*Selected Letters of Winifred Holtby and Vera Brittain (1920–1935)*, edited by Vera Brittain and Geoffrey Handley-Taylor, London and Hull: A. Brown & Sons, 1960.
TF	Vera Brittain, *Testament of Friendship*, London: Virago, 1980.
TY	Vera Brittain, *Testament of Youth*, London: Virago, 1978.

Introduction: The clear stream

1 WH to VB, 3 February 1935, Hull.

2 I have taken the decision to use the familiar first name, Winifred, throughout this biography. The alternatives, Winifred Holtby or Holtby, are either cumbersome or overly impersonal and academic.

3 *CF*, 229. It was on the advice of her husband, Gordon Catlin, that Vera changed the title to *Testament of Friendship*.

4 *LF*, 462.

5 It was a flagship book for Virago Press, who reissued it in 1978. It has been taught on numerous Women's Writing courses in universities and colleges.

6 *TF*, 1. It is not known who the other publishers were.

7 *LF*, 226.

8 The bulk of the Holtby papers are in the Local History section of Hull Central Library, having been donated to 'the citizens of Hull' by Vera Brittain from 1946 to 1965. They are undergoing cataloguing and preservation. There is a small collection in Bridlington library, separately donated by Vera Brittain in 1948. There are also papers in the William Ready Division of Archives and Research Collections, McMaster University Library, Hamilton, Canada, and in the University of Cape Town (Ballinger Papers).

9 A heavily edited selection of these was put together by Vera in a privately printed edition, *Selected Letters*, in 1960 (London and Hull: A. Brown & Sons). In the Introduction to this, Vera explains that there are a few 'extensive gaps' in the correspondence between her and Winifred, 'due to the destructive effect of a flying bomb which brought down the ceiling of my Chelsea study in 1944'.

10 There had been rumours that their friendship had been a lesbian one: 'Too, *too* Chelsea', Winifred apparently remarked of them (*TF* 118). Vera's nervousness at these rumours, and desire to repudiate them, was due to several causes but one of them was possibly the threat of the criminalisation of lesbianism during the inter-war period. In 1921 the House of Commons approved an amendment to the Criminal Law Amendment Act which would have made sexual acts between women illegal, as they were for men. In the event the amendment failed, although for legal reasons rather than from want of support.

11 *TF*, 165.

12 Vera Brittain, *Testament of Experience*, London: Fontana, 1957, in association with Virago Press. 133–40.

13 *CF*, 228.

14 VB to St John Ervine, 18 February 1939, Hull.

15 WH to VB, 7 March 1932, Hull.

Chapter 1 '. . . to be the daughter of Alice Holtby'

1 WH to AH, Hull. Alice Holtby's letter to Winifred does not survive.

2 *LF*, 362.

3 She had been diagnosed as having angina in 1935. Margaret Ballard believed the appendectomy was mismanaged and that Alice could have lived longer. She died in Harrogate, having moved there from Cottingham in 1936.

4 WH to PB, 18 March 1934, Hull.

5 Much information concerning the village and the Winns was helpfully given to me by Mrs Hutchinson, of East Witton.

6 This anecdote was told to me by Gillian Brooke whose mother, Dorothy, was married to William Holtby, a cousin of David Holtby. Alice had been William's governess.

7 The spelling of the name of the village has varied, sometimes spelt with an 'e', Rudstone, but on the Ordnance Survey map of 1910, the time of Winifred's girlhood, it is Rudston. I have used this spelling, unless the alternative spelling is in a quotation.

8 Hull.

9 The mosaics of Rudston were acquired by Hull City Council in 1963 and are presently housed in the City's Museum of Transport and Archaeology in the High Street. Winifred's short story, 'Pavements at Anderby', traces the past, present and future of the pavements and provides the title for the posthumously published collection of short stories, *Pavements at Anderby*, 1937.

10 'England, Whose England', the *Schoolmistress*, 7 June 1934.

11 Hull.

12 Many of these recollections of Winifred and of the Holtby establishment were told to me by Mrs Carr and also by Mr Wade, both of Rudston and both having worked for the Holtbys in their young days.

13 Letter to unknown correspondent, 1927, Hull.

14 Ibid.

15 *Passing Show*, 22 July 1933.

16 *Manchester Guardian*, 'Bored Children', 9 April 1928.

17 *CF*, 202.

18 George de Coundouroff, Margaret's father, was 'adopted' by the Holtbys when he came, as an orphan, to Bridlington School. When he married his wife, Edith, lodged with them too and when George disappeared, presumed dead, in Russia in 1919, Edith and her daughter Margaret stayed on with the Holtbys, making Bainesse at Cottingham their home. When Alice Holtby moved to Harrogate, Edith divided her time between Margaret, by this time in London, and Alice in Harrogate.

19 *LF*, 427.

20 *TF*, 116.

21 *Manchester Guardian*, 7 June 1927.

22 *Virginia Woolf*, London: Wishart, 1932, 16.

23 Paul Berry Collection.

24 *LF*, 24.

25 *LF*, 203.

26 WH to GEGC, 30 March 1928, McMaster.

27 *TF*, 284.

28 *LF*, 203.

29 Quoted in Geoffrey Handley-Taylor, *Winifred Holtby, A Concise and Selected Bibliography, together with Some Letters*, Hull: A. Brown & Sons, 1955. Even to the end of her life, Winifred would write 'celibasy', 'sists' (for cysts) and 'exhillerating'.

30 The *Schoolmistress*, 15 June 1933.

31 The *Schoolmistress*, 2 July 1931.

32 Hull.

33 Queen Margaret's School left the Woodard Society in 1986.

34 Winifred sometimes wrote under a pseudonym, Corbin H. Wood, during her early career. One of Wood's stories, 'The EGS Society', is an account of a society for the Extermination of German Spies. This is probably from the same time as a school speech opposing the proposition that disputes should be settled by arbitration rather than war. Hull.

35 The school, which is now at Escrick Park, near York, has retained many of these books.

36 *Hull Times*, 1 June, 18 July 1918.

37 *LF*, 56.

38 Hull.

39 21 August 1918.

40 WH to VB, July 1923, Hull.

41 Vera Brittain (*TF* 103) wrote that 'Bainesse' was 'an Indian word meaning "welcome".' But I have not been able to verify the existence of this word in any of the main Indian languages.

42 *LF*, 362.

43 *LF*, 49.

44 When he died, David Holtby's capital was estimated at £54,000, an indication of his success as a farmer and his substance as a householder, in spite of various investment failures during his retirement. As a trustee of his estate, Winifred immediately inherited £100, which, along with £250 inherited from her uncle Robert Holtby, allowed her to pay off what debts she owed, mostly incurred in connection with the Ballinger fund. WH to VB, 24 April 1933.

45 Hull.

46 The 'about 1923' is in Vera's hand.

47 *TF*, 107.

48 *LF*, 301.

49 *Pavements at Anderby*, 270–7.

50 WH to AH, 25 May 1933, Hull.

51 WH to VB, 24 February 1933, Hull.

52 WH to VB, 12 March 1933, Hull.

53 *CF*, 208.

54 *CF*, 216.

55 *Yorkshire Post*, 9 October 1935.

56 *CF*, 251.

57 The film of *South Riding*, produced by Victor Saville and released in 1938.

58 AH to Hilda Reid, 11 October 1937, Hull. Hilda Reid was one of Winifred's college friends.

59 *CF*, 208.

Chapter 2 'A war casualty of the spirit': Harry Pearson

1 'A Distinguished Yorkshirewoman', *Yorkshire Post*, 20 October 1928. WH was writing Jane Harrison's obituary.

2 Brian Gardner, *The Public Schools*, London: Hamish Hamilton, 1973, 166–7.

3 Quoted Peter Parker, *Ackerley: A Life of J.R. Ackerley*, London: Constable, 1989, 16.

4 *TF*, 53.

5 Everard Wyrell, *The West Riding Regiment in the War*, [1924–1927], vol. 1, 183–4.

6 *TF*, 100–5.

7 According to Jeremy Wilson, in *Lawrence of Arabia*, the official biography of T.E. Lawrence (London: Heinemann, 1989), Lawrence went to Peshawar on the North East Frontier on 26 May 1928 but stayed for only two days (p. 828) before being sent to Miranshah, near the Afghan border. He was busy at this time translating the *Odyssey*. Because of rumours that he was a spy, he was recalled to England in January 1929. There is no mention of Harry in the biography, nor in Lawrence's published letters.

8 WH to GEGC, 12 January 1927, McMaster.

9 *LF*, 449.

10 Quoted Robert Pitman, 'Now the Man Adored by Winifred Holtby Turns to Religion', *Sunday Express*, April 1958.

11 John Catlin, *Family Quartet*, London: Hamish Hamilton, 1987, 47.

12 The *Schoolmistress*, 5 April 1934. The review was of a biography by Captain Liddell Hart.

13 WH to VB, Easter vacation 1921, Hull.

14 nd, Hull.

15 *TF*, 100.

16 *LF*, 325.

17 WH to VB December 1925, Hull.

18 The play was never completed.

19 *LF*, 422.

20 WH to VB 2 December 1932, Hull.

21 7 April 1933, Hull.

22 11 April 1934, Hull.

23 The *Quiver*, April 1934.

24 WH to PB, 29 December 1932, Hull.

25 WH to VB, 23 November 1934, Hull.

26 WH to VB, 25 October 1934, Hull.

27 WH to VB, 4 November 1934, Hull.

28 WH to VB, 24 October 1934, Hull.

29 WH to VB, 7 March 1935, Hull.

30 WH to VB, 12 April 1935, Hull.

31 *CF*, 212.

32 *CF*, 213.

33 *CF*, 216.

34 *Time and Tide*, 5 October 1935.

35 *Time and Tide*, 6 January 1940.

36 WH to VB, 23 November 1934, Hull.

37 Hull.

38 Harry Pearson to VB, McMaster, quoted PB & MB, 339.

39 Hilda Reid to Paul Berry, 10 March 1976.

Chapter 3 Celia and Rosalind: Jean McWilliam

1 *TF*, 47.

2 Evelyne White, *Winifred Holtby As I Knew Her*, London: Collins, 1938, 41. Evelyne White was the editor of the *Schoolmistress* for whom Winifred wrote a 'Weekly Journal' in the 1930s.

3 Hull.

4 Winifred Holtby, 'Would I like my daughter to be a nurse?', the *Quiver*, December 1933. The article is written in protest at the over-long hours, poor pay and restrictions – 'a kind of lay nunnery' – of a nurse's life.

5 The *Quiver, September* 1934.

6 WH to VB, 14 April 1933, Hull.

7 Vera Brittain, *The Women at Oxford*, London: Harrap, 1960, 60.

8 *Yorkshire Post*, 12 January 1929.

9 Hilda Reid, 'Winifred Holtby', the *Oxford Magazine*, 14 November 1935.

10 Rosamond Lehmann, *Dusty Answer* [1927], London: Penguin, 1982. *Dusty Answer* was a critical success when it was published in 1927, and formed one of a group of novels to discuss women's university experience during the inter-war period, of which the most famous is

Dorothy L. Sayers's *Gaudy Night*, London: Gollancz, 1935, and the most notorious Vera Brittain's *The Dark Tide*, London: Grant Richards, 1923.

11 *LF*, 444.

12 *LF*, 21.

13 Hilda Reid to WH, Hull.

14 Hilda Reid to WH, April 1933, Hull.

15 Letter to Ethelreda Lewis, 5 March 1925, Hull.

16 Hull.

17 *Time and Tide*, 19 May 1934.

18 The *Schoolmistress*, 5 October 1933.

19 *TY*, 332.

20 Vera Brittain, *The Women at Oxford*, London: Harrap, 1960, 137.

21 *TF*, 183.

22 *LF*, 5–8.

23 WH to Alice Holtby, 9 April 1919, Hull.

24 'Sports or Games', *Manchester Guardian*, 17 July 1930.

25 *LF*, 381.

26 Alice Holtby to VB, February 1936, Hull. No originals of Winifred's letters to Jean remain. Jean's papers appear to have been dispersed although a small number of letters to Winifred are at Hull.

27 See, for example, the letter of 2 June 1935, 336–41.

28 *SL*, 326.

29 St John Ervine agreed to write an introduction to *LF* in spite of having a bad eye at the time, but nothing apparently came of this.

30 *LF*, 226.

31 *LF*, 102–3.

32 This presumably refers to political writing. Jean was a keen socialist and may at one time have even belonged to, or at least been sympathetic towards, the Communist Party.

33 *LF*, 257. It seems unlikely that Winifred succeeded in placing any stories by Jean but, according to the record in Somerville College's *Register*, she did publish a short book, 'On the Teaching of Verse Composition'.

34 *LF*, 187.

35 *LF*, 225.

36 She returned to England in 1938 and spent the war years lecturing to

troops in the north of England, then taking up a post as an English teacher in Tonbridge, visiting South Africa on several occasions. She appears to have retired in 1945. Her last visit to South Africa was in 1963, only months before her death in Edinburgh. I am indebted for this information, and for other advice on Jean McWilliam's work in Pretoria, to Mrs Laurel Becker, who, with Sonja van Putten, has written the official history of Pretoria High School for Girls, *We Work in Hope* (Pretoria, 1992). The Librarian of Somerville College, Miss Pauline Adams, has also most helpfully supplied information.

37 Since 1991, a small number of black girls has begun to be admitted to the school each year. The school's charter quoted here, as formulated by Edith Aitken, now hangs in the foyer.

38 *LF*, 108.

39 *LF*, 213–4.

40 *TF*, 183.

41 *LF*, 235.

42 *LF*, 262.

43 *LF*, 303.

44 *LF*, 324.

45 *LF*, 341.

46 *LF*, 399.

47 'The Third-Class Adventurer' typescript, Hull.

48 WH to VB, 8 March 1926, Hull.

49 *TF*, 188.

50 Jean was frequently short of money and Winifred seems to have helped her out on several occasions. After Winifred's death, perhaps to rectify the omission of Jean in Winifred's will, Vera Brittain transferred the 10 per cent income due to her from Winifred's unpublished writings (the other 90 per cent would go to Somerville College) to Jean for her lifetime.

51 *LF*, 419.

52 *LF*, 442.

53 WH to VB, 29 March 1929, Hull. 'Since journeys end . . .' was the title Vera gave to the penultimate chapter of *Testament of Friendship*, in relation to Harry, of course, and not Jean.

54 *Manchester Guardian*, 12 February 1929.

55 Jean McWilliam to WH, 21 March 1934, Hull.

56 WH to VB, 29 September 1934, Hull.

57 WH to VB, 26 October 1934, Hull.

58 *LF*, 455–6.

59 *LF*, 461.

Chapter 4 'Very small, very dear love': Vera

1 Private conversation between Hilda Reid and Paul Berry in 1975, transcript kindly made available to me by Paul Berry.

2 Vera Brittain, *The Women at Oxford*, London: Harrap, 1960, 139.

3 *LF*, 187, 339.

4 *TY*, 508.

5 *LF*, 20.

6 *TY*, 487.

7 *CF*, 210.

8 WH to VB, 2 August 1923, Hull.

9 WH to VB, 14 April 1933, Hull.

10 *TF*, 93.

11 *CF*, 210.

12 WH to VB, Easter vacation 1921, Hull.

13 *TF*, 108.

14 WH to VB, 19 October 1921, Hull.

15 Clare Leighton was an artist and illustrator. Vera knew her because she was the sister of Roland Leighton, Vera's fiancé who was killed in the war. Clare later became the companion of Noel Brailsford.

16 Hull.

17 *LF*, 55.

18 WH to VB, 30 June 1921, Hull.

19 *LF*, 136–7.

20 VB to WH, 21 August 1922, Hull.

21 PB & MB, 181.

22 *LF*, 125.

23 *LF*, 130.

24 *LF*, 111.

25 *LF*, 164.

26 *TY*, 553–5.

27 Leonard Woolf, *Beginning Again: An Autobiography of the Years 1911 to 1918*, New York: Harcourt Brace Jovanovich, 1963, 189.

28 *LF*, 112.

29 *TY*, 521.

30 *LF*, 87–8.

31 In September 1923 Greece was protesting to the League about the Italian invasion of Corfu the month before.

32 Vera Brittain, *Testament of a Peace Lover: Letters from Vera Brittain*, ed. Winifred and Alan Eden-Green, London: Virago, 1988, 6.

33 *LF*, 260.

34 Winifred Holtby Collection, Bridlington Public Library.

35 *South African Lady's Pictorial*, April 1926.

36 *Time and Tide*, 14 September 1928.

37 WH to VB, 16 April 1924, Hull. Nursie stayed until the autumn of 1925 when she returned to Yorkshire, to nurse Aunt Jane.

38 *LF*, 246–7.

39 *LF*, 245.

40 *LF*, 301.

41 *TF*, 179.

42 Catlin was known to friends and family as Gordon, to distinguish him from his father, George, until 1936 when his father died and he took the name George. Since Vera and Winifred refer to him in their letters during the time of Winifred's life as Gordon, or sometimes as G., I have used this name which is not, of course, the one he came to be known by later in life. See PB & MB, 189.

43 WH to VB, Christmas 1923, Hull.

44 WH to VB, April 1924, Hull.

45 WH to VB, April 1924, Hull.

46 It is also reproduced in *Selected Letters* but in an edited version which gives a much more restrained and moderate impression than the original.

47 WH to VB, 27 August 1924, Hull.

48 *LF*, 289–90.

49 GEGC to WH, 31 July 1924, McMaster.

50 GEGC to WH, 18 August 1924, McMaster.

51 WH to GEGC, 1 October 1924, McMaster.

52 WH to GEGC, 11 February 1925, McMaster.

53 Gordon's mother, Edith Catlin, had declared suffragette sympathies in opposition to her husband's wishes and after numerous and bitter

quarrels she decided to leave him and Gordon, her only child, in 1915 when Gordon was nineteen. She died of kidney failure in 1917. Vera used the story of her mother-in-law's life for the first part of *Honourable Estate* (1936).

54 WH to GEGC, 11 February 1925, McMaster.

55 WH to GEGC, 7 March 1925, McMaster.

56 GEGC to WH, 25 February 1925, McMaster.

57 WH to GEGC, 3 April 1925, McMaster.

58 WH to GEGC, 24 April 1925, McMaster.

59 GEGC to WH, 28 June 1925, McMaster.

60 WH to GEGC, 24 December 1924, McMaster.

61 · LF, 263.

62 VB to WH, 28 June 1925, Hull.

63 WH to VB, 29 June 1925, Hull.

Chapter 5 'Leader . . . Editor . . . Friend': Margaret Rhondda

1 *TF*, 133.

2 First printed in the *Yorkshire Post*, 26 July 1926, reprinted *Time and Tide*, 6 August 1926, 714.

3 This was a higher death-rate than in any other occupation, including mining and deep-sea fishing.

4 '. . . the substitution [of women for men in industry] has proved successful in a great majority of cases; the women have shown a capacity to take up many of the more skilled processes reserved for men and have carried them out completely and well, and have displayed unexpected readiness for work which at first sight seemed wholly unsuitable for them.' Quoted in Sylvia Anthony, *Women's Place in Industry and Home*, London: Routledge, 1932, 75.

5 In later editions it was published as *Women*.

6 *TY*, 583.

7 *LF*, 118–9.

8 *LF*, 240.

9 Her father, David Alfred Thomas, afterwards Lord Rhondda, coal magnate, Liberal MP, and President of the Local Government Board in the two years before his death in 1918.

10 Viscountess Rhondda, *This Was My World*, London: Macmillan, 1933, 295.

11 Ibid., 301–3.

12 *Time and Tide*, 31 October 1924.

13 Shirley M. Eoff, *Viscountess Rhondda, Equalitarian Feminist*, Columbus: Ohio State University Press, 1991, 128.

14 Ibid.,144.

15 Lady Rhondda had spent over a quarter of a million pounds on *Time and Tide* (Eoff, 145).

16 *Time and Tide,* 14 May 1926.

17 *CF*, 104.

18 1. Satisfactory legislation on child assault.

    2. Satisfactory legislation for the widowed mother.

    3. Satisfactory legislation for the unmarried mother and her child.

    4. Equal guardianship.

    5. Equality of pay for men and women teachers.

    6. Equality of pay and opportunity for men and women in the Civil Service.

    When one point was carried, another would be substituted. These points later evolved into six general points of equality for women: political, occupational, moral, social, economic and legal. The Six Point Group went into abeyance in 1980 and was dissolved in 1983.

19 *Time and Tide,* 19 January 1923.

20 *TY*, 586.

21 See Vera Brittain's account of the attempts to unseat Dennis Herbert, Conservative MP for Watford and a persistent opposer of the Criminal Law Amendment Bill and the Matrimonial Causes Bill: *TY*, 589–92.

22 *TY*, 582.

23 Quoted Eoff, 87. Peeresses were not admitted to the House of Lords until after the passing of the Life Peerages Act in 1958, some months after Lady Rhondda's death. She had continued to campaign on the issue since her defeat in 1922.

24 See Martin Pugh, *Women and the Women's Movement 1914–1959*, London: Macmillan, 1992, 111–13.

25 *This Was My World*, 299.

26 Ray Strachey (ed.), *Our Freedom and Its Results*, London: Hogarth Press, 1936, 153. See also Margery Spring Rice, *Working-Class Wives*, Harmondsworth: Penguin, 1939, for an account of the continuing

poor health and lack of access to maternity and child welfare benefits and birth control information of working-class women.

27 Monica Whateley, for instance, secretary of the Six Point Group, was
very critical of *Time and Tide*'s refusal in the late 1930s to give coverage to the League of Nations' 'Status of Women' report.

28 *Time and Tide*, 22 February 1924. This was Winifred's first acceptance of an article by any paper.

29 *Women*, 192.

30 Eleanor Rathbone, *The Disinherited Family*, London: Allen & Unwin,
1924, 145.

31 Quoted in Martin Pugh, *Women and the Women's Movement
1914–1959*, London: Macmillan, 1992, 238.

32 *Time and Tide*, 12 March 1926.

33 *Time and Tide*, 11 June 1926.

34 *Time and Tide*, 6 August 1926.

35 *Manchester Guardian*, 11 October, 1928.

36 The *Quiver*, December 1933.

37 n.d. Hull. Although 'M Guard' is scribbled at the top of this typescript I can find no record of it being published.

38 Originally published in 1934, reprinted in *Testament of a Generation:
The Journalism of Vera Brittain and Winifred Holtby*, ed. Paul Berry
and Alan Bishop, London: Virago, 1985.

39 'Too Much Talk about Romance', *Daily Herald*, 12 September 1930.

40 *News Chronicle*, 9 March 1934.

41 Havelock Ellis, *The Psychology of Sex*, New York: Enerson, 1933, 18.

42 Winifred Holtby, *The Astonishing Island, Being a Veracious Record of the
Experiences undergone by Robinson Lippingtree Mackintosh from Tristan
da Cunha during an Accidental Visit to Unknown Territory in the Year of
Grace MCMXXX – ?*, London: Lovat Dickson, 1933. The illustrations
were by Batt.

43 'Mothers – Train Your Daughters', *Sunday Dispatch*, 29 January 1933.

44 *TF*, 55.

45 *Manchester Guardian*, 12 September 1929.

46 *Nation and Athenaeum*, 23 June 1928.

47 *Passing Show*, 2 June 1934.

48 Lecture notes probably from 1933 on 'Women in the 1930s', Hull.

49 The *Schoolmistress*, 14 February 1935.

50 Introduction, *Our Freedom and its Results.*

51 Margaret Storm Jameson, *No Time Like the Present*, London: Cassell, 1933, 229–31.

52 Review of Mrs O'Malley's *Women in Subjection*, *Daily Telegraph*, 28 September 1933.

53 *Passing Show*, 22 July 1933.

54 Review of Friedrich Sieburg's *Germany: My Country.* The *Schoolmistress*, 30 November 1933.

55 Tyrone Guthrie, later producer at the Old Vic, who had taken out an option on the play, arranged to meet Winifred for lunch on 4 September 1935 to discuss it, perhaps with a view to producing it in London late in the autumn (*TF*, 429). Nothing came of this meeting at the time. The manuscript was (very slightly) revised and edited by Norman Ginsbury and published by Jonathan Cape in 1939, with the title *Take Back Your Freedom.* There were unsuccessful attempts to get the play performed in Hull in 1962; it was performed in Hull by amateurs in 1935 to commemorate the half centenary of Winifred's death.

56 *The Letters of Virginia Woolf*, edited by Nigel Nicolson and Joanna Trautmann in 6 volumes, vol. 6, 1936–1941, London: The Hogarth Press, 1980, 464.

57 *LF*, 336.

58 *LF*, 387.

59 Hull. The letters are from the period 1930 to 1932.

60 WH to VB, 5 August 1931, Hull.

61 MR to WH, 27 January 1931, Hull. Margaret Rhondda also admitted that she was 'a trifle hurt that St John Ervine should get one of the first batch & I come in amongst the also-rans with the second.' Winifred had met St John Ervine in 1925 at Lady Rhondda's house and he had become one of her fiercest critics and warmest admirers.

62 *Time and Tide*, 4 April 1936.

63 MR to WH, 29 January 1931, Hull.

64 MR to WH, 17 July 1932, Hull.

65 MR to WH, 16 November 1933, Hull.

66 Shirley M. Eoff, in *Viscountess Rhondda, Equalitarian Feminist*, Columbus: Ohio State University Press, 1991, 108, states that of these relationships the one with Winifred 'was probably the deepest

and most intense of her life'. There isn't a great deal of evidence to support this claim, and it also unjustifiably disregards Margaret Rhondda's many years with Theodora Bosanquet.

67 Letter from VB to St John Ervine, 18 February 1937, Hull.

68 *The Diary of Virginia Woolf*, vol. 4, 1931–35, ed. Anne Olivier Bell, London: Penguin, 1983, 149.

69 WH to VB, 27 July 1926, Hull. The quotation continues: 'I neither embarrassed her nor she me. . . . Your [Vera's] manner may make her feel gauche. She feels gauche very easily & it is a damnable feeling.'

70 MR to WH, from Cairo, 9 December 1933, Hull. Two days before Winifred died, she and Margaret discussed her engagement to Harry. *Time and Tide*, 6 July 1940.

71 *SL*, 251. Winifred replied, with more hope than realism that 'I feel she too someday will learn to understand you'. WH to VB, 7 April 1933, Hull.

72 MR to WH, 22 August 1931, Hull. Margaret Rhondda was referring mostly to the time Winifred devoted to the paper but she had also put money into it (letter 10 May 1930), probably some of the 'small income left her under some trust or other' which Margaret Rhondda mentions in *Time and Tide* (11 August 1936) and which she 'for some quixotic reason of her own felt obliged to pass the whole of this on to charity'.

73 *CF*, 338.

74 WH to MR, 11 March 1935, Hull. *Women* was one in a series of books on topical subjects published by John Lane and the Bodley Head. Others in the series included *Art* by Eric Gill, *Communism* by Ralph Fox, *Broadcasting* by Raymond Postgate and *The Home* by Naomi Mitchison.

75 WH to VB, 14 April 1934, Hull.

76 WH to VB, 26 November 1934.

77 'The Reluctant Feminists', Naomi Mitchison, *Left Review*, December 1934.

Chapter 6 'The goal of all men's longing': South Africa and William Ballinger

1 Letter to Ethelreda Lewis, 4 March 1925, Hull. Like many white colonial novels of this period, *The Harp* is obsessively concerned

with miscegenation. Winifred contrasted its integrity with the 'perversions' of writers like D.H. Lawrence, Aldous Huxley and James Joyce who 'blaspheme the spirit of beauty itself'. Mrs Lewis was best known as the author/editor of the 'autobiography' of the traveller Trader Horn.

2 Quoted in Edward Roux, *Time Longer Than Rope*, London: Gollancz, 1948,160.

3 Ballinger Papers, University of Cape Town.

4 WH to VB, 20 April 1926, Hull.

5 WH to William Ballinger and Margaret Hodgson, 28 August 1933, University of Cape Town.

6 WH, 'White Man Fights for the Black', *Clarion*, 3 June 1933.

7 'The Native Workers of South Africa', Johannesburg, May 1927. The pamphlet was, however, printed in Leicester and may well have been promoted and financed by Winifred and Creech Jones. A copy is in Winifred's papers.

8 Ethelreda Lewis to WH, 4 April 1928, Hull.

9 Leonard Woolf, *An Autobiography*, vol. 2, 1911–1969, Oxford: Oxford University Press, 1980, 351–2. Woolf was for thirty years secretary of the ILP Advisory Committee on Imperialism. He met Winifred several times in this capacity.

10 WH to Mrs Lewis, 9 November 1933, Hull.

11 Quoted P .L. Wickins, *The Industrial and Commercial Workers' Union of South Africa*, Cape Town: Oxford University Press, 1978, 104.

12 Reprinted in *Testament of a Generation: The Journalism of Vera Brittain and Winifred Holtby*, ed. Paul Berry and Alan Bishop, London: Virago, 1985.

13 WH to VB, January 1926, Hull.

14 WH to VB, 6 March 1926, Hull.

15 Clements Kadalie, *My Life and the ICU*, London: Frank Cass, 1970, 85.

16 Ethelreda Lewis to WH, 14 December 1927, Hull.

17 WH to VB, 6 June 1926, Hull.

18 'Winifred Holtby', the *Oxford Magazine,* 14 November 1935.

19 Hull.

20 The Imperialism Committee had been founded in 1924.

21 Kadalie to Creech Jones, Hull.

22 See Wickins, 105.

23 He later became Secretary of State for the Colonies (1946–50). He was affectionately known to friends, including Winifred, as Jon.

24 WH to Mabel Palmer, Hull.

25 Leornard Woolf, *Autobiography*, vol. 2,1911–1969, 204.

26 Creech Jones to Kadalie, Hull.

27 The document appears to have been typed on her typewriter and there are annotations in her hand.

28 Ethelreda Lewis to WH, 26 April 1927, Hull.

29 Clements Kadalie, *My Life in the ICU*, 107.

30 *My Life in the ICU*, 137. Margaret Bondfield was a well-known trade unionist and at the time was Minister of Labour in the Labour government under Ramsay MacDonald.

31 Hull.

32 WH to Ethelreda Lewis, July 1927, quoted Wickins, 139.

33 Memorandum, ILP Imperialism Committee, Hull.

34 Ballinger to WH, 11 February 1928, Hull.

35 Ethelreda Lewis to WH, 4 April 1928, Hull.

36 Ethelreda Lewis to WH, 28 September 1928, Hull.

37 Ballinger told this to Etaine Eberhard, one of the librarians at the University of Cape Town. She recalls that 'he said that he had been in love with [Winifred] and had asked her to marry him. She had turned his proposal down, giving her poor state of health as her reason for doing so . . . the proposal took place in a London park . . . not long after he left for S.A. in 1928.'

38 WH to William Ballinger, University of Cape Town.

39 But Mrs Lewis sent a bankers' draft of £60 to Winifred in November 1928. It is not clear where this came from, possibly from Mrs Lewis herself and her friends.

40 Hull.

41 'White Man Fights for the Black', *Clarion*, 3 June 1933. According to Mrs Lewis, the collapse of the ICU's finances was the result of malpractice and mismanagement by one of Kadalie's assistants, Allison Champion, encouraged by Glass, during Kadalie's absence in Europe. Mrs Lewis to WH, 3 September 1928, Hull.

42 WH to Ballinger, 8 April 1929, University of Cape Town.

43 Champion headed a break-away section in Natal, and Kadalie set up

a rival organisation, the Independent ICU. Neither faction enjoyed anywhere near the same success as the original ICU. Kadalie died in 1951.

44 Hull.

45 Hull.

46 *TF*, 248.

47 Creech Jones to WH, Hull.

48 Frederick Livie-Noble was a psychologist who had worked in Africa.
    He remained Honorary Secretary of the LGAA until its dissolution in
    1940.

49 A Fabian, Sydney (First Baron) Olivier had served in the Colonial
    Office. During the inter-war period he was active in African affairs.
    After a period in the Colonial Office, Leonard Barnes became a jour-
    nalist and farmer in South Africa from 1921 to 1925, before
    returning to England and an academic career. He probably met
    Winifred when she was in South Africa. Mrs Lewis thought Winifred
    would have made him a good wife: 'You would have set him on fire,
    which is what he needs.' He wrote *Caliban in Africa*, London:
    Gollancz, 1930.

50 WH to VB, 6 October 1934, Hull. Norman Leys, a medical doctor,
    was the author of *A Last Chance in Kenya.*

51 Its secretary was Julius Lewin, a South African lawyer, founder of the
    South African ILP and the Cape Fabian Society before coming to
    England in 1933. The Treasurer was F. Horrobin, MP.

52 Margaret Hodgson was a lecturer in History at Witwatersrand
    University. She married Ballinger in 1934. In 1937 she became a
    member of the South African Senate, with interests in Native affairs,
    and in 1969 she published *From Union to Apartheid*. Ballinger became
    a Senator in 1948. She was dismissed from her post on marriage; six
    weeks before her death Winifred was offering to take up the matter
    with the British Commonwealth League, and was also trying to place
    articles by 'Peg' Hodgson. WH to Margaret Hodgson, 6 August 1935,
    Ballinger Papers, University of Cape Town.

53 'Native Co-operation in South Africa', *The Co-operative Review*,
    January 1935.

54 Hull.

55 Alex Hlubi came to London as an ICU student in 1930, on the
    recommendation of William Ballinger. Winifred stood security of

£50 for him. He wished to stay on in Britain but Ballinger and Howard Pim rejected this. He seems to have been always short of money and always begging from Winifred.

56 Hull.

57 Chief Tshekedi of Bechuanaland was tried and sentenced to banishment for flogging a white youth. British liberal opinion was incensed and the sentence was revoked. The incident highlighted the tense relations with South Africa over the Protectorates.

58 Hull.

59 Hull.

60 'Timeo Danaos . . .', *Time and Tide*, 19 January 1935.

61 WH to Phyllis Bentley, 28 August 1935, Hull.

62 *CF*, 200.

63 Ethelreda Lewis to WH, 26 November 1930, Hull.

64 'White Man Fights for the Black Man', *Clarion*, 3 June 1933.

65 *Time Longer than Rope*, 204. Edward Roux was a leading figure in the South African Communist Party to 1931. He was very critical of the Ballingers' activities.

66 WH to Ballinger, 20 April 1928, University of Cape Town.

67 Hull.

68 Hull.

69 From one of the poems in WH's sequence 'For the Ghost of Elinor Wylie'.

70 Hull.

71 The Johannesburg Public Library possesses numerous papers relating to the founding of the library, including inventories of its holdings and an account of its move to Soweto in 1963.

Chapter 7 'We are both here, Gordon and I'

1 VB to WH, 4 July 1925, Hull. This is contradicted, however, by an entry in Vera's journal in 1932 describing a conversation between Vera, Winifred and Phyllis Bentley 'about sex & sex experience. We all seemed to imagine we were all highly sexed, but this is almost certainly only true of Winifred' (*CF*, 49).

2 WH to VB, 7 July 1925, Hull.

3 GEGC to WH, 25 June 1925, McMaster.

4 WH to VB, 7 July 1925, Hull.

5   WH to VB, 2 May 1926, Hull.

6   WH to VB, October 1925, Hull.

7   WH to VB, September 1925, Hull.

8   WH to VB, 4 October 1925, Hull.

9   WH to VB, August 1931, Hull.

10   VB to WH, 16 July 1926, Hull.

11   PB and MB, 218–9.

12   *TF*, 261.

13   WH to VB, 27 July 1926, Hull.

14   WH to VB, 18 July 1926, Hull.

15   Deborah Gorham, *Vera Brittain: A Feminist Life*, Oxford: Blackwell, 1996, 166.

16   'Exit Papa', *Manchester Guardian*, 26 October 1929.

17   For a discussion of the productive rivalry existing between Vera and Winifred, see unpublished thesis by Diana Wallace, 'Sisters and Rivals: The Theme of Female Rivalry in Novels by Women 1914–1939', Loughborough University, 1997. See also Jean Kennard, *Vera Brittain & Winifred Holtby: A Working Partnership*, Hanover and London: University of New Hampshire Press, 1989, for an excellent account of the friendship of Vera and Winifred, particularly its effect on their development as writers.

18   VB to WH, 30 July 1926, Hull.

19   WH to VB, 27 July 1926, Hull.

20   *TF*, 274. The Earl's Court Road maisonette was the two upper floors of 6 Nevern Place.

21   VB to WH, 21 May 1927, Hull.

22   WH to VB, 27 August 1926, Hull.

23   WH to GEGC, 12 May 1933, McMaster.

24   *CF*, 168.

25   John Catlin, *Family Quartet*, London: Hamish Hamilton, 1987, 111.

26   Hilda Reid, conversation with Paul Berry, September 1975.

27   VB to GEGC, 27 April 1927, McMaster, quoted PB & MB, 235.

28   According to the listing in *Eutychus* of volumes in preparation, Rebecca West's volume was to be on *The Future of the Sexes*. It is not clear that she did in fact complete this. Vera's volume was *Halcyon, or the Future of Monogamy*, 1929.

29   *LF*, 366.

30 Joy Grant, *Stella Benson, A Biography*, London: Macmillan, 1987, 220.

31 *TF*, 172. Stella Benson, who had suffered from tuberculosis for many years, died in December 1933 and was buried on an island off the China coast. Winifred went to a memorial service for her at St Mary Abbott's Church in Kensington.

32 *LF*, 454.

33 Joy Grant, 247.

34 See Perry Anderson's account of his father's career in China, *London Review of Books*, 6 and 20 August 1998.

35 *TF*, 359.

36 *Time and Tide*, December 1931.

37 WH to GEGC, 16 May 1929, McMaster.

38 WH to VB, 6 October 1934, Hull. It is a measure of Winifred's liberality of mind that she continued on amiable terms with Wells during this episode, perhaps even trying to act as mediator between them. Odette was threatening to publish his letters, a threat he took lightly – 'As for the letters I don't give a rap' – although he was worried about Odette's state of mind and in March 1934 was asking for Winifred's advice on what to do (Hull).

39 WH to VB, 27 July 1926, Hull.

40 GEGC to WH, 7 June 1926, McMaster.

41 GEGC to WH, 29 October 1926, McMaster.

42 Gordon later commented on this to Vera: 'It may be that an agreement to ignore all warmer emotion was a necessary condition of being in the same house . . . God knows what would have been the consequences of any other line.' GEGC to VB, 18 March 1937, McMaster, quoted PB & MB, 280.

43 GEGC to WH, 28 February 1932, McMaster.

44 WH to GEGC, 30 March 1928, McMaster.

45 WH to GEGC, 3 April 1929. The *Realist*, a journal of scientific humanism, lasted only six months before it folded from editorial disagreements and lack of funds (PB & MB, 282).

46 WH to GEGC, 12 February 1933, McMaster.

47 WH to GEGC, 1 March 1933, McMaster.

48 WH to GEGC, 11 April 1933, McMaster.

49 WH to VB, 11 April 1933, Hull.

50 GEGC to VB, 11 October 1937, McMaster, quoted PB & MB, 342.

51 PB & MB, 280–5.

52 After frenzied activity during the early 1930s to get him established as a political figure, in which Winifred was inevitably involved, Gordon was selected to contest (unsuccessfully) a Labour seat for Brentwood and Chiswick in the General Election of 1931. He was selected again for Sunderland in 1935 but was again defeated.

53 WH to VB, 23 February 1933, Hull.

54 WH to VB, 4 August 1933, Hull. A brief passage had to be omitted from the notice, because she had mentioned that the four young men died, which might 'destroy the readers' suspense'.

55 Hull.

56 Phyllis Bentley, O Dreams, O Destinations, London: Gollancz, 1962, 153.

57 CF, 35.

58 CF, 45.

59 VB to WH, 16 April 1933, Hull.

60 O Dreams, O Destinations, 178–9.

61 WH to PB, 12 April 1933, Hull.

62 WH to PB, 13 July 1933, Hull.

63 WH to VB, 4 August 1933, Hull. After Winifred's death, Vera intensified her friendship with Storm Jameson but this too did not last.

64 WH to VB, 10 April 1933, Hull.

65 PB to WH, undated, Hull.

66 I am grateful to Diana Wallace for pointing out the resemblance between the two self-descriptions.

67 The Letters of Virginia Woolf, edited by Nigel Nicolson and Joanna Trautmann in 6 volumes, vol. 6, 1936–1941, London: The Hogarth Press, 379.

68 Martin Ceadel, Pacifism in Britain 1914–1945, London: Oxford University Press, 1980, 1–8.

69 Margaret Storm Jameson, Journey from the North, New York: Harper & Row, 1969, 326–7.

70 Quoted in Sybil Oldfield, Women Against the Iron Fist, Oxford: Blackwell, 1989, 64.

71 Kingsley Martin, Editor, London: Hutchinson, 1968, 157.

72 TF, 376–7.

73 Constable, the publisher, initially refused Winifred's chapter because they feared it was libellous. Winifred removed references to individuals.

74 Her letter to *The Times* on 16 November described the presentation in which the Archbishop expressed 'deep concern lest equality for Germany might be attained by her rearmament rather than by the disarmament of other Powers'.

75 'Collective Security and Party Politics', Hull.

76 For a discussion of Vera's pacifist activities after Winifred's death, see PB & MB, especially chapters 12 and 13.

Chapter 8 A reformer-sort-of-writer: Virginia Woolf and the woman's novel

1 WH to PB, 24 December 1933, McMaster.

2 *TF*, 129 and 139.

3 The author of three experimental fictions, May Sinclair, was one of these exceptions. Highly esteemed in literary circles, May Sinclair published three novels heavily influenced by psychoanalytic theories: *The Three Sisters*, London: Hutchinson, 1914, *Mary Olivier: A Life*, London: Cassell, 1922, and *Life and Death of Harriet Frean*, London: Collins, 1922. Her long illness from Parkinson's Disease was a contributory factor in the decline of her reputation after the early 1920s.

4 Schreiner's influential novel, *The Story of an African Farm*, London: Chapman & Hall, 1883. Its impact was kept alive by the publication of her feminist polemic, *Woman and Labour*, London: Fisher Unwin, 1911. A later novel, *From Man to Man*, London: Fisher Unwin, 1926, was unfinished at the time of her death.

5 Nicola Beauman, *A Very Great Profession: The Woman's Novel 1914–39*, London: Virago, 1983, 6. Beauman quotes West's comment from 1922 in the *New Statesman*. See also Anthea Trodd, *Women's Writing in English, Britain 1900–1945*, London: Longman, 1998.

6 *LF*, 55.

7 WH to VB, 25 August 1932, Hull.

8 Phyllis Bentley, *The Regional Novel*, New York: PEN Books, 1966, 13.

9 WH to VB, 5 December 1932, Hull.

10 St John Ervine to WH, 29 September 1933, Hull.

11   For a full discussion of the recommendations, see John Sheail, 'South Riding: A Portrayal of Local Government Between the Wars', *Local Government Studies*, January/February 1985, 65–74.

12   *Hull Daily Mail*, 3 June 1932.

13   Winifred herself wrote an article about 'Crumbs in the Bed' for the *Manchester Guardian* in March 1929. It has pretty much the same to say as Julia Stephen's passage, but does so more robustly.

14   *TF*, 308.

15   Winifred Holtby, *Virginia Woolf*, London: Wishart, 1932, 27–9.

16   Ibid., 183.

17   Her collections of critical essays, *The Common Reader*, London: The Hogarth Press, 1925, and *The Common Reader: Second Series*, 1932.

18   Leonard Woolf, *Autobiography*, 2 vols, London: Oxford University Press, 1980, vol. 1, 401.

19   *The Letters of Virginia Woolf*, edited by Nigel Nicolson and Joanne Trautmann, 6 vols, London: The Hogarth Press, 1979, vol. 5, 114.

20   There are apparently no surviving letters from Winifred to Virginia Woolf.

21   Virginia Woolf to WH, Hull.

22   *The Diary of Virginia Woolf*, edited by Anne Olivier Bell and Andrew McNeillie, 5 vols, London: Hogarth Press, 1977–84, vol. 4, 6.

23   'My husband says that you are coming to see him on Tuesday afternoon. I wonder if it would suit you to come after dinner on Tuesday instead? . . . I should like so much to see you but it can't be in that afternoon,' Woolf wrote in early 1933 in a letter to WH, Hull.

24   Virginia Woolf, *The Pargiters: The Novel-Essay Portion of 'The Years'*, edited by Mitchell A. Leaska, London: The Hogarth Press, 1978, 100.

25   The Epistle of St Paul the Apostle to the Ephesians, 4. 25: 'Wherefore putting away lying, speak every man truth with his neighbour: for we are members one of another.'

26   For a fuller discussion of the relation between the two writers see Marion Shaw, ' "Alien Experiences": Virginia Woolf, Winifred Holtby and Vera Brittain in the Thirties,' in *Rewriting the Thirties: Modernism and After*, edited by Keith Williams and Steven Matthews, Harlow, Essex: Addison, Wesley & Longman, 1997, 37–52.

27   *Letters*, vol. 6, 379.

28 *Letters*, vol. 6, 382.

29 Alison Light, *Forever England: Femininity, Literature and Conservatism between the Wars*, London: Routledge, 1991, 11.

30 WH to PB, 19 December 1932.

31 Dorothy McCalman was a teacher 'who went late to Somerville after earning her living . . . and died after only a year as a tutor at the Oxford Training College' (Vera Brittain, *Testament of Experience*, London: Fontana, 1979, 145). The history of the bequest to Somerville is complicated; after the unexpected financial success of *South Riding*, it became possible to establish more than one fund and scholarship.

32 Somerville Council minutes v 14, 21.

33 See Jeffrey Richards and Anthony Aldgate, *The Best of British: Cinema and Society, 1930–1970*, Chapter 3, 'The Age of Consensus: *South Riding*', Oxford: Blackwells, 1983, 32.

34 *Testament of Experience* [1957] London: Fontana, 1980, 188.

Chapter 9 A woman in her time

1 *TF*, 315.

2 WH to VB, 5 March 1932, Hull.

3 WH to VB, 4 April 1932, Hull.

4 *CF*, 110.

5 This was standard treatment for nephritis at the time. Winifred's renal failure was probably caused by glomerulonephritis. The bacteria that causes scarlet fever is associated with this condition which often causes high blood pressure. Her blindness, in the late stages of the disease, was most likely due to accelerated hypertension, and her death due to uraemia and pulmonary oedema, related to fluid overload and hypertension. I am indebted for this medical information about Winifred's condition to Dr Cassidy of Nottingham City Hospital.

6 St John Ervine to VB, 23 December 1939, McMaster.

7 *LF*, 462.

8 WH to PB, 17 February 1935.

9 Hilda Reid, the *Oxford Magazine*, 14 November 1935.

10 WH to PB, 26 August 1935, Hull.

11 *CF*, 200.

12 'Sentence of Life', in *Truth Is Not Sober*. The story was written in 1933.

13 Vera amalgamates two biblical quotations: 'When thou passest through the waters, I will be with thee' from Isaiah 43.2, and 'I will not fail thee, nor forsake thee' from Joshua 1.5.

14 Vera had never been to Rudston before this occasion.

15 The pavements are now in the Transport Museum in Hull.

16 'The Legend of Rudston', in *Pavements at Anderby*.

17 *CF*, 224–5.

18 *TF*, 437.

19 Letter to Hilda Reid, in Paul Berry collection, quoted PB & MB, 331.

20 *CF*, 248.

21 *CF*, 11.

22 *CF*, 217; also *TF*, 435.

23 *CF*, 220–1.

24 *CF*, 229.

25 *TF*, 2 and 117.

26 VB to St John Ervine, 18 February 1937, Hull. The letter was not sent until March 1939.

27 *CF*, 330.

28 Vera had left Gollancz, having reached a point of 'fundamental incompatibility' with him following his pro-war propaganda at a Left Book Club meeting in March 1939, on the same day that she began writing *Testament of Friendship*. Howard Lewis painted the portrait from 'Various photographs wh. I gave him.' According to Vera, it 'gives a remarkable impression of her personality; her vitality, eagerness, intellectual alertness, & even has the right lines of her face & the crookedness of her nose' (*CF*, 350 and 362). The portrait is now in Somerville College and is reproduced by kind permission of the College.

29 Quoted in 'Books for the Summer and Autumn' by James Milne, the *Scotsman*, 21 June 1937.

30 *Testament of Experience*, 133–4.

31 *TF*, 260.

32 Freud himself did not unreservedly value such a character: 'A love that does not discriminate seems to me to forfeit a part of its own value, by doing an injustice to its object; and secondly, not all men

are worthy of love.'

33 Prelude to George Eliot's *Middlemarch*.

34 Corinthians, 6.10: 'As having nothing, and yet possessing all things.'
    Winifred described the experience in a letter to Vera whilst staying in
    Monks Risborough in 1932. She used it in *South Riding* in relation to
    Miss Sigglesthwaite, and Vera used the incident in *Testament of
    Friendship*, 325.

35 WH to VB, 21 August 1928.

36 *TF*, 143.

37 Hilda Reid, 'Winifred Holtby', the *Oxford Magazine*, 14 November
    1935.

38 *TF*, 330.

39 Wells to WH, Hull. Wells's letter has a postscript, 'Odette sends her
    love.' This was at the time when he and Odette were still lovers.

Index

Note: Except where otherwise indicated, titles of novels, articles, poems, stories, etc, are by Winifred Holtby.

Abbreviations: VB = Vera Brittain; WH = Winifred Holtby

REMEMBER, REMEMBER!

Selected Stories of Winifred Holtby

Edited by Marion Shaw and Paul Berry

This selection of Winifred Holtby's short stories is drawn from her two published volumes, *Truth is Not Sober* and *Pavements of Anderby*, which were published posthumously by her two friends, Vera Brittain and Hilda Reid and have been collected here in one volume for the first time.

Brightly written, in an unselfconscious, matter-of-fact style, these stories are irreverent and entertaining, fulfilling what she saw as the short story's purpose in a reader's life: 'nice for chance guests – easy to pick up and more tantalising for one's bedside than a novel'.

Many of these stories are autobiographically based, and feature the Yorkshire farming community in Rudston where she was brought up. This was the setting for her most famous novel, *South Riding*, also published posthumously. Some of the stories relate to the last years of her life when she was contending with the incessant headaches and nausea of Bright's disease.

ANTONIA WHITE
A Life
Jane Dunn

'One of our best biographers' – *Sunday Times*

'Oh I DID want to be happy as a woman . . . But I'm a monster and must accept being one. Not all writers are monsters. But my kind is.'

Antonia White is best known for her masterpiece *Frost in May*, for having come back from 'Bedlam' hospital and madness, and for the public feud between her daughters over the editing of her diaries. This is the first biography to tell the complete story of a life courageously lived against most difficult odds.

This is the story of a woman who – two generations too soon – attempted to live the modern female life of single parent and working mother but longed for the artistic and intellectual stage. Antonia White wrestled throughout with the large questions of faith, the attractions and repulsions of Catholicism, the problems of being a woman and an artist. And over it all hovered the threat of madness. This book reveals her as a woman unafraid of extreme experience and honest enough to accept the consequences: self-obsessed, funny, fascinating, tragic – and ultimately heroic.

Now you can order superb titles directly from Virago

☐	Remember, Remember!	Marion Shaw and Paul Berry (eds)	£6.99
☐	Antonia White	Jane Dunn	£9.99
☐	The Haunting of Sylvia Plath	Jacqueline Rose	£8.99
☐	Flesh and the Mirror	Lorna Sage (ed)	£9.99
☐	Christina Rossetti	Frances Thomas	£8.99
☐	Willa Cather	Hermione Lee	£8.99
☐	Bloomsbury Pie	Regina Marler	£7.99

Please allow for postage and packing: **Free UK delivery.**
Europe; add 25% of retail price; Rest of World; 45% of retail price.

To order any of the above or any other Virago titles, please call our credit card orderline or fill in this coupon and send/fax it to:

Virago, 250 Western Avenue, London, W3 6XZ, UK.
Fax 020 8324 5678   Telephone 020 8324 5516

☐ I enclose a UK bank cheque made payable to Virago for £ ....

☐ Please charge £.............. to my Access, Visa, Delta, Switch Card No.

☐☐☐☐☐☐☐☐☐☐☐☐☐☐☐☐☐☐☐

Expiry Date ☐☐☐☐   Switch Issue No. ☐☐

NAME (Block letters please) ....

ADDRESS ....

....

....

Postcode ....Telephone ....

Signature ....

Please allow 28 days for delivery within the UK. Offer subject to price and availability.

Please do not send any further mailings from companies carefully selected by Virago ☐